About this book

Can developing countries trade their way out of poverty? International trade has grown dramatically in the last two decades in the global economy, and trade is an important source of revenue in developing countries. Yet, many low-income countries have been producing and exporting tropical commodities for a long time. They are still poor. This book is a major analytical contribution to understanding commodity production and trade, as well as putting forward policy-relevant suggestions for 'solving' the commodity problem.

Through the study of the global value chain for coffee, the authors recast the 'development problem' for countries relying on commodity exports in entirely new ways. They do so by analysing the so-called coffee paradox - the coexistence of a 'coffee boom' in consuming countries and of a 'coffee crisis' in producing countries. New consumption patterns have emerged with the growing importance of specialty, fair trade and other 'sustainable' coffees. In consuming countries, coffee has become a fashionable drink and coffee bar chains have expanded rapidly. At the same time, international coffee prices have fallen dramatically and producers receive the lowest prices in decades.

This book shows that the coffee paradox exists because what farmers sell and what consumers buy are becoming increasingly 'different' coffees. It is not material quality that contemporary coffee consumers pay for, but mostly symbolic quality and in-person services. As long as coffee farmers and their organizations do not control at least parts of this 'immaterial' production, they will keep receiving low prices. *The Coffee Paradox* seeks ways out from this situation by addressing some key questions: What kinds of quality attributes are combined in a coffee cup or coffee package? Who is producing these attributes? How can part of these attributes be produced by developing country farmers? To what extent are specialty and sustainable coffees achieving these objectives?

About the authors

Benoit Daviron is a French economist at the Centre de coopération internationale en recherche agronomique pour le développement (CIRAD), in Montpellier. He has published widely on issues of food policy, trade in foodstuffs, as well as tropical commodity chains, international agreements and agriculture in developing countries. He has been a Visiting Scholar at the University of California, Berkeley.

Stefano Ponte is Senior Researcher at the Danish Institute for International Studies, Copenhagen. He is co-author (with Peter Gibbon) of *Trading Down: Africa, Value Chains and the Global Economy* (Temple University Press, 2005) and author of *Farmers and Markets in Tanzania: How Policy Reforms Affect Rural Livelihoods in Africa* (James Currey, 2002). He has published extensively on commodity trade (especially coffee) and development, global value chains, the political economy of standards, agro-food markets, and rural livelihoods in developing countries.

The Coffee Paradox

Global markets, commodity trade and
the elusive promise of development

Benoit Daviron and Stefano Ponte

Zed Books
LONDON & NEW YORK

in association with the CTA

The Coffee Paradox was first published in 2005 by
Zed Books Ltd, 7 Cynthia Street, London N1 9JF, UK and
Room 400, 175 Fifth Avenue, New York, NY 10010, USA
www.zedbooks.co.uk

in association with the ACP–EU Technical Centre for Agricultural and
Rural Cooperation (CTA), Postbus 380, 6700 AJ Wageningen, The Netherlands
www.cta.int

Cover designed by Andrew Corbett
Set in 10.5/13 pt Bembo by Long House, Cumbria, UK

Distributed in the USA exclusively by Palgrave Macmillan, a division of
St Martin's Press, LLC, 175 Fifth Avenue, New York, NY 10010

A catalogue record for this book
is available from the British Library

US Cataloging-in-Publication Data
is available from the Library of Congress

ISBN   978-1-84277-457-1

Transferred to Digital Printing in 2008

Contents

Tables, figures and boxes

Tables

Figures

Boxes

Abbreviations

AAFN	alternative agro-food network
ABA	American Birding Association
ACE	Alliance of Coffee Excellence
ACP	Africa–Caribbean–Pacific (countries)
ACPC	Association of Coffee Producer Countries
AOC	Appellation d'Origine Contrôlée
ATO	alternative trade organization
CAFE	Coffee and Farmer Equity Practices Programme
CAP	Common Agricultural Policy
CBK	Coffee Board of Kenya
CDR	Centre for Development Research (Copenhagen)
CEPCO	Coordinadora Estatal de Productores de Café (Oaxaca, Mexico)
CFC	Common Fund for Commodities
cif	cost, insurance, freight (as being included in the price)
CIRAD	Centre de Coopération Internationale en Recherche Agronomique pour le Développement
CMB	Coffee Marketing Board
CQI	Coffee Quality Institute
CQP	Coffee Quality Improvement Programme
CSCE	(New York) Coffee, Sugar and Cocoa Market
CTA	Coffee and Tea Authority (Ethiopia)
DFID	Department for International Development (UK)
DOC	Denominazione di Origine Controllata
ECEA	Ethiopian Coffee Exporters Association
EPZ	export-processing zone
EU	European Union
EUREP–GAP	European Retailer Group Good Agricultural Practices
FAO	Food and Agriculture Organization
Fedecafé	Federación Nacional de Cafeteros de Colombia
FLO	Fair Trade Labelling Organizations International

fob	free on board (cost exclusive of freight and insurance)
GATT	General Agreement on Tariffs and Trade
GCC	global commodity chain
GDP	gross domestic product
GLAF	Globalization and Economic Restructuring in Africa
GVC	global value chain
HACCP	Hazard Analysis and Critical Control Point
IBC	Instituto Brasileiro do Café
ICA	international coffee agreement
ICO	International Coffee Organization
IFAD	International Fund for Agricultural Development
IFOAM	International Federation of Organic Agriculture Movements
IGO	indication of geographical origin
IIED	International Institute for Environment and Development
IISD	International Institute for Sustainable Development
IMF	International Monetary Fund
INAO	Institut National des Appellations d'Origine
IRSG	International Rubber Study Group
ISEAL	International Social and Environmental Accreditation and Labelling
ITC	International Trade Centre
ITL	Italian lira
KPCU	Kenya Planters Cooperative Union
LDC	least-developed country
LIFFE	London International Financial Futures and Options Exchange
MNC	multinational corporation
NGO	non-governmental organization
NIC	newly industrialized country
NOP	National Organic Program (US)
NYBOT	New York Board of Trade
OCA	Organic Coffee Association
OECD	Organization for Economic Cooperation and Development
OFPA	Organic Foods Production Act (US)
OTA	Organic Trade Association
PDO	Protected Designation of Origin
PGI	Protected Geographical Indication
PSP	preferred supplier program
SAI	Sustainable Agriculture Initiative
SCI	Sustainable Coffee Initiative
SCAA	Specialty Coffee Association of America

SCCF	Sustainable Coffee Cooperation Forum
SMBC	Smithsonian Migratory Bird Center
SMI	supplier-managed inventory (system)
SMR	Standard Malaysian Rubber
STABEX	Stabilization of Export Earnings
TCB	Tanzania Coffee Board
TRIPs	trade-related intellectual property rights
UCDA	Uganda Coffee Development Authority
UK	United Kingdom
UN	United Nations
UNCTAD	United Nations Conference on Trade and Development
US	United States
USAID	United States Agency for International Development
USDA	United States Department of Agriculture
WHO	World Health Organization
WTO	World Trade Organization

To Zeno William

Preface

Every day, about 2.25 billion cups of coffee are consumed in the world (Dicum and Luttinger 1999: ix). Yet the act and symbolic associations of coffee drinking are not the same as they were twenty years ago. New consumption patterns have emerged with the growing importance of specialty, fair trade, organic and even 'bird-friendly' coffees. Coffee bar and café chains have spread dramatically, although the relative coffee content of the final consumption 'experience' in these outlets is extremely low. Café chains sell an ambience and a social positioning more than just 'good' coffee. The coffee market has gone through a '*latte* revolution', where consumers can choose from (and pay dearly for) hundreds of combinations of coffee variety, origin, brewing and grinding methods, flavouring, packaging, 'social content', and ambience. Retail coffee prices continue to rise in the specialty market, and even in the mainstream market they have not decreased nearly as much as international coffee prices have. Roasters capture increasing profit margins. At the same time, coffee farmers receive prices below the cost of production.

The global value chain for coffee[1] is currently characterized by a 'coffee paradox': a 'coffee boom' in consuming countries and a 'coffee crisis' in producing countries. A paradox within this paradox is that the international coffee market is awash in coffee of 'low quality', while there is a dire shortage of 'high quality' coffee – and it is the latter that is generating sales growth. How can we explain such divergent dynamics?

Some analysts have depicted the current market situation in terms of the law of demand and supply: there is simply too much coffee in the global market. They argue that chronic oversupply – facilitated by the breakdown of the International Coffee Agreement in 1989 – arose from increased production in Brazil and Vietnam. Other analysts have explained the coffee crisis in terms of market power. They argue that the growing gap between the price of the raw material (the coffee bean) and the final product is the result of oligopolistic rents captured by an increasingly concentrated roasting industry.

In this book, we propose an explanatory framework that considers market power not simply on the basis of controlling market share, but also in relation to the ability to define the 'identity' of a coffee – in other words the ability to set the language and the reference values that determine production norms and quality standards. We argue that the coffee boom in consuming countries and the coffee crisis in producing countries can coexist because the coffee sold on the international market and the coffee sold as a final product to the consumer are becoming increasingly 'different'. This happens because it is not the *material quality* 'content' that roasters, retailers and cafés are selling, but mainly *symbolic* and *in-person service quality* attributes. As long as coffee farmers and their organizations do not control at least parts of this 'immaterial' production, they will be confined to the 'commodity problem' – even though coffee may be moving away from 'commodity status' in consuming countries.

Rather than conceptualizing coffee in different markets as beans 'more or less roasted', we propose to treat coffee as the sum of attributes produced in different geographical locations and by different actors along the value chain. Thus 'market power' is a question not only of market share but also of capturing the most valuable attributes while undermining the value of the attributes that need to be purchased.

A new consensus is emerging in both the North and the South among donor communities, policy makers, academics, and even some civil society groups – developing countries should 'trade their way out of poverty'. If tariff barriers were removed, market access would improve. If we stopped subsidizing developed country farmers, poor farmers in the South would benefit. If technical assistance was provided, non-tariff barriers such as food safety standards would be overcome. If only trade rules were fair, poverty in the world would be reduced. If producers in the South were included in global value chains, they would learn from their buyers and upgrade. There is a grain of truth in each of these statements, and some problematic aspects. For decades (and sometimes centuries) low-income countries have been producing and exporting tropical commodities, such as coffee, that encountered small tariff and non-tariff barriers, little or no competition from farmers in the North, and have been part of global value chains. They are still poor.

International trade has indeed grown dramatically in the last two decades in the global economy, and trade is an important source of revenue in developing countries. These countries are estimated to generate more than thirty times more revenue *per capita* from exports than they receive in aid – and aid flows are decreasing (Oxfam 2002a: 47; OECD/DAC database). Yet most low-income countries still depend heavily on exports of primary commodities – which have lagged behind the growth of global income. As a result, low-income countries account for only 3 per cent of income generated through exports in the global economy (UNCTAD 2002).

Coffee is produced in more than 50 developing countries and involves several million small farmers. Historically, coffee exports have been linked to several development 'success stories': Brazil at the end of the nineteenth century, Colombia and Costa Rica in the 1920s, Kenya and Côte d'Ivoire in the 1960s and early 1970s. Some of these stories have been time-bound, others have provided the basis upon which further growth and diversification occurred. In many other stories, the promise of development has been elusive. Furthermore, there has been no equivalent success story in recent decades.[2] In the governance of the global value chain for coffee, producing countries used to play an important role. Since the late 1980s, this has not been the case. Governance is firmly in the hands of actors based in the consuming countries of the North, especially roasters.

The key issue is not that these producing countries are not trading, but rather that they are not gaining much from trade. In other words, these countries are stuck in a commodity problem that has made development an elusive target. They produce similar agricultural products and labour-intensive manufactures that are flooding global markets and depressing prices. The classical questions that have been asked in relation to solving the commodity problem are: Can the gains from commodity exports be increased? Otherwise, how can low-income countries break away from relying on exports of primary commodities?

These pertinent questions have been at the centre of commodity trade analyses for at least half a century. In this book, we seek a shift in emphasis. We argue that the promise of development is an elusive one partly because global value chains are increasingly driven by large actors based in the North, and partly because low-income countries are stuck in producing and exporting goods that are valued only for their material quality attributes. Symbolic and in-person service quality attributes which provide higher value-added gains are generated in consuming countries in the North – or by Northern actors. We explain this discrepancy in value through a combination of historical political economy, global value chain analysis, and convention theory.

Throughout the book, we use the terms 'commodity' and 'primary commodity' interchangeably. Most authors dealing with the relation between commodity exports and development do not actually provide a definition of 'commodity', nor do they explain the identity of a commodity as compared to other goods, and particularly to industrial goods. Rather, they use the proxy distinction between agriculture and manufacturing, or primary and secondary sectors, instead. Others, while acknowledging that markets for labour-intensive manufactures behave like the ones for agricultural products, and that high-value fresh produce value chains are substantially different from, for example, the cocoa value chain, still have a process-based definition of commodity. In our approach, commodities are goods with a world market where most participants and transactors use the same standards to discover the same quality attributes, and for the most part only measurable attributes. At the extreme, these are goods where transactions are organized around a single global quality standard. In much of the literature, standards are determined by technology and the constraints and opportunities it generates. The history of agricultural markets suggests the opposite: standards are created to allow the existence of market transactions; they also impose their constraint on downstream transformation processes.

This kind of approach has implications in terms of what we do not cover in this book. Many of the contributions on the commodity problem and/or the coffee crisis have placed emphasis on the impact of low international prices on the livelihoods of producers in the South. That decreasing commodity prices have had a severe impact on farmers and their communities is without dispute, and has been accepted by the mainstream agro-food industry as well. Therefore, it is not our intention to focus on producer livelihoods, although we do not intend to undermine the significance of this topic. Our main aim in this book is to use the case study of coffee to recast the development problem for countries relying on commodity exports. What is the value given by the consumer to different attributes that are combined in a coffee cup or a coffee package? Who is producing these attributes? How can part of these attributes be produced in developing countries? Can developing countries capture the value of in-person service activities at all? To what extent are specialty and sustainable coffees helping achieve these objectives? In other words, what are the upgrading opportunities for developing countries and for small producers within these?

In Chapter 1, we provide a historical background to current debates on the role of commodity trade in promoting and sustaining economic growth and development in the South. First, we lay out a brief history of changes in models of commodity production and trade, starting in the fifteenth century when the long era of slave plantations began. Within this discussion, we pay particular attention to the role played by standards in creating 'commodity markets'. Second, we review the academic and policy debates on commodity trade and development. Once we have highlighted the limitations of these debates, we introduce the global value chain (GVC) framework, which is the main analytical tool used in this book. Finally, we develop a typology of quality based on material, symbolic and in-person service attributes that helps in unpacking issues of governance and the distribution of value-added increments along global value chains.

In Chapter 2, we start analysing the coffee industry. First, we provide a brief overview of how coffee flows from producer to consumer – including its material transformations. Second, we analyse historical trends in production and exports. Third, we examine various systems of coffee labour mobilization and organization of production. Fourth, we analyse a succession of different forms of market organization, including their constitutive elements such as contracts, grades and standards. Finally, we examine changes in retail and consumption patterns, focusing in particular on the *latte* revolution that has taken place in the last 25 years with the emergence of the specialty coffee industry.

In Chapter 3, we examine issues of regulation and governance in coffee value chains. In the first two sections, we analyse these issues in relation to the global value chain for coffee, following two broad periods: (1) the period before 1989, when producing countries had influence in its regulation and governance – first through the dominance of Brazil, and later through international regulation in the form of international coffee agreements (ICAs); and (2) the period following the demise of ICAs, when private sector actors based in consuming countries (especially roasters) have become the 'drivers' of the global value chain; ICAs still exist but, as we will see, have no regulatory 'bite'. In this context, particular attention is paid to the corporate strategies of key actors, especially large roasters. In the third section of this chapter, we provide in-depth case studies of regulatory changes in coffee value chains originating in four East African countries (Ethiopia, Kenya, Tanzania and Uganda). These countries have liberalized their domestic markets to different extents and with different trajectories, leading to different local outcomes of global transformation. In the final section of this chapter, we look at international coffee prices in a historical perspective. We show that the historical cycle of coffee booms and busts has become much less pronounced since the 1970s – and thus that the current coffee crisis is quite different from those in the 1930s and the 1960s. We also show that changes in the ownership of coffee stocks (and their different degrees of availability) have much to say about the current crisis, which is characterized for the first time in history by low international prices *and* low levels of stocks.

In Chapter 4, we apply the analytical framework provided in Chapter 1 to coffee quality. We follow coffee quality from farm to cup, not only in its material attributes, but also in its symbolic and in-person service attributes. As in Chapter 3, the focus in terms of producing countries is on East Africa. In consuming countries, we cover both mainstream and specialty markets. Because types and patterns of consumption vary from country to country, more detailed information is provided in relation to the US and Italy.

In Chapter 5, we examine the new frontier of coffee quality: sustainability. Sustainability certifications, codes of conduct, and sourcing guidelines are multiplying and becoming mainstream. They are extending the content of symbolic quality attributes beyond brand, ambience of consumption and packaging design (among others) by embedding environmental and socio-economic preoccupations in the description of coffee. They are also re-framing governance, away from state-controlled processes and towards more hybrid public/private dynamics, if not outright private ones. First, we evaluate the impact on supposed beneficiaries of four groups of coffee certifications: organic, fair trade, shade-grown and Utz Kapeh. Then we analyse private and public/private initiatives in the realm of sustainability, such as the Starbucks Coffee and Farmer Equity Practices (CAFE) Programme and the Common Code for the Coffee Community.

Chapter 6 is structured in two main parts. In the first part, we provide empirical evidence of value distribution along the global value chain for coffee and specific value chains (various combinations of Uganda and Tanzania coffees on the one side, and mainstream retail, bar consumption, and sustainability coffees in the US and Italy on the other). This analysis provides a stark picture of inequalities along coffee value chains. However, singling out what attributes are valued at what points of value chains also helps to identify possible solutions to the commodity problem. We examine the more theoretical underpinnings of these solutions in the second part of this chapter. Four aspects are covered in some depth: (1) the role of quality conventions in changing the governance of value chains; (2) whether the purported transparency of alternative commodity networks helps producers; (3) territoriality as a vehicle for linking responsibility with specific places; and (4) the potential and real roles of consumers and retailers in stimulating social change.

We lay out the more practical and policy-oriented aspects of solving the commodity problem in Chapter 7. We first examine what regulation can and cannot do for producers given the changes in governance of value chains that have taken place in the last 25 years. We also critique business- and donor-oriented solutions to the coffee crisis that have been proposed thus far. Second, we provide an eclectic menu of possible solutions, with specific focus on unorthodox approaches that have received less attention in policy circles so far: (1) how to improve sustainability initiatives so that they really benefit producers; (2) how to facilitate producers' control of symbolic quality attributes through indication of geographic origin (IGO) systems; and (3) how to 'make hedonism work for the South'. While these approaches, at first sight, seem to relate mostly to niche markets, we will show that they have broad implications for the future of mainstream markets as well.

Benoit Daviron's contribution to this book is the product of two decades of research and study dedicated to coffee and other tropical commodities. Most of this time has been spent as a researcher at the Centre de Coopération International en Recherche Agronomique pour le Développement (CIRAD), Montpellier. Some of the ideas and arguments presented in this book have been discussed with several CIRAD colleagues, more specifically with Tancrède Voituriez and Bruno Losch, and with François Lerin from the Institut Agronomique Méditerranéen. He would like to thank them for their support and friendship. Benoit started some of the background work for this book during a one-year stay as a visiting scholar at the University of California, Berkeley. He is grateful to Alain de Janvry for his kindness and hospitality. He would also like to thank Vinod Aggarwal, Peter Evans and Andrew Janos for the stimulating seminars they offered during this time.

Stefano Ponte's contribution to this book is based on work he has been carrying out on agro-food markets and rural livelihoods in Africa since the mid-1990s. More specific research on coffee took place between 1999 and 2003 under a research programme on Globalization and Economic Restructuring in Africa (GLAF) at the Centre for Development Research (CDR), Copenhagen (from 2003, Danish Institute for International Studies). The programme was funded with contributions from the Danish Social Science Research Council (SSF) and the Danish Development Studies Research Council (RUF), which he gratefully acknowledges. The programme involved Peter Gibbon, Britt Noehr Jensen, Marianne Nylandsted Larsen, Poul Ove Pedersen and Lotte Thomsen from CDR; Niels Fold from the Institute of Geography, University of Copenhagen; and Michael Friis Jensen from the Institute of Economics, Danish Royal Veterinary and Agricultural University. Stefano is deeply indebted to his colleagues for their intellectual stimulation, social companionship and hard work during these years.

In connection to the GLAF programme, Stefano carried out fieldwork in Ethiopia, Kenya, Tanzania, Uganda, Italy and the USA. He received support and cooperation from too many people to be listed here. However, special thanks are due to Henry Ngabirano of the Uganda Coffee Development Authority, Leslie Omari of the Tanzania Coffee Board, Tsegaye Berhane of the Coffee and Tea Authority (Ethiopia), and Karega Mutahi of the Coffee Board of Kenya. While in East Africa, Stefano was affiliated to the Development Studies Institute,

Sokoine University of Agriculture, Morogoro (Tanzania) and the Economic Policy Research Centre, Makerere University, Kampala (Uganda). He would like to acknowledge the support received at these two institutions.

Invaluable feedback and constructive criticism on earlier drafts of this book and related papers were provided by many scholars, policy makers and activists. The authors would like to thank Henry Bernstein, Andy Carlton, Mette Christensen, Kathrine Fjendbo, Martin Fowler, Deepa George, Gary Gereffi, Daniele Giovannucci, Alberto Hesse, Raphie Kaplinsky, Paul Katzeff, Fred Kawuma, Alf Kramer, Anders Riel Muller, Wim Pelupessy, James Pletcher, Jason Potts, Colin Poulton, Lisa Richey, Peter Robbins, Anne Marie Tallontire, Pauline Tiffen, Joni Valkila and Bill Vorley. Special thanks go to Peter Baker, Lawrence Busch, Emmanuelle Cheyns, Peter Gibbon, Diego Pizano, Laura Raynolds, Bertrand Sallée, and Morten Scholer, who read the whole manuscript and provided essential comments.

All errors and omissions are entirely our responsibility. Finally, the listing of the authors' names is strictly alphabetical. They have both contributed equally to the book and are equally responsible for its limitations.

Notes

1 In this book, we use both the terms 'global value chain for coffee' and 'coffee value chains'. The first term is used to analyse general features in relation to the movement of coffee from production to consumption. The second term is used when a specific strand of the global value chain for coffee is examined (either at the production or consumption ends, or both). Thus, we will talk about one global value chain for coffee, but also about distinct coffee value chains, such as the Uganda-to-Italy chain for Robusta coffee, or the Tanzania-to-US chain for specialty Mild Arabica coffee.

2 From the point of view of economic growth, the performance of Vietnam could be seen as a success story. However, it was not one mainly based on coffee. The maximum share of the value of coffee exports over total exports was 11 per cent in 1995 (and 30 per cent of agricultural exports during that year). In the early 2000s, it was around 2 per cent (and 10 per cent of agricultural exports). The share of coffee in the past exports of Brazil, Colombia, Costa Rica, Kenya and Côte d'Ivoire was much higher.

1

Commodity trade, development and global value chains

In this chapter, we provide some essential historical and analytical elements for interpreting the 'commodity problem' and its development implications in the South. This analysis, in turn, will introduce the reader to the case study of coffee presented in the following chapters. The first part of the chapter is dedicated to a brief history of the evolution of labour mobilization systems, forms of coordination and the use of standards in tropical commodity production and trade. The second part builds upon this history to analyse the debates on the relationship between commodity trade and development that emerged after the Second World War – debates that are still at the core of international policy discussions, most recently in relation to World Trade Organization (WTO) negotiations. The third part introduces the reader to global value chain (GVC) analysis. It lays out its methodological and theoretical contribution (and limitations) in understanding the development-relevant issues of governance, power, equity and upgrading. The fourth and final part of this chapter takes the discussion of commodity trade and development in a new direction. Here, the commodity problem is linked to the ability/inability of producers to create and control the value embedded in *material, symbolic* and *in-person service* quality attributes of a product. In following chapters, this typology, and its related quality focus, will help understanding the distribution of value along coffee chains and its dynamics.

Division of labour and coordination in commodity production and trade: historical background

During the last century, value chains for tropical products have been organized around a fairly stable division of labour based on the following succession of independent agents: producer, primary processer/middle person, exporter, international trader, industrial processer, wholesaler, retailer and consumer. This specific division of labour supposes the existence of market transactions between each of these agents. One of these transactions (the one between exporter and international trader) entails the exchange of a specific category of good called 'commodity' – the description, identity and price discovery mechanism of which are internationally recognized. In international trade, the description of a commodity is incorporated in a grade – within the framework of a standard. The identity of this commodity is based on national origin, sometimes coupled with a generic regional identity, rather than on a brand or a specific *terroir* (a smaller region with specific and unique agro-ecological traits). Finally, the price of the commodity is defined in relation to the price set in a futures market, where transactions are not about the physical exchange of actual products, but about paper contracts. The purpose of futures markets is to provide hedging against risk. Futures prices are short-term syntheses of market fundamentals (production, consumption and stocks) and technical factors (hedging, trend following, reactions to trigger signals). This organization, which we call the 'classical organization' of tropical value chains, emerged between the middle of the nineteenth century and 1920 (depending on the product).

In the rest of this section, we first highlight the historical transition between the plantation model, which characterized production and trade in tropical commodities between the fifteenth century and the second part of the nineteenth century, and the classical organization. Second, we explain how the latter system evolved as a result of the development of standards.

Value chains for tropical commodities: from the plantation complex to the classical organization

Invented in the fifteenth century for sugar cane, the plantation model dominated the production of tropical commodities until the last quarter of the nineteenth century (Curtin 1990). The planter – or *planteur, fazendeiro, finquero* – was a central actor in this model. Owner of the land and of the processing equipment, the planter was the entrepreneur of tropical export agriculture. For centuries, African slaves supplied almost all the labour for the plantations. After 1830, in response to the abolition of slavery in the British colonies of the Caribbean, a new

indenture labour system was developed. This system brought contracted Indian labour to work in the sugar plantations (Northrup 1995).

According to Chandler (1977: 64) 'until the nineteenth century, in
both the United States and Europe there were many more large-scale
enterprises in agriculture than in industry'. However, tropical plantations differed from manufacturing enterprises in the US and Europe not
only in terms of scale (the former were larger) but also in terms of
labour organization. As Fogel (1989: 25–6) notes,

> the plantation success was closely related to the development of a new
> industrial labour discipline.... The industrial discipline, so difficult to bring
> about in the factories of free England and free New England, was achieved
> on sugar plantations more than a century earlier – partly because sugar pro-
> duction lent itself to a minute division of labour, partly because of the
> invention of the gang system, which provided a powerful instrument for the
> supervision and control of labour, and partly because of the extraordinary
> degree of force that planters were allowed to bring to bear on enslaved black
> labour.

According to Sheridan (1969: 8) '[s]lave labour called for large-scale
units of production and control, partly to take advantage of specialization and division of labour, partly to minimize the cost of supervision,
and partly to distribute fixed capital cost over a wide range'. In addition
to these factors, the emergence of large-scale units was also linked to
the marketing system of the product. As argued by Weber (1927), the
distance from the production site to the consumer market was an
important variable in the organization of production. Access to the
consumer market for tropical products was particularly problematic and
entailed longer distances and transit times. For the agent owning the
product during its transportation from the tropical region to the
consuming country, distance and time implied risk and need for credit.
Until the middle of the nineteenth century, in most cases, the planter
owned the product until its point of sale in a European country, and
therefore assumed the related risk. The operation of bringing the
product from the plantation to the European market was centrally
organized by a specific actor: the factor.

The factorage system had its origin in the West Indies sugar
economy. 'The factor was the home agent of the colonial planter. He
was at once his merchant and banker. He bought the goods which the
planter has to purchase at home and sold for him the product return in

exchange' (Holt Stone 1915: 557). In practice, the factor was much more than an agent of the planter in the European market. The factor dealt with: (1) the transportation of the product by contracting with the railway company and the shipper; (2) the storage of the product by contracting with warehouse facilities owners in the country of destination; (3) insurance and payment of taxes and harbour fees; (4) the sorting of the product in grades; and (5) the broker in charge of the sale. The factor could also arrange the supply of new slaves for the plantation, provide equipment and consumer goods to the planters, and even act as a guardian of the planter's children while they were schooled in England. Later, in the Southern United States, the factor also kept the account book of the cotton plantation.

The factor did not own the product. He/she received the product, sold it in auction markets on behalf of the plantation owner, and received a commission.[1] The provision of credit to the planter was also an important activity carried out by the factor. Credit was initially conceived as an advance on consignment but in fact, as a way to secure product supply, the factor provided credit well before he received the product and even before the beginning of the harvest. Moreover, most of the goods the factor supplied to the planter were provided on credit. Based initially in Europe, and above all in England, the factor system partly moved to the producing territories, such as the US.

It was around the middle of the nineteenth century in the US that the classical organization of commodity markets appeared. Two innovations played a decisive role in this evolution: (1) the introduction of a standard to grade products; and (2) the development of a futures market. These two institutions emerged first in the grain trade in Chicago. They resulted in the transformation of the commission merchant into a buyer merchant. Later, these innovations spread to cotton and other products. In the case of cotton, changes were not limited to marketing technologies, but also involved a radical transformation of labour organization that followed the Civil War and the abolition of slavery. Former slaves became small-scale tenants. Thus, the previous gang system and the extreme division of labour in the plantations disappeared.

Cronon (1991) offers a fascinating account of the historical process that led to the creation of grains standards and the Chicago Board of Trade. Until the middle of the nineteenth century, grains (mostly corn and wheat) produced by the prairie farmers were sold in New Orleans or in the East Coast cities under a marketing system that was similar to the one seen above for tropical products. The ownership rights to grain remained with its original shipper until it reached the point of final sale. A commission merchant, the equivalent of the planter's factor, organized the transportation, storage and sale of the grain and sometimes provided credit and insurance to the shipper. Using the river, the grain was transported in sacks and remained untouched from the farm to the flour mill. According to Cronon (*ibid*.: 109) '[a] farm family, sending a load of wheat from Illinois to New York, could still have recovered that same wheat, packed with a bill of lading inside its original sacks, in a Manhattan warehouse several weeks later'.

The first impulse for change came from the expansion of railroads. Grain flows were reoriented from St Louis and New Orleans to Chicago and the Great Lakes. New incentives to achieve 'economies of speed' appeared. The response to these incentives was the development of a specific technical innovation: the steam-powered grain elevator. Built in the 1850s, these elevators changed the whole organization of marketing. The ability to handle and transport grain without the use of sacks, and to mix grains from several farmers in the bin of an elevator, meant that the ownership could not remain with the farmer during handling and transport as before. Here the response was institutional rather than technical, and led to the creation of the Chicago Board of Trade (Cronon 1991).

The Chicago Board of Trade was initially a voluntary association of grain traders aimed at promoting the city and at dealing with the day-to-day problems of the grain market. In 1856, however, the Board created a uniform wheat standard for the city – based on three grades. This act was decisive for the reorganization of the grain trade in the US. Cronon states that

> [a]s long as one treated a shipment of wheat or corn as if it possessed unique characteristics that distinguished it from all other lots of grain, mixing was impossible. But if instead a shipment represented a particular 'grade' of grain, then there was no harm in mixing it with other grain of the same grade. Farmers and shippers delivered grain to a warehouse and got in return a receipt that they or anyone else could redeem at will. Anyone who gave the receipt back to the elevator got in return not the *original* lot of grain but an equal quantity of *equally graded* grain. A person who owned grain

could conveniently sell it to a buyer simply by selling the elevator receipt, and as long as both agreed that they were exchanging equivalent quantities of like grain – rather than the physical grain that the seller had originally deposited in the elevator – both left happy at the end of the transaction. (1991: 116)

After 1848, the building of the telegraph network led to the synchronization of price movements between Chicago, the hub of prairie grain supply, and the East Coast – its major consumer market. The emergence of the telegraph and the grain standard enabled the sale of a grain lot *before* it moved from Chicago to New York (on the basis of a so-called 'to arrive' contract). The standard enabled the buyer to know exactly what would be received. The telegraph enabled the two parties to build a contract on a common price basis. According to Cronon, the '"to arrive" contract in combination with standardized elevator receipt made possible Chicago's greatest innovation in the grain trade: the futures market' (1991: 124). Indeed, from then on, a trader could sell a 'contract to arrive' without owning the grain. The trader would then hope to buy the grain, just before the time of delivery, by buying elevator receipts at a cheaper price than the one stipulated in the contract. Until delivery, or just before delivery, this contract could be resold several times between traders.

Based initially on the 'contract to arrive', this speculative activity was subsequently (after 1865) organized by the Chicago Board of Trade through a 'future contract'. This contract defines a specific grade of grain, a specific volume and a specific date of delivery. This contract 'could be bought and sold quite independently of the physical grain that might or might not be moving through the city' (Cronon 1991: 146). The last step in the building of a modern commodity market was the invention of hedging. Hedging emerged and spread along with futures markets in the third quarter of the nineteenth century (Rothstein 1983). Hedging means using future contracts as insurance. In practice, it entails the buying (or selling) of a future contract simultaneously with the selling (or buying) of 'real' grain. Hedging enables operators, anxious to buy grain and to keep it for a while before selling it in the same form (or in a transformed form, flour for example), to protect themselves against price fluctuation (specifically, a price fall). Because the fluctuations in the future contract are linked to the fluctuation on the 'real' grain market, carrying out the inverse operation in the futures market enables the trader to minimize the loss (or the gain) realized in the 'real' grain market.

Hedging seems to have been first used by traders who bought grain in Chicago and sold it to exporters in New York (Rothstein 1983). The diffusion of hedging, as an insurance against price fluctuation, occurred simultaneously with a change in the merchant function, where merchants increasingly bought grain on a cash basis rather than on consignment. Being protected against the risk of selling at a lower price than the price paid at purchase, the merchant could now become the owner of the product and hold it for a long time. Because of this new ability, previously distant market transactions were suddenly brought close to small towns or even the farm gate. Subsequently, the necessity for the farmer to hold the product for months before selling disappeared.

The organization of cotton marketing in the US followed more or less the same evolution observed in grains. With the emergence of the new railway and telegraph network, cotton factors were substituted by traders buying the fibre directly in the countryside (Woodman 1966; Woodman 1968). As a consequence, in 1870 the New York Cotton Exchange opened its doors. The New Orleans exchange opened one year later. The major organizational change in the cotton sector was the emergence of tenants that displaced the plantation system. Related to this was the replacement of the gang system by a labour organization system based on kinship. As soon as the North defeated the South, the former slaves refused all labour organization that in any way resembled that of the former slave plantations. The wage-earning system promoted by planters that were seeking to conserve their previous organization was widely rejected. Furthermore, the abandoning of any agrarian reform project strongly limited the establishment of direct farming systems. Although the percentage of black families (as categorized by Kolchin) in the South purchasing farmland increased from 2 per cent in 1870 to 21 per cent in 1890, it reached only 24 per cent in 1910 (Kolchin 1993).

After a brief trial period, the former plantation owners massively opted for sharecropping. First, just after the Civil War, owners paid sharecroppers in kind (a sixth or an eighth of the harvest in the early years, rising later to a quarter) and provided them with a house, draught animals and sometimes seeds. However, the share rental system soon became dominant. In this system, the harvest was divided in equal parts but the sharecroppers had to find their own food, tools, livestock and accommodation. Even if sharecroppers were largely dependent on (and exploited by) plantation owners, the end of the gang system entailed no centralized coordination of labour in terms of cultivation and harvesting times. This constituted a revolutionary change in tropical crop production.

The process initiated in the middle of the nineteenth century for grains and cotton in the US spread to other products during the following decade. Between the end of the nineteenth century and 1920, most tropical products switched from the plantation model to specialized household cultivation. The Ghanaian smallholder displaced the São Tomé *roça* (estate). The 'native' cultivating 'jungle rubber' displaced the European rubber estate. As we will see later, Colombian peasants provoked the crisis of the Brazilian *fazendeiros*. This process created a sort of inversion in industrial organization between agriculture and manufacturing. Starting with a situation of large-scale enterprises in agriculture and small-scale manufactures, the nineteenth century ended with small-scale production and low vertical integration in agriculture and large and vertically integrated firms in manufacture. As the managerial revolution took place in manufacturing (see Chandler 1977), a 'specialized household' revolution occurred in agriculture. The two revolutions took place first in the US, then spread to the rest of the world.

Standardization and the organization of production

A vast amount of academic literature has examined the relative efficiency of large-scale versus small-scale units in agricultural production. In the course of the twentieth century, the dominant preference among economists (except in the Soviet Union and in China) broadly shifted from large-scale to small-scale production. In both camps, the core arguments were related to technological constraints. Whereas in the past pro-large-scale economists referred to the benefits of economies of scale (Kautsky 1988), current pro-small-scale economists underline the diseconomies of labour monitoring deriving from uncontrolled biological processes and spatial dispersion (Binswanger and Rosenweig 1986; Hayami 1996). Although the latter arguments are correct in explaining the current predominance of small-scale family labour units, they cannot account for the historical shift from large-scale to small-scale units of production. They also underestimate the diversity of technology available to different producers and regions for the same crop.

To prove their efficiency *vis-à-vis* large-scale units, small-scale units needed to operate in an environment of open competition. Open competition means first and foremost equal access to the market. Equal market access occurred during the last quarter of the nineteenth century with the transformation of the merchant function, from commission merchant or factor to trader. Equal market access was also facilitated by the creation of global standards that organized full interchangeability between producers independently of their size. Thus, for agricultural products, and in particular for tropical products, the household production revolution was accompanied – if not caused – by the emergence of traders and the creation of standards (Daviron 2002).[2]

The first standard for cocoa was created in 1925 to enable the functioning of the New York futures market. The standardization of rubber started in 1913 with the founding of the London Rubber Trade Association. This association set up a Standard Quality Committee during its first year of operation with the purpose of defining a standard and providing arbitration for sales concluded with reference to this standard. However, in 1928, the US Rubber Manufacturers Association published its own standard (Rondet 1997). Like the cotton standard, it was based on the distribution of sets of reference samples to operators. It soon became the dominant standard in the market, reflecting the influence of US tyre manufacturers in the international rubber market. This standard was subsequently renegotiated by producers, users and traders at conferences organized by the International Rubber Study Group (IRSG). In 1952, these negotiations resulted in the so-called Green Book, a globally agreed document defining the various smoked sheet and crepe[3] classes recognized in international trade.

During the early stages, the standardization of tropical products was accompanied by a gradual broadening of the area of operation of standards, starting from the basis of national-level standards of dominant producing countries. Cotton, the best illustration of this process, experienced a transition from the overlap of local standards, to the development of a national standard, and then to the formulation of an international standard. International standards progressively emerged for all the traditional tropical products: in 1925 for cotton, 1952 for rubber, and 1963 for cocoa. Generally, this happened at the instigation of the dominant producing country, using its standard as a model – the United States for cotton, Malaysia for rubber, Ghana for cocoa.

However, these international standards were rarely adopted in unchanged form by other producing countries, and constituted a reference for the drafting of national standards. Standardization was therefore mainly conducted at the national level. As a result, reference to the national origin became, and remains, to a large extent an essential component of the qualification system for tropical products.

Yet, the product characterization criteria laid down in various standards remains extremely generic. Cleanliness and absence of damage (mould or insect damage) are the main variables considered. The different grades are defined according to the amount of impurities present in a sample (foreign matter or deteriorated product). The standard for sheet and crepe rubber laid down in the Green Book is limited solely to cleanliness.[4] A further factor in the case of cocoa is the presence of slaty or violet beans, indicating possibly inadequate fermentation and hence a potentially weak chocolate aroma. The general appearance and staple length of cotton is added to cleanliness criteria. These criteria allow simple methods of testing and product acceptance. Visual inspection is dominant, even though it might be preceded by a knife cut (the cut test for cocoa) or by stretching the product between the thumbs (pulling cotton). In this situation, product qualification is based mainly on the know-how of the person performing the visual inspection and does not require any special equipment.

The generic standards used to qualify tropical commodities are thus characterized on the one hand by the absence or minor role of processability criteria, and on the other hand by the absence of interest in their local specificities. Finally, these standards reflect the comparative weakness of the quality requirements of the user industries and above all the absence of demand for variety. From this point of view, standards were developed to define quality in a mass production economy. The reduction of the diversity available that accompanied the creation of national standards can be seen as the price that consumers paid for the development of low-cost, small-scale production (in comparison to the costs incurred by large plantations).

The discussion carried out so far has direct implications for what will be discussed in the next chapters. The trend towards product differentiation, and the proliferation of standards that goes with it, has shaped the organization of value chains for tropical commodities – and the feasibility of small-scale production in particular. To the extreme, this could lead to the re-emergence, in a different guise, of the plantation model of commodity production and trade. In the next section, we trace the debate on commodities and development. As we will show, standards and quality issues do not feature prominently in the present form of this debate. To partially address this shortcoming, in the rest of this chapter we take a quality/standards reading of upgrading in GVCs. We will come back to quality and standards issues in all the other chapters of the book: in Chapter 2, in relation to the historical emergence of standards in coffee; in Chapter 3, as a tool to understand changes in governance in the global value chain for coffee; in Chapter 4, in particular, we analyse the dynamics of quality evaluation as coffee moves from production to consumption; in Chapter 5, we examine the present and future role of sustainability standards; in Chapters 6 and 7, we use a quality reading to understand the distribution of value added along coffee value chains, and to highlight overall conceptual and policy implications.

Commodities and development: the debate

The relation between commodity trade and development has been the subject of debates and analyses for several decades. The issue of management of commodity markets, however, dates back to the nineteenth century, before the advent of the development project of the post-Second World War era. From the end of the nineteenth century to 1920, the management of international commodities was considered a private problem. Associations of farmers or estate owners tried to influence price formation by organizing collective infrastructure to store commodities. Collective action of this kind was attempted in cocoa (Clarence-Smith 2000), rubber, tea and coffee (see Chapter 3). After the First World War and the Great Depression, the management of commodity markets became increasingly an affair of the state. The commodity problem moved from being a farmers' problem to being an issue of national wealth and growth (McMichael 2000). With the adoption of import substitution strategies and a central focus on industrialization in the 1960s and 1970s, this version of the national interest dominated policy making to the detriment of farmers' interests.

The counter-revolution in development economics of the 1980s and the increasing concern for poverty introduced a new shift, with a focus on deregulation, market liberalization and export-oriented growth. In this framework, primary commodities did not have a special place in trade and development policy. Countries were advised to export whatever product they had a comparative advantage in – whether that was primary commodities, labour-intensive manufactures, high technologies, or services (but not labour). More recently, new preoccupations have been raised in relation to 'unfair' trade practices in commodity trade, especially in terms of subsidization of agriculture in developed countries and skewed distribution of value added along value chains. New attention has been placed on commodities, from the cotton and commodity initiatives presented during the WTO Doha Round negotiations, to fair trade and related certifications and codes of conduct guaranteeing the sustainability of commodity production and trade. Table 1.1 summarizes the main features of these debates. The headings in the first column (debate and period) are also the titles of each subsection that follows.

The agricultural crisis

For about 20 years following the end of the First World War, the debates and actions on commodity management turned around the agricultural market crisis or, in other words, how to deal with the structural – and apparently permanent – oversupply of agricultural products. At that time, supporting farmers' incomes was the main objective of state intervention in commodity markets – at least in industrialized nations. Many analysts argued that, because of the excess of labour in agriculture, agricultural supply did not respond to price decreases and did not follow the business cycle (Schultz 1945). Others (Means 1935, among others) underlined the contrast between the working of markets for manufactured goods and for agricultural commodities. Means shows that, during the 1930s, the supply of manufactured goods decreased while prices remained stable. On the contrary, the supply of agricultural commodities remained stable while prices fell. For Means (*ibid.*), this opposite behaviour reflected different market structures – oligopoly in manufacture, perfect competition in agriculture.

In this context, state intervention in commodity markets was based on a double justification. First, a stabilization policy in agricultural markets was meant to guarantee parity between the industrial sector and agriculture. Second, a policy supporting farm incomes was meant

Table 1.1 Summary of the historical debates on commodity markets and development

Debate and period	Development problem	Key indicator	Main causes of problem
The agricultural crisis (1920s–1940s)	Farmers' income; National wealth and growth (business cycle)	Ratio of agricultural prices/industrial prices	Price inelasticity of supply; Abundance of production factors in agriculture; Market structures
Structuralism (1950s–1970s)	Import capacity; Wealth of countries exporting primary commodities	Terms of trade (ratio of export unit value/import unit value)	Unlimited supply of labour; Price inelasticity of demand
The counter-revolution in development economics (1980s–)	Rural poverty	Ratio of farmer price/export price	Direct and indirect taxation; State intervention in markets
Unfair trade (1980s–)	Export incomes of countries exporting agricultural commodities; Rural poverty; International inequalities	Amount of subsidies by export unit or production unit; Barriers to trade; Ratio of farm-gate (or export-level) price to consumer price; Levels of oligopoly	Unfair trade rules; Agricultural protectionism in developed countries; Market power of traders, processers and retailers

to stabilize the whole economy, since agriculture was not thought to follow the business cycle. In this perspective, governments sought to counteract the business cycle by taking advantage of the inelasticity of agricultural supply. This was based on the idea that price decreases in commodity markets were a problem not only for farmers, but also for society as a whole. In a Keynesian perspective, farmer income support was part of an overall macroeconomic stabilization package.

In the framework of the Keynesian policies adopted after the Second World War, foreign trade was subordinated to the domestic goals of price stability and full use of national resources – full employment in particular. Exports, like public expenditure, participated in the relaunching of the economy by increasing the outlets for a nation's companies. In agriculture, the search for stability implied a strict partitioning between domestic and international markets. Stabilization policies elaborated during the Great Depression and the Second World War included instruments that ensured the disconnection between domestic prices and international prices, such as import quotas, variable levies and export subsidies. World markets were fragmented into a sum of disconnected national – or imperial – markets. In a sense, international markets operated like canal locks between national markets, handling the transfer of products without calling into question the level or the stability of prices at the national level (Johnson 1973). Except for 'exotic products', countries traded only surpluses and deficits in international markets – in quantities required to ensure the equilibrium and hence the stability of the domestic market. Dumping policies illustrate the use of the international market as an overflow outlet. Starting in the 1930s, the US Department of Agriculture used dumping to eliminate surplus production from the domestic market (Wallace 1934).

To limit the strong trend toward world market fragmentation, two different projects emerged during and in the years after the Second World War (Daviron and Voituriez 2003). The aim of the first project was to reproduce, at the world level, the policies existing at the national levels. The supporters of this project wanted a planned integration of the world market. They promoted a world-level coordination mechanism that would ensure coherence between import and export needs as defined in national plans.[5] Part of the US administration (including the Department of Agriculture) supported this project of an 'organized international trade'. On the basis of the inter-war experience, the Department of Agriculture promoted the creation of international agreements that would organize supply control policies – as the 1938 Agricultural Adjustment Act had done.

The second project promoted a gradual reunification of the world market through the implementation of trade liberalization policies. This project was promoted, among others, by the US State Department. Economists like Schultz proposed to liberalize agricultural trade and to use deficiency payments instead of trade barriers. The famous Keynes proposal to create an international organization 'for steadying the price of primary products and the holding of buffer stocks' is part of the same project (Keynes 1942/1980). Presented in 1943, during the Hot Springs Anglo-American Conference, the proposal made sense only in view of eventually opening up the world market. The argument was summarized by a US economist some years later: '[t]he real argument for stabilization is that, without it, trade and production restrictions that almost invariably outlast the crisis which evokes them are likely to be imposed by governments' (Mason 1952: 19). In other words, the main objective of national agricultural policies implementing barriers to trade was to stabilize domestic prices. Thus, if these barriers were to be dismantled then international prices would have to be stabilized – otherwise such a dismantling would have faced strong political opposition.

Both projects were defended in 1947 at the Havana Conference dedicated to the creation of an International Trade Organization. However, neither of them survived. The idea of international commodity agreements was inserted in the Havana Charter, but only as a provisional tool to manage temporary crises in agriculture. Liberalization of agricultural markets was not implemented. The International Trade Organization was not created. Its much more modest substitute, the General Agreement on Tariffs and Trade (GATT), recognized the legitimacy of agricultural protectionism (this continued until the end of the Uruguay Round in 1994). As a result, the international economic regime of the post-Second World War period did not have any general framework for organizing international cooperation in the field of commodity markets.

Structuralism

The end of the Second World War witnessed the emergence (presaged by the Atlantic Charter) of the development project, or 'the adoption of the European model across the formerly colonial world' (McMichael 2000: 7). In this context, the impact of commodity exports on the 'wealth of nations' became a key issue. Attention shifted from farmers' incomes to export revenues, the international division of labour, and the gains or advantages to be expected from commodity exports.

In the 1950s, several works converged around a negative vision of commodity exports. Singer (1950) and Prebisch (1950) are the most famous representatives of this line of thought. They elaborated three arguments against specialization in primary commodity exports. First, primary commodity export sectors were considered to be external to 'underdeveloped areas'. According to Singer, 'they are really an outpost of the economies of more developed investing countries' (Singer 1950: 475). The production of primary commodities for export was thus viewed as the result of foreign investment by firms (plantations, mines). Second, primary commodity exports were seen as using resources that could have been better used in manufacturing. The latter was thought not only to create immediate benefits but also to have a positive impact on 'the general level of education, skills, lifestyles, inventiveness, habits, store of technology, creation of new demand, etc.' (*ibid.*: 476). Third, the terms of trade between primary commodities and manufactured goods was thought to be deteriorating over time.

This third argument will be the longest-lasting in future debates, as well as the most controversial one. According to Singer and Prebisch, the main explanation for the deterioration of terms of trade for primary commodities lay in the inability of exporting countries (the periphery) to benefit from their productivity gains – contrary to what happened in countries that exported manufactured goods (the centre). In the periphery, productivity gains caused declining primary commodity prices; in the centre, productivity gains led to higher salaries for labour and higher profits for capitalists. For Singer, this unequal distribution of productivity gain was to be interpreted in relation to demand elasticity, lower for raw materials than for manufactured goods. For Prebisch, this was primarily the result of the low collective action capacity of workers in the South compared with those in the North.

In terms of the solution to the commodity problem, these authors converged to endorse the objective of industrialization. For commodity-exporting countries, the creation of a manufacturing sector was seen as the way of escaping the international division of labour. As a result, import substitution strategies, aiming at substituting the domestic supply of manufactures for imports, became a major component of development strategies. To finance the process of industrialization, developing countries taxed the primary sector heavily. In the 1950s and the beginning of the 1960s, most of these analysts were in favour of a high rate of taxation on agricultural producers. This was justified by the view that farmers, and even more African farmers, were relatively

Table 1.2 The causes of deterioration of terms of trade for primary
commodities, according to different authors

Cause of deterioration of terms of trade	Authors
Supply side	
• Wages for unionized workers in developed countries rise; monopolistic pricing	Prebisch (1949; 1950), Singer (1950), Myrdal (1956; 1957), Emmanuel (1972), Kaldor (1963a), UNCTAD (1982)
• Wages and earnings in developing countries' export sectors remain stable because of unlimited supply of labour	Lewis (1954), Prebisch (1950)
• Lack of flexibility for economic adjustment in developing countries; structural rigidity in primary production	Kindelberger (1956), Myrdal (1956; 1957)
Demand side	
• Falling demand in developed countries due to (1) technological progress that reduces primary inputs in manufactured output and (2) artificial substitutes	Bernstein (1960), Singer (1950), Kaldor (1963a), UNCTAD (1982)
• Protectionism in developed countries that reduces imports from less developed countries	Prebisch (1964), UNCTAD (1982)
• Engel's law (the income elasticity of demand for food decreases with increasing income)	Kindelberger (1943; 1950), Prebisch (1964), Schultz (1961), Nurkse (1959), Porter (1970)

Source: Adapted from Dialosavvas and Scandizzo (1991).

price-insensitive and had a low propensity to save (see, for example, Kaldor 1963b).

Discussions on possible international cooperation for managing commodity markets returned to the fore in the 1950s, and even more prominently in the 1960s with the organization of the first United Nations Conference on Trade and Development (UNCTAD) and the creation of its permanent secretariat. UNCTAD, promoted by

Prebisch, represented the most ambitious and coherent attempt to solve the development implications of the primary commodity problem. What was new in the 1960s, in comparison to the 1940s, was the link between commodity management and the import substitution policies adopted in developing countries.

In spite of high taxation, the primary sector maintained a predominant place in developing country exports. Moreover, primary commodity exports tended to be concentrated on a limited number of products with a 'natural' competitive advantage. On the contrary, manufacturers were not able to export. These factors must be interpreted in relation to the economic instruments used to encourage the growth of the manufacturing sector: currency overvaluation and high import tariffs for final industrial goods. Currency overvaluation was aimed at lowering the price of imported equipment goods necessary for the manufacturing sector. At the same time, it acted as an indirect taxation on the export sector – operating a financial transfer from the export sector to the domestic manufacturing sector. Yet the latter supplied a small domestic market and thus could not benefit from the scale economies that developed country manufacturers had. As a result of their high cost structure, local manufacturers could not be competitive in world markets. At the same time, import needs increased because of rising demand for equipment goods and machinery. Thus, when the Korean War ended in 1953, and international prices for commodities began to drop dramatically, countries following import substitution strategies started to experience massive deficits of their balance of payments (see Furtado 1970; Hirschman 1968; Cardoso and Faletto 1979).

The main objective of UNCTAD was to help these countries in reducing their balance of payment deficits. Negotiations between developing and developed countries turned on four main issues: aid, regional trade agreement between developing countries, market access in developed countries for manufactured and agricultural goods exported by developing countries, and international commodity agreements. But while the Havana Charter had viewed these agreements as provisional and exceptional tools devoted to the management of particular disequilibria between world supply and demand, UNCTAD saw international commodity agreements as permanent tools for maximizing export incomes by supporting prices (UNCTAD and Prebisch

1964). Therefore, negotiations and related projects covered only products exported exclusively by developing countries, mostly tropical agricultural products (such as coffee, cocoa and rubber).[6]

The counter-revolution in development economics

During the 1970s and especially the 1980s, a major change took place in development thinking. According to its supporters, this was a revolution (Dorn, Hanke and Walters 1998); according to its critics, it was a counter-revolution (Toye 1987; Leys 1996; Desai 2002). This counter-revolution produced three major shifts. First, the objective of development was transformed from increasing national wealth to alleviating poverty (Finnemore 1996). Second, the macroeconomic model was not based on a nationally centred economy anymore, but on the global market where every country had to find its right place (McMichael 2000). Third, the ability of the state to promote development was first questioned and then dismissed. The counter-revolution rediscovered the 'truths' promoted by liberal thinkers in the nineteenth century – that individual initiatives coordinated by the market are better than the state at promoting growth.

In relation to commodity exports, the 1980s and the beginning of the 1990s saw a reversal of policy approaches. Import substitution was replaced by the promotion of an export-led growth strategy. Export growth was not linked to any sector in particular, but needed to take place in whatever sector a country had a comparative advantage (primary, secondary or even tertiary). International commodity agreements were abandoned and liberalization policies adopted. At this time, three arguments were used against the traditional developmentalist perspective. First, the hypothesis of deterioration of terms of trade was questioned. Based on new series of price data, and the consideration of changes in transport costs or product quality, new contributions yielded results that were opposite to Prebisch's and Singer's analyses – or at least mitigated their affirmations (Spraos 1980; Bleaney and Greenaway 1993; Hadass and Williamson 2001). Second, other authors argued that developing countries were unable to control international prices by collective action and that the costs of price stabilization actually exceeded the gains (Newbery and Stiglitz 1981). Third, 'new political economy' and rent-seeking scholars (Gorter and Swinnen 2002) developed a case against any form of public intervention in agricultural markets. Analysing agricultural policies in developed countries, the 'new political economy' framework examined the role of private interest groups (cereal farmers, for example) in shaping national policies (for a recent illustration, see Sheingate 2001). In relation to developing countries' agricultural policies, the role of state bureaucracies and politicians was highlighted. The vision of the state as a predatory and clientelist machine progressively came to dominate these studies. Robert Bates's *Markets and States in Tropical Africa* (1981) exemplifies this perspective – to the point that almost any public intervention in agricultural commodity markets came to be seen as taxation. 'New political economy' arguments were used by aid agencies to promote the liberalization of agricultural markets. One indicator was especially used to evaluate the success of liberalization: the ratio 'producer price' over 'export unit value'. Many contributions have compared this ratio between 'liberalized countries' and 'non-liberalized countries' (Akiyama *et al.* 2001) and argued that it was higher in the former than in the latter.

Agricultural market liberalization promoted in developing countries included three components: (1) privatization of public enterprises that processed or marketed commodities; (2) deregulation and promotion of competition in input and output markets; (3) elimination, or large reduction, of subsidies and taxation – including the elimination of domestic price stabilization devices.

Accompanying liberalization, several aid agencies started to promote the use of risk management tools by developing countries' traders and even farmers. The World Bank, back in its *1986 World Development Report* dedicated to agricultural policies, argued that, '[r]ather than try (and certainly fail) to eradicate price movements, it may be more useful to find ways of alleviating their effects. One obvious remedy is to encourage traders to use forward, future and options markets .... These markets are not at present suited to the needs of small commodity producers, but they could be adapted and developed' (World Bank 1986 : 92). Since this publication, several reports have been dedicated to the issue of risk management (Claessens and Duncan 1993; Varangis and Larson 1996). In 1999, an International Task Force for Risk Management in Developing Countries was created with World Bank support and the objective of assisting producing countries – particularly least-developed countries (LDCs) – to use futures markets. Since its creation, however, discussion on the use of futures markets as the main instrument of price risk management has been replaced by a combination of 'put options', price insurance schemes and financing based on warehouse receipts. Developing country actors are encouraged to engage in arrangements with international traders and local credit institutions (the limitations of this approach are spelled out in Chapter 7).

Unfair trade

Achieving fairness in trade is an old quest. It has always been related to a denunciation of the abuse of market power. In theory, a well-functioning market (a pure and perfect competition market) is a market without power – a market where nobody is influencing price formation in voluntary ways. Real markets, however, are far from being the ideal markets of economic theory. In international commodity markets, two actors have regularly been denounced as culprits of unfair trade: states and large firms. The arguments against agricultural protectionism of developed countries that characterize current discussions on commodity trade go back to the first UNCTAD in 1964 – when the problems of market access and export subsidies had already been highlighted. This debate was reactivated during the GATT Uruguay Round of trade negotiations by the Cairns Group of countries that favoured agricultural trade liberalization. More recently, during the Doha Round of negotiations, an influential alliance of developing countries' governments, Cairns Group members and non-governmental organizations (NGOs) emerged to press for the reform of agricultural policies in developed countries.

For the last thirty years, a series of shocks – oil price and dollar fluctuations, debt and financial crises, the rise of newly industrialized countries (NICs) – has shaken the nation-centred model of growth. In response, developed countries have begun to reform their own economies. The neoliberal regimes adopted in these countries have been based on privatization, deregulation and the opening of national markets. However, developed country agricultural sectors escaped most of these reforms. In spite of the inclusion of agriculture in the agenda for trade negotiations during the GATT Uruguay Round, a large majority of developed countries continued to protect their domestic agricultural markets and support their agricultural production. According to the Organization for Economic Cooperation and Development (OECD) secretariat, '[i]n 2002, the level of support provided to farmers (the

Producer Support Estimate) was US$235 billion, which represented 31 per cent of total farm receipts in the OECD area, compared with an average of 38 per cent between 1986 and 1988. Output-based support and input subsidies accounted for 76 per cent of support to farmers in 2002, compared to 90 per cent in 1986–88' (OECD 2003: 1). This picture, however, hides considerable disparity between countries. Oxfam has produced a Double Standard Index to compare 'the level of protectionist trade policies employed by the richest and more powerful trading nations against exports from developing countries' (2002a: 99). According to this index, the European Union (EU) comes first in the level of protection that affects exports of developing countries, followed by the US and then Japan. The European Common Agricultural Policy (CAP) is being reformed at an extremely slow pace. The objective of promoting 'multifunctionality' in agriculture, which is linked to commodity production support, looks more like a new way of justifying protectionism than a new project. For its part, in 2002 the US adopted a new farm bill, the Farm Security and Rural Investment Bill, that provided producer and export subsidies to a higher extent than the act it replaced.

The criticism of agricultural policies in developed countries has given new impetus to the primary commodity debate. WTO negotiations in the Doha Round have centred around agriculture, especially after the July 2004 framework agreement. Special initiatives on cotton and on commodities have been brought forward during the negotiations. The cotton initiative has proved to be more resilient, although it was eventually folded into the overall agriculture negotiations, but with a special status. The victories of Brazil and other countries in cases brought before the WTO dispute settlement process against US cotton subsidies and the EU sugar regime have raised expectations that developing countries would finally rise out of poverty through exports of commodities to developed countries. This euphoria has partially obscured other existing problems: supply-side rigidities in developing countries, especially in LDCs; the hurdles posed by sanitary and phytosanitary standards and technical barriers to trade; the power exerted by retailers in global agro-food value chains; and the impact of the erosion of preferences that the US and EU already accord to least-developed and/or Africa–Caribbean–Pacific (ACP) countries. In other words, the liberalization of agricultural policies in developed countries, while probably benefiting more advanced developing countries, is unlikely by itself to raise LDCs out of poverty.

In addition to pressure exerted within WTO negotiations for the elimination of subsidies in developed countries, a number of organizations have also been promoting the marketing of so-called fair trade products (for more detail, see Chapter 5). One of the concerns that the fair trade movement raises is the low share of consumer prices received by exporting countries and their farmers. According to the Fairtrade Foundation, 'of the £1.75 charged for a cappuccino in a London coffee shop, the grower will be lucky to receive the equivalent of 5p' (Fairtrade Foundation 2002: 4). Furthermore, this share has decreased during the last decades. In its study of the international coffee market, Oxfam (2002b) notes that the share of the final price filtering down to producing countries dropped from 30 per cent in 1992 to 10 per cent in 2002 (see Chapter 6 for more details and other examples).

In a more academic fashion, Morisset (1997), analysing price series for the 1970–95 period, shows a growing spread between consumer and international prices for six products (coffee, sugar, wheat, beef, gasoline and fuel). This evolution can be interpreted in relation to the asymmetric response of domestic prices to changes in international prices. According to Morisset (*ibid.*), the elasticity of transmission (the percentage of variation transmitted from international prices to consumer prices) is on average more than three times higher when international prices are increasing than when they are decreasing. Morisset (*ibid.*) suggests that there is a power imbalance in world commodity markets. In other words, the low and decreasing share of consumer prices received by farmers is explained by the market power of large private actors in consuming countries, and in particular the market power of large trading companies able to influence the transmission of world commodity prices to domestic prices (but see our analysis of coffee in Chapter 6, where it appears that it is not international traders that are able to influence this transmission).

Oxfam (2002b) reported that profit margins for roasters may be as high as 17 per cent for roasted coffee and 30 per cent for soluble coffee. Coffee roasters in consuming countries used their brand power to limit price competition and, during the last 15 years, have adopted new technologies enabling them to use substitutes for coffee origins and qualities more easily. Talbot (1997a: 86) shows that 'after about 1986, there was a major shift of surplus from the coffee-producing countries to multi-national corporations (MNCs) at the core of the world system, who used their market power to hold the price of green coffee while inflating the price of coffee processed for final consumption'. These arguments are part of a fast-growing body of work that has focused on oligopolistic behaviour at the retail level, but also among food and beverage processors, in explaining unfair distribution of value along global chains (see, among many others, Vorley 2003).

Yet most econometric studies on price transmission in coffee roasting and roasting/retailing in various consuming countries carried out in the last 20 years (Roberts 1984; Bettendorf and Verhoven 2000; Feuerstein 2002; Koerner 2002; Durevall 2003) reject the hypothesis that market power determines price transmission, with the exception of a study of US roasters in the 1972–87 period (Bhuyan and Lopez 1997). At the same time, these do suggest that markets function imperfectly, and that price behaviour may not be an appropriate indicator of market power – given that highly concentrated sectors may be characterized by high price competition. Furthermore, few of these studies cover both periods of increasing and decreasing international coffee prices. When they do (as in the case of Durevall 2003), it appears that increases in international coffee prices are more fully transmitted to the retail level than decreases (although the finding is not statistically significant) (see Gibbon 2004 for an overview).

Whether large companies are the culprits of unfair trade or not, arguments for fairer rules of trade are also built upon evidence of the adverse impacts of commodity price shocks on the economies of exporting countries and on the livelihoods of their citizens. This is especially the case where commodities represent a large proportion of export earnings. In the late 1990s, for example, nine developing countries relied on coffee exports for 23 per cent or more of export earnings (FAO 2001; Gibbon 2004). Low-income countries are also more likely than other developing countries to experience both price shocks and terms-of-trade shocks (Humphrey 2004). Price shocks are important because they affect growth; deteriorations in terms of trade affect balance of payments. According to Kruger, Mason and Vakis (2003), the international coffee price decline of 1999–2001 alone led to a drop of 1.2 per cent in GDP in the five main coffee-producing countries of Central America as a group,[7] even without taking multiplier

effects into account (see Gibbon 2004). As for the effects on the livelihoods of coffee producers, it is fairly clear from the evidence available
that there is a positive correlation between coffee prices and income
levels. This has been documented in a period of increasing coffee prices
in Uganda (Deininger and Okidi 2003) and in a period of decreasing
prices in Nicaragua (Kruger, Mason and Vakis 2003).

Although examining market power and abuse of market power in
commodity markets is not a new idea, recent contributions seek to
unpack better the combined role of regulation (and deregulation) and
of business strategies in determining openings to developing country
producers. Much of this kind of discussion has taken place in work
more or less explicitly linked to GVC analysis. Here, openings for
developing countries are examined not only in terms of market access
in general, but in relation to specific demands on quality, timing of
supply response, flexibility, and functions performed that are determined by powerful buyers (retailers, industrial processors, brand-name
food manufacturers). In the next section, we examine the main feature
of GVC analysis in relation to issues of commoditization and possibilities for upgrading in developing countries.

Global value chains, commoditization and upgrading

The share of manufactured goods in developing countries' exports has
increased tremendously during the last 25 years. According to
UNCTAD (2002: 198), this share increased from about 20 per cent at
the end of the 1970s to 70 per cent at the end of the 1990s. Increasingly,
developing countries (except for sub-Saharan Africa) are exporting
manufactured goods instead of primary commodities. Between 1980
and 2000, the percentage of primary commodities in total non-oil
exports dropped from 60 per cent to 40 per cent in Brazil, from 80 to
43 per cent in Colombia, from 41 to 7 per cent in Mexico, from 75 to
33 per cent in Morocco, from 75 to 10 per cent in Malaysia and from
41 to 19 per cent in India (Kozul-Wright and Rayment 2004). Some
authors explain this tendency in relation to the building of global value
chains and production networks, which involve actors in a large
number of localities in the production/transformation process.
According to these authors, the current growth of international trade is
not characterized mainly by exchange of final consumer products, but

rather by exchange of components and intermediary products (see, among others, Feenstra 1998).

Yet various studies carried out in the 1990s and early 2000s have also shown that increases in exports of manufactures by developing countries have been accompanied by price falls in labour-intensive manufactures. In other words, prices for these manufactures seem to behave like prices for primary commodities. Kaplinsky (1993), examining apparel exports from the Dominican Republic and Central America, was one of the first authors to document this phenomenon. The Dominican Republic, like many other developing countries, adopted policies promoting the creation of export-processing zones (EPZs), characterized by no taxation, no restrictions in the labour market, currency devaluation and un-restricted access to foreign exchange. Kaplinsky argues that the com-moditization of export-oriented manufacturing produces 'immiserizing employment growth' – that is, 'employment growth which is contin-gent upon wages falling in international purchasing power' (ibid.: 1861). His argument depends mainly on the observation of declining terms of trade for exported manufactured goods. The use of unskilled labour and the adoption of the same export strategy by several countries (the fallacy of composition) are seen as the causes of declining terms of trade. They are also seen as the very reason for classifying industrial products of this kind as commodities.

But is this the whole story? Are developing countries and their labour forces and farmers doomed to increased competition with each other that drives down prices and wages? What are the possible paths for upgrading in primary commodity production? How can producers get better prices for improved quality content of what they sell? Is quality just a matter of material goodness? In what value chains do they get better returns? Working with which intermediaries? For which final markets?

GVC analysis addresses some of these questions, disaggregating the international structure of production, trade and consumption of com-modities into stages that are embedded in a network of activities con-trolled by firms.[8] This approach allows the identification of the 'place' where specific 'quality attributes' are produced, and the examination of how value is distributed between different actors. GVC analysis also discusses the dynamics of upgrading into 'higher' positions (in terms of technology, value added, or operational scale) in global markets –

which involves acceptance of terms, rules and measuring devices defined by key agents or institutions.

GVC analysis examines the diversity of insertion of developing countries in international trade and seeks to identify the opportunities they offer. It first appeared in the literature under the term 'global commodity chain' (GCC) analysis. The notion of a commodity chain as 'a network of labour and production processes whose end result is a finished commodity' comes from Hopkins and Wallerstein (1986; 1994), where it is used to discuss a variety of international chains for agricultural (and timber) products, from the beginning of the early modern era. If Hopkins and Wallerstein introduced the notion of commodity chains, the beginning of GCC analysis as a relatively coherent paradigm can be traced to a collection edited by Gereffi and Korzeniewicz (1994).[9] Although the book starts with a brief version of Hopkins and Wallerstein's argument (1994), Gereffi and most of his collaborators are concerned specifically with industrial commodity chains. They largely ignore the historical/cyclical context, and focus on the emergence of a new global manufacturing system in which economic integration goes beyond international trade in raw materials and final products, to encompass centrally coordinated but internationally dispersed production of many of the activities along the chains of given commodities or manufactured products. This emergence is seen to be related to the internationalization of manufacturing chains and to the externalization of functions that were previously carried out 'within the organizational boundaries of vertically integrated corporations' (Gereffi, Korzeniewicz and Korzeniewicz 1994: 7) and, to a large extent, within specific nation states.

In his original formulation, Gereffi identified three key dimensions of commodity chains: their input–output structure and geographical coverage; their form of governance; and their institutional framework (Gereffi 1994a; 1995). Input–output structure and geographical coverage were used mainly descriptively to outline chain configuration. The form of governance of global commodity chains introduced the key notions of entry barriers and chain coordination. The GCC literature originally distinguished broadly between 'producer-driven' and 'buyer-driven' types of governance. Producer-driven chains were said to be found usually in sectors with high technological and capital requirements, where capital and proprietary know-how constitute the main entry barriers. In these chains, producers tend to keep control of capital-intensive operations and subcontract more labour-intensive functions, often in the form of vertically integrated networks. Buyer-driven chains were said to be found in generally more labour-intensive sectors, where market information, product design and marketing/advertising costs set the entry barriers. In these chains, production functions are usually outsourced and key actors concentrate on branding, design and marketing functions (for further elaborations of the concept of value chain governance, see Gereffi, Humphrey and Sturgeon 2005; Ponte and Gibbon 2005).

The institutional framework surrounding a global value chain was meant to delineate the conditions under which key (or 'lead') agents incorporate subordinate agents through their control of market access and information − both technological and regarding markets. Under the rubric of 'institutional framework', Gereffi also discussed how subordinate participation in a GVC could provide indirect access to markets at lower costs than individual small-scale producers would otherwise face, and how technological information and 'learning by doing' allow (the more favoured) producers to move up the chain hierarchy (also known as 'upgrading'). This suggested that participation in a global commodity chain is a necessary, but not sufficient, condition for subordinate agents to upgrade. Participation also involves acceptance of terms defined by key agents or institutions, especially for those aiming to progress towards higher positions in the chain (see Gereffi 1999).

In recent years, the GCC literature has abandoned the term 'commodity chain' and has taken up that of 'value chain' in its place. The latter is thought to better capture a wider variety of products, some of which lack commodity features. As a result, the GCC approach is now known as global value chain (GVC) analysis. A large part of the development implications of the GVC framework is related to the notion of upgrading. Based on the historical evolution of the global chain for apparel and electronic devices, Gereffi and others argue that the continuous process of externalization driven by large marketers and/or retailers provides opportunities for developing countries. These opportunities are linked to a progressive control in developing countries of an increasing number of transformation stages. For developing-country subcontractors, participation in global value chains brings benefits in terms of organizational and technological learning, technology transfer, and positive backward linkages with local supply industries.

In this perspective, Gereffi (1994b) sees specific upgrading opportunities arising particularly from participation in buyer-driven value chains. He classifies different regions in the world in relation to the kind of product exported – distinguishing five categories from primary commodity to original brand-name products. An increase in the number of categories of goods exported by one region is an illustration of the upgrading process. East Asia is the region exporting the widest range of goods. This demonstrates, in Gereffi's perspective, the possibility and reality of the upgrading process.

In the GVC literature, the upgrading process is examined through the lenses of how knowledge and information flow within value chains from 'lead firms' to their suppliers (or buyers) (Gereffi 1999). Upgrading is then seen as the process of acquiring capabilities and accessing new market segments through participating in particular chains (Humphrey 2003). The argument is that upgrading in various forms can be effectively stimulated through learning from lead firms rather than through interactions between firms in the same functional position (horizontal transfer in clusters) or within the frameworks of common business systems or national systems of innovation.

Although much of the early GVC literature privileged one kind of upgrading (functional), subsequently other categories of upgrading have been highlighted. Humphrey and Schmitz (2002), for example, use four categories of upgrading: (1) process upgrading (achieving a more efficient transformation of inputs into outputs through the reorganization of productive activities); (2) product upgrading (moving into more sophisticated products with increased unit value); (3) functional upgrading (acquiring new functions, or abandoning old ones, that increase the skill content of activities; and (4) intersectoral upgrading (applying competences acquired in one function of a chain and using them in a different sector/chain).

More recent analyses (Gibbon and Ponte 2005) give greater recognition to the importance of achieving greater economies of scale as a means of securing a stable and profitable supplier position in buyer-driven contexts. They also suggest a focus on identifying structures of rewards available to suppliers within specific chains, on the one hand,

and concrete roles releasing these rewards on the other. In specific reference to upgrading opportunities in global value chains for primary commodities, Gibbon (2001; 2003) argues that, albeit limited, upgrading options are present in three forms: (1) capturing 'higher margins on exports of existing forms of unprocessed raw material by moving up the quality grade ladder, increasing volumes and reliability of supply, securing more remunerative contracts through forward sales and becoming active in hedging risk, via utilizing futures and options instruments' (2001: 352); (2) producing 'new forms – as opposed to higher grades – of unprocessed raw materials' (*ibid*.: 353), for example 'user-specified' commodity forms; and (3) localizing commodity processing, since 'intermediate processing is still a technologically irreducible stage of many commodity chains and within these it usually remains a necessary economic and learning precondition for entry to final processing' (*ibid*.: 354).

In this book, we continue to explore this approach to upgrading through the analysis of the global value chain for coffee and its local ramifications (both in producing and consuming countries). The case study of coffee – with its twin tendency for standardization in the mainstream market and increasing differentiation in the specialty market – illustrates both opportunities and constraints for upgrading in developing countries. However, rather than using the vocabulary of 'upgrading', we will focus on its components. In other words, we will frame the issue of upgrading in terms of the ability of producers to create and control the value embedded in various coffee quality attributes. In the next section, we lay out the analytical framework upon which this approach is based.

The quality issue: material, symbolic and in-person service attributes

Approaches to quality
Contesting the liberal perspective claiming that free trade is the best way to get rich for everyone, whatever a country exports, the structuralists tried to demonstrate that specialization in primary commodity exports was not a good choice. However, their discussion did not include any clear definition of what a primary commodity is. Their analysis was based on a dichotomy between primary and secondary

sectors, or agriculture and manufacturing. Prebisch and Singer argued that relations between productivity and prices were opposite in the two sectors. This was because of different constraints on labour mobility (high in agriculture and low in manufacturing), different abilities of firms to build power in product markets (high in manufacturing and low in agriculture), and differences in demand elasticity.

Current analyses highlighting the unfairness of trade and the commoditization of manufactured goods share some of the same weaknesses. In the unfair trade perspective, primary commodities are seen simply as less transformed than manufactured goods. The imbalance of power within global markets is related to different degrees of concentration and competition at the production level: pure and perfect in agriculture; oligopolistic or even monopolistic in manufacturing. In the 'commoditization of manufactured goods' perspective, low barriers to entry – such as simple technologies – are supposed to be the main characteristics of the commodity sector, which incorporates massive quantities of easily replaceable low-skill labour. Once again, technological determinism predominates.

The definition of what is a primary commodity – or more generally a commodity – cannot be based simply on production characteristics or consumer preferences. Although there is a substantial literature on quality, and several classifications of quality, to our knowledge there have been no attempts to draw a clear link between quality and value (or price). This requires a theoretical framework that goes beyond traditional approaches to quality evaluation in commodity trade and beyond mainstream epistemologies in economic analysis of the global economy (see Levy 2002 for an overview).

Most economic analyses of quality still assume that agents have an objective idea of quality, which entails predetermined preferences that do not change in relation to the behaviour of others. In these formulations, quality attributes are often classified depending on the ease with which they can be measured. *Search* attributes are those that can be verified at the time of the transaction (the colour of a coffee bean, for example). *Experience* attributes can be assessed only after the transaction has taken place (the taste of brewed coffee). *Credence* attributes cannot be objectively verified (or it is very expensive to verify them) and are based on trust (whether coffee is organic) (Darby and Karni 1973; Nelson 1970; Tirole 1988). Attributes are also linked to the product itself (for example, coffee appearance, taste, cleanliness, absence of taints) or to production and process methods. These methods may include aspects related to authenticity of origin (geographical indication), safety (pesticide residues, levels of toxins) and environmental and socio-economic conditions (organic, fair trade, shade-grown coffees).

These classifications assume that the evaluators of attributes have identical capacity to assess them. In reality, these capacities vary dramatically between individuals, and across time, countries and cultures. Also, economic agents (especially consumers) make quality decisions also on the basis of imitation and/or the achievement of 'distinction' (Bourdieu 1979). Finally, the way attributes are measured varies, depending on what convention is used to set accepted reference values and measurement methods.

Convention theory can help unpack some of these issues. This is not the appropriate place for an extensive discussion of the features of convention theory (see Wilkinson 1997; Raikes, Jensen and Ponte 2000; Gibbon and Ponte 2005; Ponte and Gibbon 2005). What needs to be highlighted here is that the concept of convention can help us to understand how quality is valued at different points in value chains, and in different consumption markets (both geographically and in terms of kind of consumption).[10] It also helps to delineate how the evaluation of quality attributes (which leads to a certain price) changes historically in different contexts. Finally, it helps us to think through what strategies (marketing, PR-related, political) could be adopted to actively seek a change in quality conventions that can be beneficial to coffee (and other commodity) producers.

Boltanski and Thévenot (1991) claim that all action is justified in relation to common sets of principles. The authors develop six historically based 'worlds' (also known as cités) of 'legitimate common welfare' that draw on particular paradigms of moral philosophy: thus we have inspirational, domestic, opinion-based, civic, market and industrial worlds. Each of these worlds is organized around different forms of justification and counter-justification. These correspond to different norms of qualification of people (employees, for example) and objects, and to different conventions for organizing the activities of firms (see also Ponte and Gibbon 2005). Conventions are neither permanent nor linked directly to specific social interests. At any particular time and locality, there may be multiple justifications of action operating at the same time. Finally, although there is an internal coherence in each world, different worlds can also overlap.

The consequences of Boltanski and Thévenot's heuristic framework for the concept of quality are far-reaching: first, it suggests that there is no universal understanding of quality; and, second, that quality is cognitively evaluated in different ways depending on what 'world' is used to justify evaluation and action. These lines of thinking have been taken further by Eymard-Duvernay (1989), who developed a typology linking quality conventions to different forms of coordination that arise in relation to various types of information asymmetry.[11]

Eymard-Duvernay (1989) argues that price is the main management form of a particular market only if there is no uncertainty about quality. If this is the case, differences in price directly express known differences in quality. This characterizes what convention theory calls *market* coordination. When, for whatever reason, price alone cannot evaluate quality, actors set up conventions linked to three other 'forms of coordination'. In *domestic* coordination, uncertainty about quality is solved through trust (long-term relationships between actors, or use of private brands or geographical indications which signal the reputation of products). In this case, the definition of quality is established interpersonally, and the identity of a product is guaranteed or institutionalized 'in the repetition of history' (*ibid.*) by its region or country of origin or brand name. In *industrial* coordination, uncertainty about quality is solved through the actions of an external party who determines common norms or standards and enforces them via instrument-based testing, inspection and certification. More recently, an additional category has been added, *civic* coordination, where there is collective commitment to welfare, and the identity of a product is related to its impact upon society or the environment. As in other strands of convention theory, it is acknowledged that different forms of coordination may exist side by side at the same time, and even for the same product, sometimes (see Allaire and Boyer 1995) in a state of tension where one is trying either to resist or encroach on other modes.

Thévenot (1995) highlights some of the major historical changes in the forms of economic organization and conventions of quality that have taken place in the twentieth century. He argues that the dominant form in the post-war era was a compromise between industrial and market coordination – with a tendential predominance of industrial norms of productivity, economies of scale and technical progress. This configuration is said to have tilted to the side of market coordination, and its underlying norm of competitiveness, as a result of the processes of market liberalization and deregulation of the 1980s. Thévenot also claims that, at the same time, market coordination coexists with domestic forms of coordination such as geographical indication and branding – as well as with the underlying civic content of environmental and socio-economic standards and labels.

Convention theory has been criticized for its speculative character, its multiplication of typologies and the accuracy of its historical periodizations. It has also been taken to task for its exclusive micro-focus and lack of explicit discussion of power relations. Yet, at the same time, its 'worlds' seem to embody implicit but powerful constraints on behaviour. In other words, despite its limitations, convention theory provides an innovative way of looking at quality, which encompasses cognitive, and not only material, preoccupations.

In the rest of our discussion, we apply this theoretical framework as an interpretive tool for understanding changes that have taken place in the coffee value chains examined in this book. Yet convention theory, along with other approaches, does not examine how value is created and why a certain quality attribute of a product receives a higher price (or generates a higher value for the seller). In the rest of this section, we present a tentative typology based on *material, symbolic* and *in-person service* quality attributes.

Material attributes, physical transformations and measurement

Many economists see material attributes of a product as embedded within the product. These qualities are usually referred to as 'intrinsic' and/or 'objective', and are seen as independent from the identity of sellers and buyers. They result from previous physical, chemical or bio-chemical processes that create and/or select some specific physical parameters. Yet, in a market transaction, the value of material quality attributes relates first and foremost to the existence of measurement operations and devices, and to the accuracy of these measurements. Therefore, qualities are attributed to products based on measurement that itself creates objectivity.

Material attributes can be measured by using the human senses (vision, taste, smell, hearing, touch), or by mobilizing sophisticated technological devices such as spectrographs. The measurement of attributes can be direct or indirect. Often, an attribute cannot be measured directly, or only in a costly manner. Sometimes, another attribute can be used as a proxy for the one to be measured (the colour of a piece of fruit to measure taste, for example). The use of proxies supposes a previous building of equivalences between the different measured values of the proxy and the values of the 'real' attribute. The ability to measure an attribute will depend on the resources (equipment and skills) owned by the transactors at the time and place(s) of transaction. Asymmetric resource endowment between actors is a first and basic source of specific distributions of value along a chain. As a buyer, a potential source of profit is being able to identify the existence of a specific and valued attribute that the seller cannot evaluate. As a seller, masking a quality defect that the buyer cannot discover at the time of transaction can also be a source of profit. However, it is likely that the buyer will eventually discover the problem (most likely, through price discounting from his/her own buyer, who is able to measure the defective attribute). If this happens, he or she will not buy from the same seller next time, or will apply a quality risk discount.

Historically, standards in agricultural markets have been based on measurable attributes (see Chapter 2). These attributes could be the attributes valued by the user/consumer or they could be proxies. According to Kindelberger (1983), standards are public goods because everyone can use them without reducing the availability to others. From an economic point of view, standards are a public good because they are codified knowledge, and knowledge, according to economists, is a public good. However, knowledge can also be a private good and standards can be privately owned. At the same time, standards are not just knowledge, they are collectively agreed knowledge. Even when they are privately used within a firm, they are based on an agreement – whether between the different parts of the workshop floor, for example, or with the purchasing department, or with the machine manufacturer. Standard elaboration entails negotiations, meetings and committees. As suggested in convention theory, standards are a specific type of investment, an 'investment in form' (Eymard-Duvernay 1989). This means 'operations that must be undertaken so that goods gain generality (objectivity) by the establishment of relations of equivalence' (*ibid.*: 334).

For agricultural products, '[s]tandardization means making uniform among buyers and sellers, and from place to place and time to time, the quality specifications of grades' (Thomsen 1951). The core of the standardization process is the adoption and the diffusion of the same rules to define the identity of products prior to market transactions. The existence of a public standard for agricultural products (the use of the same rules to grade a product by all market participants) is based on achieving at least four agreements: (1) on a limited list of measurable attributes (preferred attributes or proxies); (2) on the way to measure these attributes; (3) on a classification or a grading system, which itself presupposes agreement on a limited number of grades and the upper and lower limits of the value of different attributes for each grade; and (4) on the names by which the different grades are known.

The setting of such agreements and the necessary funding to elaborate the associated technical knowledge clearly raise a problem of collective action for different users of a standard. Trader associations have often provided support for such a collective action. The Chicago Board of Trade is certainly the best example of such a collective action (Odle 1964). The key role of trader associations suggests a certain degree of specificity of standards for agricultural products. In manufacturing, standardization is necessary to guarantee interchangeability, and interchangeability is necessary to guarantee compatibility between the different components in the assembly line. For agricultural products, as for components in manufactures, interchangeability is also the key issue. But the working of market transactions is more important. Because of the existence of standards, products coming from different places, at different times and from different agents can be exchanged without difficulty for the buyer and the seller. In other words, the submission of standard definition to the technical constraint of the assembly line is displaced by the submission to the constraint of anonymous market transactions.

Cronon (1991) highlights the arbitrary character of the boundaries that are set to define different grades and standards, and consequently the conflictive nature of these boundaries. From a technical point of view, there was no reason for these boundaries to exist. Some criteria like the density of the grain could be important for the milling operator. But density can take different values. Nevertheless, the definition of a grade, necessary to organize interchangeability, is essential for the market: '[b]y imposing their own order and vocabulary on the world of first nature, the city's traders invented a world of second nature in which they could buy and sell grain as commodity almost independently from grain as crop' (*ibid.*: 146)

Most of the literature explains the possibility of market transactions between two stages of a value chain by the existence of standards. Implicitly or explicitly, standards are determined by the constraints and opportunities generated by technology. This is the interpretation proposed by the new institutional economics. This is also the interpretation given by most of the authors working in a GVC perspective (see, for example, Gereffi, Humphrey and Sturgeon 2005). The history of the agricultural markets suggests the opposite: standards are created to allow the existence of market transactions (see also Busch and Tanaka 1996); they also impose their constraints on the downstream transformation process. In our approach, we consider this the very nature of commodities – that is, goods with a world market where most participants and transactors use the same definition of quality attributes, and for the most part only measurable attributes. At the extreme, these are goods giving rise to transactions organized around a single world quality standard.[12]

Symbolic quality: trademarks, geographical indications and sustainability labels

Symbolic quality attributes cannot be measured by human senses or complex technological devices. They are based on reputation and often embedded in trademarks, geographical indications and sustainability labels. Trademarks enable the 'consumption of an enterprise'. Geographical indications facilitate the 'consumption of place'. Sustainability labels make it possible to 'consume ethics'.

According to economic theory, the quality of a product that bears a trademark is not measured directly, but is identified with the name of a firm or a brand. Trademarks are distinctive signs. Consumers use them to identify products with specific attributes. Trademarks are socially useful because they reduce information asymmetries between producer and consumer when the valued attributes cannot be measured easily. Reputation is the key determinant of value creation (or destruction) in this case. Reputation is acquired through repeated consumption experiences and advertising. According to Chamberlin (1933) and the industrial organization school (see for example Scherer 1970), price formation for brand name goods can be analysed in relation to monopolistic competition. From this perspective, the promotion of a brand name is part of the differentiation strategies enterprises adopt. The objective is to decrease price elasticity of demand in order to control selling prices.

In everyday life, trademarks, firm names and related reputations that build consumer confidence acquire value to some extent independently of the product's material attributes. They are not just proxies for difficult-to-measure material attributes. Consuming specific branded goods distinguishes the consumer from some people and identifies him/her with others. To designate these goods, economists use the expression 'status goods'. Grossman and Shapiro (1988) define status goods as those 'goods for which the mere use or display of a particular branded product confers prestige on their owners, apart from the utility deriving from their function' (*ibid.*: 82). However, the expression – status good – and the definition proposed are confusing. Every good owns a status dimension, contributing to defining and identifying the social membership of a consumer. The value given to trademarks exemplifies the increasing role of ideas and symbols in consumption and the importance of consumption in the definition of identities (see a critical review of the large literature on consumption in Fine 2002).

Trademarks can only acquire value when there is a legal framework protecting their use: intellectual property rights. Without legal protection, other firms would use the reputation associated with the brand name of a specific firm. According to Rangnekar (2004), the legal protection of brand names has two objectives – to enable the appropriation of investment made in developing a brand name and to maintain the information role of the brand name as an indicator of source. To these, we would add a third one – to guarantee the capture of rents. This takes place when an enterprise buys a good with quality defined by easily measurable attributes and sells, after some transformation, another good qualified by a brand name.

An indication of geographical origin (IGO) is in some ways similar to a brand name. It creates differences within consumer opinion and makes it possible to organize a differentiation strategy in term of price and quality. Its existence and value also depend on the creation of a protective legal framework limiting the use of the quality sign. The rationale for the legal framework is the same that applies to brand names: protection against misleading use and against the dilution of meaning. The main difference between brands and IGOs lies in the collective nature of property for the latter. This entails that all the enterprises present in the area protected by an IGO can use the indication as long as they meet the required technical specifications.

In France, a first law enabling the organization of appellation for top-quality wines was voted in 1935. This law gave birth to the Institut National des Appellations d'Origine (INAO). Within this legal framework, any Appellation d'Origine Contrôlée (AOC) is confirmed by a ministerial decree defining the geographical area for production, the technical specifications and the assent conditions. A 'defence association', representing the producers of the area, must exist for every AOC. This association is in charge of elaborating, jointly with the INAO, the text that will serve as a basis for the ministerial decree. This association is also in a position to control the maximum quantity produced – through the use of planting rights and by setting a maximum yield per hectare. This initial legal framework was complemented in 1955 by a law enlarging the appellation system to cheese, and in 1990 by a new law that allows appellations to be developed for any agro-food product (Lagrange, Briand and Trogon 2000).

The main instrument protecting geographical origin in Europe is EU legislation (2081/92). Before its publication, this legislation was fiercely discussed. The French system was seen as incompatible with the creation of a unified market in Europe. Many European actors (public and private) wanted to limit any regulation about quality to food safety and fraud issues. For these actors, regulation protecting geographical appellation would be disguised protectionism limiting competition and innovation. On the contrary, the so-called 'Latin countries' (France, Italy and Spain) were arguing that it was necessary to create a European regulation to limit the use of geographical names that qualify specific products (Valceschini and Mazé 2000).

EU legislation protects agro-food products that have either quality characteristics 'essentially due to' a particular production, processing and preparation environment linked to a geographical area (Protected Designation of Origin – PDO), or that are 'attributable' to a particular area and to production, processing and/or preparation that take place in that area (Protected Geographical Indication – PGI) (Ilbery and

Kneafsey 1999: 2210–11). In this system, no reference is made to the actual quality of the product itself. The (unwarranted) assumption is that quality is guaranteed by the geography of production. In terms of territoriality, PDOs are clearly stronger than PGIs. With a PDO, the whole value chain, from the production of the raw material to packaging, must be done in the origin region. Moreover, the product characteristics must be linked not only to the natural attributes of the region (such as climate and soil) but also to some cultural attributes. In a PGI, just one part of the value chain must be located in the region giving its name to the product, and no cultural attribute of the region is considered.

One of the agreements concluded in Marrakech at the end of the Uruguay Round in 1994, the so-called TRIPS (Trade-Related Intellectual Property Rights) agreement, deals with indications of geographical origin. Agricultural quality signs are just one of the components of the TRIPS agreement, which covers a broad range of topics (including patents, trademarks and rights of authors). In similar ways to what happened in the European debate, the TRIPS negotiations mobilized a strong opposition against any international legal acknowledgment of geographical appellations. For the opponents, among them the US, geographical appellations are an example of non-tariff barriers to trade. Another key issue is whether the system of trademarks can be used to protect 'locality' (as the US argues) or whether these labels belong to a collectivity – in which case, individual companies or persons cannot own the intellectual property right attached to the name of the territory (as argued by the EU) (Barham 2003: 129). Under the latter system, no individual entity is allowed to move its production outside the region and retain the label of origin. In the French tradition, *terroir* refers to a specific area in which environmental, climatic and soil conditions impart a distinctive quality to an agro-food product (*ibid.*: 131). The AOC label embeds this concept and connects it to a regulatory system through its status as a geographical indication. In order to qualify for an AOC label, a link between a certain area and the distinctiveness of a product needs to be demonstrated through justificatory claims in relation to natural factors, human capacity (*savoir faire*) and history. Implicit in this system is a quality message that is tied to the processes and specific environmental conditions of a particular place, not one that is about product quality itself.

Article 22 of TRIPS is dedicated to the protection of geographical indications. It states that '[g]eographical indications are, for the purposes of this Agreement, indications which identify a good as originating in the territory of a Member, or a region or locality in that territory, where a given quality, reputation or other characteristic of the good is essentially attributable to its geographical origin'.[13] According to Boy (2001), the TRIPS agreement institutes a weaker version of geographical indication, the one illustrated in European legislation by the PGI, not the PDO. This version protects the consumer more than the product or the producer. Under the PGI system, a firm not located in the concerned area can be interdicted from using the geographical indication only if it can be demonstrated that it creates confusion among consumers.

According to Valceschini and Mazé (2000: 36), the allocation of property rights on geographical designations contributed to guaranteeing the accuracy of the information given to the consumer on the basis of three mechanisms. The first is an institutional mechanism, based at the national level, designed to approve which products can hold the rights of using a particular denomination. This is done to oversee respect of the rules by the beneficiary organizations and to guarantee the reputation of the entire denomination system. The second is an organizational mechanism, based at the local level. Here, a producer association defines the rules regarding the characteristics of the production process and makes sure that each member respects them. The third mechanism consists in monitoring and certification by a third-party independent expert.[14]

Because of the collective nature of the property rights defining the use of IGOs, small farmers and small manufacturers located in areas covered by geographic indications may be able to generate and control extra value for 'symbolic production'. However, the existence and utility of IGOs as means for farmers to capture value is related to two conditions: an existing legal framework supporting and protecting them; and the ability to build vertical alliances with other actors in the value chain (see Barjolle and Sylvander 2000, 2002; Réviron, Chappuis and Barjolle 2003). At present, the legal framework being elaborated within the WTO is less protective of farmers' interests than the historical framework created in France around AOC wines. Moreover, the ability to build vertical alliances is clearly weakened or contested by the current process of spatial disintegration of value chains. Both tendencies are limiting the possibility of using IGOs to increase farmers' incomes and to provide a stimulus for building stronger producer organizations. We will come back to this point later when we discuss the IGO issue in relation to coffee (see Chapters 6 and 7).

In addition to trademarks and IGOs, a third kind of sign can provide information on products to consumers: sustainability labels. These labels are awarded to products provided by enterprises or organizations that meet specific criteria. These criteria concern the technical process and/or the management methods. They can define the characteristics of inputs (as the organic label does), the characteristics of labour (child-labour-free labels, for example) and/or the characteristics of machinery and equipment used in transformation processes (as in the case of sanitary labels). They can also define rules regarding the way decisions are taken or profits are distributed (as the fair trade label does), and the procedures for segregating certified products from non-certified products. In other words, labels are based on process-oriented standards, a kind of standard previously used to coordinate production *within* firms. These process-oriented standards can be elaborated by a large number of entities: a group of enterprises (such as the European Retailer Group), associations and NGOs (fair trade), and a combination of public administration and associations (organics in the US and EU). Most of them include a sustainability dimension: that is, they are conceived in relation to current definitions of sustainable development.

To be able to use a label, enterprises or organizations must be inspected by a third party – the certifier. The certifier guarantees that the enterprise respects a set of predetermined criteria. Any label supposes inspection of the technical process and/or the management methods. For agricultural producers, the implementation of labels is introducing a radical change in the relations with the enterprises buying their products. Suddenly, product control is replaced by control of production and process methods, including labour monitoring. Labels ensure control of the production process without the need for vertical integration. Like historical agricultural standards before them, the new standards and certification processes supporting these sustainability labels allow the existence of market transactions. They authorize a much more extended governance of the value chain without the use of formal hierarchical relations.

A distinction should be made at this point between process-oriented standards and labels dedicated to: (1) organizing relations within a value chain; and (2) providing distinctive signs for consumers. Retailers and/or the food industry can use the latter for differentiation strategies and to get higher prices – as long as the use of these standards is not generalized. With the diffusion of common codes and standards, the social, environmental or sanitary practices cease to be a differentiation variable. As this happens, retailers cannot use them to set higher prices at the consumption level.

Labels are distinctive signs, but access to them is much less restrictive than with trademarks and IGOs – as long as standards are met. Thus, at least in theory, any enterprise or farm can apply to use a label, irrespective of its location and identity (with some exceptions, such as fair trade coffee, where estates are not certified). Nevertheless, the contents of the standard (the list of criteria and their value) are defined by a specific enterprise/organization or a group of such bodies. From this point of view, the standard supporting a label is similar to the new industrial standards described by Borrus and Zysman (1997) as 'open-but-owned' standards. The actors in position to define the standard place themselves in a key governing position in the value chain (see also Ponte and Gibbon 2005). Once more, the ability to mobilize collective action is decisive.

In-person service quality

Material goods are sold increasingly in association with in-person services. In the course of the last decade, many publications have been dedicated to the 'immateriality' of consumption and the service component that comes with it. However, confusion arises in the discussion of what is and what is not a service. For example, Rifkin (2000) includes in the service category every economic activity that differs from material production or construction that: (1) is of transitory nature; (2) is characterized by consumption occurring simultaneously with production; and (3) is creating immaterial value. With such a definition, Rifkin characterizes as services a large number of activities, such as liberal professions (law, accounting and consultancy), retail trade, transport, communications, health care, baby-sitting, elderly care, recreation activities and state-sponsored social programmes. He sees services as immaterial and intangible. Moreover, according to

Rifkin the increasing role of services in economic life is directly related to a major social change, from an age of private property to an age of access.

The immaterial dimension of modern capitalism is mostly discussed by other authors in terms of knowledge (see for example Vercellone 2003; Gorz 2003). Yet, according to Hill (1999), a strict distinction must be established between so-called intangible goods and in-person services. Hill starts by defining a good as 'an entity over which property rights may be established and from which its owner(s) derives some economic benefit' (ibid.: 437). From this definition, Hill infers an important characteristic: 'a good is an entity that exists independently of its owner and preserves its identity through time. If ownership rights can be established it follows that they can also be transferred from one economic unit to another, which implies that goods must be exchangeable' (ibid.: 438). In addition to material goods, there are also intangible goods, which are 'originally produced as outputs by persons, or enterprises, engaged in creative or innovative activities of a literary, scientific, engineering, artistic or entertainment nature' (ibid.: 438). Hill adds that '[a]n original is the archetypal immaterial good. It is a good because it is an entity over which ownership rights can be established and which is of economic value to its owner. It is also intangible because it has no physical dimensions or coordinates in space' (ibid.: 440; original emphasis).

From this point of view, in-person services are quite different from intangible goods. 'A service involves relationships between producers and consumers ... In contrast to a good, a service is not an entity that can exist independently of its producer or consumer and therefore should not be treated as if it were some special kind of good, namely an "immaterial" one' (ibid.: 441). For Hill, a service must be defined as 'some change in the condition of one economic unit produced by the activity of another unit. Many services consist of material changes in the persons or property of consumers, such as haircuts, surgical operations or the repainting of houses, which is wholly inappropriate, and misleading, to describe as "immaterial" just because no new entity is created' (ibid.: 441).

Albeit useful, Hill's discussion fails to cover services that do not include any material changes in the person or property of consumers. In the case of the food sector, the worker involved in the in-person service, preparing a meal for example, can perform a physical transformation process. This transformation operation involves specific technical skills, such as cooking. But often the transformation can be small or even non-existent (opening a bottle, serving a glass of wine) and no technical skill is mobilized, except one that can be acquired in a few days. How can we then explain the value of in-person services? Why is it that some in-person services provided by a specific enterprise are highly valued compared to those offered by competitors?

As a first step, we can mobilize the framework elaborated by Reich (1992). For Reich, three broad categories of work are emerging in the US, and more generally at the global level:

- *Routine production*, historically represented by the blue-collar worker in Fordist enterprises. Today, routine production is also largely present in information-processing activities (for example, entering data in computers or devising routine coding for software programmes), and also in fast food restaurants.
- *In-person services*, where workers are in direct contact with the ultimate beneficiaries; these services are not sold globally.
- *Symbolic-analytical production*. In this last category, Reich introduces a new distinction between problem solvers, who put things together in a unique way; problem identifiers, who help customers understand their needs and how these needs can best be met by a customized product; and strategic brokers, who organize teams of problem solvers and problem identifiers.[15]

This typology of work is useful but does not analyse in depth the labour-specific content of in-person services. To do so, another quality attribute must be considered: interpersonal relations. Two kinds of interpersonal relations can be distinguished: (1) the relation between the consumer and the person delivering the service; and (2) the relations between consumers. Both are important for the value of the service sold. Regarding the first interaction Hardt (see Hardt 1999; Hardt and Negri 2000) argues that among the different sorts of labour involved in service production (defined by Hardt as 'immaterial labour'), a specific kind must be distinguished – affective labour. Affective labour can be found in almost any service industry, from fast food to banking. 'This labour is immaterial, even if it is corporal and affective, in the sense that its products are intangible: a feeling of ease, well-being, satisfaction, excitement, passion − even a sense of connectedness or community' (Hardt 1999: 93). In most in-person services, affective work is neither acknowledged nor paid, even if it is embedded in the price of the service.

Relations between consumers, and the quality of these relations, are another determinant part of the price of in-person services, such as providing a meal at a restaurant, hairdressing, performing a concert, or running a holiday camp. Economists dealing with services (public or private) analysed consumer involvement in term of co-production (Ostrom and Ostrom 1977). Because in-person services imply a direct contact between the producer and the consumer, in most cases consumers are grouped in a limited space. The ambience associated with a specific place where an in-person service is delivered depends to a large extent on consumers' behaviour and on the relations among them.

In short, what is sold as coffee in an outlet such as Starbucks is a mix of three quality attributes: material, symbolic and in-person service. Material attributes relate to the taste, aroma and appearance of the espresso or the cappuccino the consumer buys and drinks. Symbolic attributes are linked to Starbucks as a brand, the conception of the bar, ambience, interior design, the spatial organization of the place, its architecture, the clothes of the employees and so on. Some of these ideas are likely to be trademarked or copyrighted. Others are determined by the aggregation of consumers' individual behaviour, which is partly determined by the organization of the bar. The in-person service is the relation between the employees and the consumer, including a component of affective labour. As we move up a value chain towards producers, the make-up of these attributes changes, and so does their evaluation. By their very nature, in-person services take place at the point of consumption. Therefore, it is difficult for producers of tropical products to capture value from them, unless consumption is brought closer to them (as in agro-tourism or ecotourism) or unless the sites of service provision are more directly controlled by producer organizations (as with the Juan Valdez coffee shop chain in the US, which is run by the Federación Nacional de Cafeteros de Colombia).

Conclusion

In this chapter, we have highlighted the limitations of various approaches that have tried to solve the commodity problem in the last

50 years or so. We proposed a more nuanced analysis of the commodity problem and its impact on development, based on two tenets. First, we proposed to see commodities as goods that are exchanged by different players using the same standards – standards mostly based on measurable attributes. Second, we argued that many developing countries are stuck in producing and exporting goods that are valued for their material quality attributes. Symbolic and in-person service quality attributes are generated and controlled elsewhere. Thus market power is a question not only of market share (and abuse of it), but also of capturing the most valuable attributes while undermining the value of the attributes that need to be purchased. In the rest of this book, we study how inter-changeability or its opposite, uniqueness, are created in specific relation to the global value chain for coffee, and how coffee quality attributes are created, valued and/or appropriated.

Notes

1 Developed in Antwerp for selling products of the Dutch East India Company, the auction market was the main device for selling tropical products from the seventeenth century until the middle of the nineteenth century – and even later for products like tea and cocoa. In the auction market, the buyer bids on discrete lots for which descriptions are presented in catalogues sent by the sellers' broker. Moreover, previous to the sale, the buyer had a direct contact with the lots stored in the warehouse (Rees 1972).

2 This was particularly the case where spot markets were the norm. Hence, palm oil production remained based on plantation crops well into the 1990s.

3 Smoked sheet and crepe are two different presentations for rubber traded in the international market. Natural rubber is produced by first coagu-lating latex collected from the trees. The coagulum is then processed by a number of roll mills. Crepes are made by air-drying the sheet obtained after this process. Smoked sheets are made through drying in smoke houses.

4 In 1965, a new rubber standard based on the Malaysian technical specifi-cation scheme somewhat changed this situation. The specification for Standard Malaysian Rubber (SMR) was based on physicochemical criteria aimed at evaluating non-rubber components. Five product classes were defined, mainly according to the proportion of foreign bodies. For the first time in the history of tropical commodities, evaluation was based on

objective indicators rather than visual inspection. The establishment of a new standard was directly related to the marketing of block rubber by Malaysia. Block rubber was a new presentation for rubber that appeared on the international market after the Second World War. Visual examination, on which the Green Book classification was based, is impossible in block rubber. Following Malaysia, other producing countries have also adopted technically specified standards.

5   Myrdal's book *Beyond the Welfare State* (Myrdal 1960) is a typical example of such a perspective.

6   To be more precise, in the 1960s, the European Economic Community tried, under French influence, to promote several international agreements for the products it exported. The sugar agreement, and the beef and cheese protocols elaborated in the framework of the GATT during the Uruguay Round, are expressions of this project. However, these agreements never really worked. They were too manifestly in contradiction with the constraints and the objectives of developed country agricultural policies, including the Common Agricultural Policy (for more details on these contradictions, see Daviron and Voituriez 2003).

7   Costa Rica, El Salvador, Guatemala, Honduras and Nicaragua.

8   In GVC parlance, movement from production to consumption is a 'downstream' process. Therefore, in this book, we use the expression 'upstream' to mean movement towards producers and 'downstream' to mean movement towards consumers.

9   GVC analysis also draws from other approaches, such as the French *filière* tradition and the commodity systems approach (Friedland 1984). For an exhaustive coverage of commonalities and divergences among these (and other) traditions, see Gibbon and Ponte (2005) and Raikes, Jensen and Ponte (2000).

10 Conventions are systems of reciprocal expectations arising from interactions whose regularities are unintended. They are mechanisms of clarification that are themselves open to challenge (Wilkinson 1997: 318). They are both guides to action and collective systems to legitimize those actions – which can also be submitted to testing and discussion. Thus, we can see a convention as a system of reciprocal expectations about the behaviour of others, including things (Salais 1989).

11 Furthermore, Salais and Storper (1992; Storper and Salais 1997) have developed a typology of 'worlds of production' as a combination of technologies and markets, product qualities, and practices of resource use. A discussion of this approach is in Gibbon and Ponte (2005).

12 According to this criterion, rubber was a commodity in the 1950s and 1960s, when the Green Book standard elaborated under the control of the

US tyre manufacturers was the worldwide dominant one (Daviron 2002). In the twentieth century, in a large majority of international markets for agricultural products, several national standards coexisted. However, these standards were similar enough to establish equivalences and organize substitutability between national origins.

13 A supplementary article provides a stronger protection to wines and spirits.

14 In France, within the AOC system, INAO embeds the first and third mechanisms.

15 This last skill is a central one and some very successful enterprises reduce their activity to pure brokering within their global networks. In a way, US business can be seen to have shifted from the visible hand of the manager to the less visible hand of the broker.

2
What's in a cup?
Coffee from bean to brew

For a variety of reasons, coffee is particularly helpful in understanding the relation between commodity trade and development, and the distribution of value along global chains. First, over 90 per cent of global coffee production takes place in the South, while consumption takes place mainly in the North.[1] The production–consumption pattern therefore provides insights into North–South economic relations that are not tainted by the possibility of hidden protectionism for the benefit of farmers in the North. Second, for most of the post-Second World War period coffee has been the second most valuable traded commodity after oil.[2] Third, attempts at controlling the international coffee trade have been taking place since the beginning of the twentieth century, making coffee one of the first regulated commodities. Fourth, a number of low-income countries, even those with a low share of the global export market, rely on coffee for a high proportion of their export earnings. Fifth, producing country governments have historically treated coffee as a strategic commodity; they have either directly controlled domestic marketing and quality control operations or have strictly regulated them – at least until market liberalization took place in the 1980s and 1990s. Sixth, during the last few decades, the post-harvest part of the coffee chain did not experience the adoption of new technology (although there has been innovation and adaptation of older technology). Thus, the analysis of value distribution and of its evolution is simplified. Finally, coffee has been the first commodity and/or the main focus in several of the 'new' forms of regulation that have emerged in the last two decades – such as socio-economic and environmental labels, certifications and codes of conduct.

In this chapter, we introduce the reader to the essential characteristics of coffee production, trade and consumption, focusing on the historical dynamics of these processes and on their technical aspects. The next section leads the reader through the flows and trans- formations that determine the movement of the coffee bean from production to consumption. The second and third sections examine historical trends in the geography of coffee production and the evolution of labour systems. The fourth presents a history of the changing organizational features of the coffee trade, and the type of contracts and grades that underpin them. Finally, the fifth section provides some background information on coffee retail and con- sumption patterns. In Chapter 3, we will revisit some of these aspects through the lenses of governance as we start unpacking the reasons behind the coffee crisis and the coffee paradox.

Coffee flows and transformations

Coffee as a drink is the output of a value chain beginning with a cherry produced by a tree. The coffee tree requires a warm climate without sudden temperature shifts, does not tolerate frost, and needs plenty of seasonal rains. These conditions are normally met between the tropics of Cancer and Capricorn. Two species are currently used in coffee cultivation for commercial purposes: *Coffea arabica* and *Coffea canephora* (also known in the trade as Robusta). At the beginning of the 2000s, *Coffea arabica* accounted for 64 per cent of global coffee production. Two other species were traded until the Second World War: *Coffea liberica* and *Coffea excelsa*. They have now almost totally disappeared from the trade.

Both species, *Coffea arabica* (hereafter, Arabica) and *Coffea canephora* (hereafter, Robusta), produce cherries that enclose two flat seeds (the bean). Arabica coffee is more susceptible to attacks by pest and diseases. Its best growing conditions are found in warmer temperate zones or in highlands of tropical zones. Robusta coffee is more resistant and can be grown between sea level and an altitude of 800 metres. The first harvest for a newly planted coffee tree usually takes place after two years, and optimal yields are reached two or three years later. The ripening period of the cherries depends on climate and soil fertility – usually 6–8 months for Arabica and 9–11 months for Robusta. Coffee is often cultivated in association with a variety of trees providing shade and helping to maintain soil fertility and humidity. In some producing regions, coffee is cultivated with minimal or no use of chemical inputs and irrigation; in others, various kinds of pesticides, anti-fungal chemicals and fertilizers are applied to the coffee trees – sometimes in addition to irrigation systems of varying complexity.

In the movement from harvest to export, coffee goes through various steps of primary processing. The main goal of primary processing is the separation of the bean from the skin and pulp of the cherry. There are two methods for doing this. In the 'wet' method, ripe cherries are harvested and then pulped, fermented, washed, and dried. The end result of these operations is 'parchment' coffee. This coffee goes to a curing plant, where the parchment is removed and the beans are cleaned and polished. Wet processing takes place mostly for Arabica coffee. Wet-processed Arabica coffee is also known as Mild Arabica. In the 'dry' method, farmers harvest ripe cherries and dry them until the coffee bean inside separates from the outer layers. The dry cherries are taken to a huller where the outer layers are removed. Almost all Robusta coffee is dry-processed. Dry-processed Arabica is also known as Hard Arabica or Natural Arabica. In both methods, wet and dry, the end result is 'green' coffee, which is the qualified product for export.

Before being exported, green coffee is cleaned, sorted and graded into lots that have differentiated quality attributes. The grading systems vary from country to country. They are based on the coffee variety; the method of processing; the size, density, shape and colour of the green bean; the number and type of defects; and, in some countries, on the aroma, colour and flavour of roasted and/or brewed coffee. Green Robusta coffee is treated as an undifferentiated commodity and few efforts are made to distinguish between different flavours within a given country or even between countries. Robusta is normally graded simply by size and number of defects. In Arabica, evaluation of the variations in aroma and taste is much more important. These variations depend on the cultivar of the coffee grown, the processing method, the type of soil, climate and altitude. 'The top quality coffees are produced in the higher altitudes where, amongst other factors contributing to quality, the ultraviolet light is stronger and growth is generally slower' (Wrigley 1988: 490).

After storing and transport to the export harbour, most green coffee is shipped to a harbour in a consuming country in 60-kilogram bags loaded in containers.[3] However, some Robusta is shipped in bulk (without bags) in containers. The most important of these harbours, which have large storage facilities, are located in Antwerp, Amsterdam and Hamburg in Europe, New York, New Orleans and San Francisco in the US. Here, green coffee is stored before being sent to various locations for roasting. Unlike cocoa beans, green coffee can be stored for a relatively long period – even in tropical countries. However, international traders tend to dispose of their stocks before the 'new' crop comes in. Thus, most green coffee is stored for periods of under one year.

Usually, blending is the first operation carried out in roasting facilities in consuming countries.[4] However, in the last decade or so, some roasters are requiring Robusta and Hard Arabica coffees to go through a process of steam-cleaning (usually carried out by international traders or specialist firms) to remove some of the defects and tame the harshness of some Robustas. Coffees from different countries or different regions are used to obtain a specific aroma in the roasted coffee, and a specific flavour and body profile when it is brewed. Blending is also used to manage the natural variability of coffee. By manipulating the composition of the blend, roasters can achieve the same profile without being overly dependent on any one origin. By changing the share of each origin, the roaster is able to stabilize the attribute value of the final product. Blending is the most important operation for a roaster, the one in which specific know-how is mobilized. Roasters use blending formulae that they adjust after sample testing. Robusta is harsher than Arabica and has twice the caffeine content. Few roasted coffees are made with pure Robusta. Robusta is used mostly in blends as a filler to reduce the price of the blend. Robusta and Hard Arabica are also key components in espresso blends to create their signature foam on top of the brew.

Green coffee beans must be roasted to release the aroma. Roasting is a relatively simple operation and roasting machines are basically a rotating drum with a heat source underneath. Yet, the production of high quality and specialty coffees requires skilled roasters and/or more advanced machinery that can control and manipulate roasting times, heat conditions and cooling. The length of roasting determines the colour and the taste of the roasted coffee. The longer the beans are roasted the darker and 'stronger', in terms of taste, they become. Sometimes, depending on local consumer taste, coffee is mixed with

The dry method (Natural Arabica and Robusta)

Labour process		State of the product
Nursery	→	Seedlings
		↓
Planting	→	Seedlings in the orchard
		↓
Seedling maintenance	→	Adult coffee trees
		↓
Weeding, fertilising, pruning, spraying	→	Coffee cherries on the trees
		↓
Harvest	→	Harvested coffee cherries
		↓
Transportation	→	Coffee cherries delivered to the farm
		↓
Drying	→	Dry cherries
		↓
Storing	→	Dry cherries
		↓
Transportation	→	Dry cherries delivered to the huller plant
		↓
Hulling	→	Bulk green coffee
		↓
Cleaning, sorting, grading, bagging	→	Bags of graded green coffee
		↓
Transportation to the harbour	→	Bags of graded green coffee in the producing country harbour
		↓
Storage	→	Bags of graded green coffee in the producing country harbour
		↓
Shipping	→	Bags of graded green coffee in the vessel located in the producing country harbour
		↓
Transportation	→	Bags of graded green coffee in the consuming country harbour
		↓
Unshipping	→	Bags of graded green coffee in the consuming country harbour warehouse
		↓
Storage	→	Bags of graded green coffee in the roasting factory
		↓
Blending	→	Bags of graded green coffee in the roasting factory
		↓
Roasting	→	Batches of blended green coffee
		↓
Grinding, packing	→	Batches of roasted coffee
		↓
Transportation	→	Bags of roasted coffee in the location of consumption
		↓
Storage	→	Packages of roasted coffee in the location of consumption
		↓
Preparation of the beverage Consumption	→	Coffee ready to drink

Figure 2.1 Flows and transformations of coffee between

The wet method (Mild arabica)

Labour process		State of the product
		Coffee cherries delivered to the pulping station
		↓
Pulping	→	Pulped cherries
		↓
Fermenting	→	Fermented cherries
		↓
Washing	→	Fermented and washed cherries
		↓
Drying	→	Parchment coffee
		↓
Storage	→	Parchment coffee
		↓
Transportation	→	Parchment coffee in the curing plant
		↓
Curing (peeling)	→	Bulk green coffee

The soluble coffee value chain

Labour process	State of the product
Extraction	Batches of blended green coffee
	↓
Concentration, drying (spray, freeze)	Liquid coffee extract
	↓
Packaging	Batch of soluble coffee
	↓
Transportation	Boxes of soluble coffee
	↓
Storage	Boxes of soluble coffee in the consumer city
	↓
Preparation of the beverage	Boxes of soluble coffee in the consumer city
	↓
Consumption	Coffee ready to drink

production and point of consumption

other inputs such as sugar, chicory (*Cichorum intybus*) or roasted cereals. Most roasted coffee is ground in the roasting facility before being packed. However, whole beans are also marketed when appearance is important to the consumer, as in some branches of the specialty coffee industry and for consumption in espresso bars. The production of soluble coffee includes two more transformation steps: the preparation of a liquid coffee extract and dehydration, which can be done by heating or freezing.

Most international coffee trade consists of 'green' coffee, but coffee is also traded in its soluble and roasted forms. Trade between producing and consuming countries consists mostly of green coffee and bulk instant coffee. Bulk instant coffee imported from producing countries is usually blended and repackaged in consuming countries. The roasted coffee trade takes place almost exclusively between consuming countries. This pattern of trade comes from the fact that green and instant coffees can be stored for a long period of time, while roasted coffee loses its freshness much more quickly.

In comparison to other commodities, there have been relatively few technological and product innovations in coffee once it reaches consuming countries. Up to the beginning of the nineteenth century, and even later in large parts of the European countryside, coffee beans were roasted at home in pans or cylinders. With the introduction of roasting machines, coffee came to be roasted in shops. As a consequence, the roaster profession was created. Thereafter, the invention of soluble coffee was the main technical innovation in processing. The soluble coffee process was invented in the US at the beginning of the twentieth century. A major step forward was the introduction by Nestlé in the 1930s of a spray technology adapted from the one used in milk drying. Following the introduction of soluble coffee in US army rations in the Second World War, soluble coffee consumption increased dramatically. During the past 20 years, in the US and Europe the image of soluble coffee has changed radically. Soluble coffee is now considered as a low-quality product and its consumption is currently decreasing in most national markets. The daily number of cups of soluble coffee drinks consumed by US consumers has fallen from 0.75 in 1974 to 0.11 in 2004 (USDA 2004).

Coffee offerings at the retail level (both in roasted and brewed forms) have diversified dramatically in the last 10–15 years, with the expansion of the specialty coffee industry, the introduction of ready-to-drink coffee-based beverages, and the proliferation of Starbucks and other café chains. Yet, in terms of end use, coffee still has a limited number of outlets. Except for soluble coffee, there have been variations around one type of product – rather than the creation of a completely new product. Coffee is still used mainly as a warm drink and to provide caffeine content for the pharmaceutical and soft drink industries. This is a relatively limited range when compared to corn (which can be used to make plastic bags, animal feed and sugar substitutes), sugar (which is used to produce gas), milk (which can be consumed as a drink, butter, cheese or yoghurt), or even cocoa (chocolate, beverages, cosmetics).

Production and export geography

At the beginning of the nineteenth century, coffee was exclusively cultivated on islands. Réunion, Martinique, Santo Domingo, Cuba, Jamaica, Puerto Rico, Java and Sri Lanka were the main coffee-producing territories. During the following decades, with the railway revolution in transportation, coffee cultivation spread to the Americas, including most of the newly independent Latin American nations. Soon after, Brazil became the first exporting country in that region. It produced 25 per cent of the world harvest around 1830, 50 per cent around 1860 and 75 per cent at the end of the century. It was not until the 1920s that the expansion of coffee production was resumed in the rest of Latin America, with Colombia emerging as Brazil's main competitor. It is also during this period that Africa progressively emerged as a new coffee-exporting continent, the British colonies (Uganda, Kenya) being the first African territories to be incorporated in the world coffee market. Within the French empire, Madagascar was the first colony with a noticeable coffee sector. But it was not until after the Second World War (between 1950 and 1965), that Franco-phone Africa became an important player in the coffee market. Eventually, during the 1980s and 1990s, coffee cultivation also spread to Asia, first with the rapid development of coffee cultivation in Indonesia and, later, an even faster development in Vietnam (see Tables 2.1 and 2.2, Figure 2.2).

In 1994, Vietnam produced 230,000 bags of coffee, while Colombia produced over 11 million. By 1999, however, Vietnam had replaced

Table 2.1 Green coffee production by main region (thousands of 60-kg bags and percentage of world total, 1830–2004)

	1830		1855–9		1880–4		1900–4	
West Indies	960	38%	264	5%	608	6%	635	4%
Indonesia–Sri Lanka	500	20%	1,779	34%	1,983	21%	550	3%
Other Asian countries	199	8%	172	3%	495	5%	210	1%
Brazil	610	24%	2,742	52%	5,290	56%	12,424	73%
Colombia	—	—	5	—	102	1%	460	3%
Other Latin American countries	200	8%	261	5%	910	10%	2,531	15%
Africa	25	1%	25	0.5%	91	1%	165	1%
World total	2,494	100%	5,248	100%	9,479	100%	16,975	100%

	1925–9		1950–4		1970–4		2000–4	
West Indies	1,400	5%	2,025	5%	1,946	3%	1,201	1%
Indonesia-Sri Lanka	1,785	6%	983	2%	2,441	3%	6,270	5%
Other Asian countries	397	1%	793	2%	2,321	3%	21,994	19%
Brazil	18,572	62%	19,083	46%	20,380	29%	36,760	32%
Colombia	2,723	9%	6,341	15%	8,120	11%	11,094	10%
Other Latin American countries	4,262	14%	6,156	15%	14,572	21%	22,032	19%
Africa	913	3%	6,335	15%	21,082	30%	15,542	14%
World Total	30,052	100%	41,716	100%	70,862	100%	114,893	100%

Source: Daviron (1994); United States Department of Agriculture (USDA) (2004).

Colombia as the world's second largest producer with a production of over 11 million bags.[5] In Vietnam, the production boom took place with the 'frontier' expansion of coffee cultivation in the Dak Lak province located in the Central Highlands. In the 1990–2000 period, the area under cultivation in this province increased by 14 per cent a year (ICARD and Oxfam 2002). Population density increased from three inhabitants per square kilometre in the 1930s to 77 in 1997. In 1940, the Kinh (the majority ethnic group coming from the plains) represented only 6 per cent of the population in the area; by 1996, they were a staggering 70 per cent (Fortunel 2000). In Vietnam, as well as in other countries, the dramatic coffee production increase was associated with a frontier. The novelty of this experience was the transposition of the 'deltaic' agricultural system[6] to coffee cultivation. In parallel to

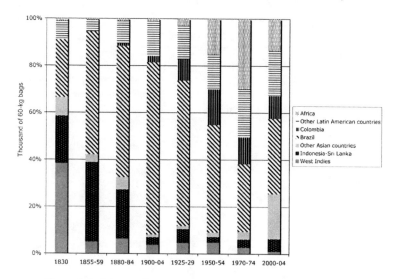

Figure 2.2 Green coffee production by main region, 1830–2004
Source: Table 2.1.

labour-intensive expansion in Vietnam, Brazil promoted the 'rebirth' of coffee cultivation, with new expansion based on a mechanized and input-intensive model of cultivation and harvesting in the centre of the country (in the so-called *cerrado*) and in the state of Espirito Santo on the Atlantic coast. The result of new expansion has been the steady decline of African production – from one third of the global coffee harvest in 1970–4 to 13–14 per cent in 2001–4. Overall, export dynamics followed a similar path, since only Brazil and Ethiopia have significant domestic consumption. Current export volumes are summarized in Table 2.3.

In specific relation to Robusta, its production and export started with the entry of African colonies into the coffee market, mostly Uganda, Angola, Madagascar, Côte d'Ivoire and Cameroon. The share of Robusta in the world harvest increased from almost zero in 1920 to 27 per cent at the end of the 1960s. Then, in the 1970s, with civil unrest in Angola and later in Uganda, and the ageing of coffee trees in other African countries, this share decreased. The 1980s and 1990s, on the contrary, witnessed a large increase in Robusta cultivation. Four countries played a decisive role: Indonesia and India during the 1980s, and Vietnam and Brazil more recently and more spectacularly. During

Table 2.2 Total production of major exporting countries, crop years 2001/2 to 2003/4 (millions of 60-kg bags)

Crop year commencing	Type of coffee	2001/2	2002/3	2003/4	2001/2–2003/4 Average	Share of world production
Total world		110.8	124.2	105.3	117.3	100%
North and Central America		17.1	16.5	16.8	16.8	15%
Mexico	(A)	4.2	4.3	4.6	4.4	
Guatemala	(A/R)	3.5	3.8	3.8	3.7	
Honduras	(A)	3.1	2.6	2.8	2.8	
Costa Rica	(A)	2.3	2.2	2.2	2.2	
El Salvador	(A)	1.6	1.3	1.3	1.4	
Nicaragua	(A)	0.9	0.8	0.6	0.8	
South America		51.7	67.9	48.6	56.0	49%
Brazil	(A/R)	35.1	51.6	32.0	39.6	
Colombia	(A)	11.9	11.7	11.8	11.8	
Africa		14.4	14.1	13.7	14.1	13%
Ethiopia	(A)	3.7	3.7	3.2	3.5	
Uganda	(R/A)	3.2	2.8	3.2	3.1	
Côte d'Ivoire	(R)	3.0	1.8	1.3	2.0	
Cameroon	(R/A)	1.2	1.1	1.2	1.2	
Kenya	(A)	0.9	0.9	1.0	0.9	
Tanzania	(R/A)	0.6	0.8	0.8	0.8	
Asia		27.4	25.7	26.1	26.4	23%
Vietnam	(R)	12.8	11.2	11.8	11.9	
Indonesia	(R/A)	6.2	6.1	5.7	6.0	
India	(A/R)	5.0	4.6	4.6	4.7	

Notes: A= Arabica: R= Robusta
Source: United States Department of Agriculture (2004).

the last few years, Robusta has accounted for almost 40 per cent of world coffee production (see Table 2.4; Figure 2.3).

Systems of labour mobilization and organization of production

Various form of labour mobilization have been applied in the history of coffee cultivation, from the exclusive use of slave labour to the current situation, in which smallholders and wage labour coexist. Between these two forms of mobilization, there have also been

Table 2.3 Coffee exports by ICO category and by main exporting countries
(2003/4, 60-kg bags)

	2003	2004
Total	85,761,701	89,310,415
Colombian Milds	11,766,557	11,355,327
Other Milds	20,919,526	20,826,368
Brazilian Naturals	23,751,846	26,605,437
Robustas	29,323,772	30,523,283
Brazil	25,693,727	26,395,188
Colombia	10,244,392	10,194,319
Costa Rica	1,701,812	1,440,939
El Salvador	1,304,030	1,322,420
Guatemala	3,820,800	3,309,581
Honduras	2,425,237	2,779,189
Mexico	2,594,508	2,360,592
Peru	2,412,192	2,951,667
India	3,706,837	3,640,817
Indonesia	4,752,972	4,440,000
Vietnam	11,631,111	14,858,991
Côte d'Ivoire	2,646,649	2,601,796
Ethiopia	2,229,143	2,490,944
Kenya	919,569	729,867
Tanzania	882,665	542,919
Uganda	2,522,128	2,627,011

Source: International Coffee Organization (ICO) database.

different 'transitional' forms – sometimes with the use of coerced labour and sometimes without.

At the end of eighteenth century, coffee was the second crop after sugar in terms of the number of slaves mobilized in plantations. Until the French Revolution, the slave coffee plantation model was exemplified by Saint Domingue (Haiti). In the late 1780s, the island was supplying half the volume of European coffee consumption (DiFulvio 1947). At that time, the population of the island consisted of 40,000 whites, 28,000 free 'coloureds' and 452,000 slaves (Curtin 1990: 161).

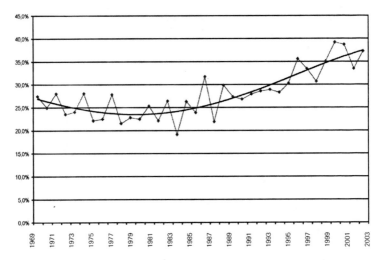

Figure 2.3 Share of Robusta in world coffee production, 1969–2003

Source: USDA (2004).

Table 2.4 Robusta production of major exporting countries, crop years 2001/2 to 2003/4 (millions of 60-kg bags)

Crop year commencing	2001/02	2002/03	2003/04	2001/02-2003/04 Average
Total world	42.4	40.9	38.6	40.7
Brazil	10.7	12.0	9.4	10.7
Uganda	2.9	2.4	2.7	2.7
Côte d'Ivoire	3.0	1.8	1.3	2.0
Cameroon	1.1	1.0	1.1	1.2
Vietnam	12.7	10.9	11.5	11.7
Indonesia	5.7	5.6	5.2	5.5
India	3.0	2.9	2.8	2.9

Source: USDA (2004).

The plantation system collapsed after a series of events, beginning in 1788 with a conflict among whites, followed by a large slave rebellion in 1791, and ending with the creation of an independent state – Haiti. In subsequent decades, Brazil became the very heart of the slave coffee plantation economy. Plantations were created first in Rio de Janeiro, close to the coast. At the beginning of the nineteenth century, coffee ousted sugar and cotton as the main crop cultivated in the Paraiba Valley. 'Brazil imported an annual average of 37,000 slaves a year between 1811 and 1850 – more than two-thirds of the Atlantic slave trade of that period' (Curtin 1990: 191). Later, one of the competitive advantages of Rio and later São Paulo was the number of slaves available in Minas Gerais (due to the decline of the gold industry there) and in the North-East (where the sugar industry was in crisis) (Vioti da Costa 1982). Because of this surplus of slave labour, Brazil was able to maintain and even develop the slave coffee production model in spite of already existing restrictions on the slave trade imposed by the British government and, later, other European countries. At the time abolition was voted in 1888, Brazil was the last country to legislate an end to slavery.

Following these events, a transitional model of coerced labour emerged, based on two variants: (1) coerced labour or pseudo-coerced labour on large plantations; and (2) coerced cultivation by smallholders. The forced labour variant preceded and outlived the abolition of slavery. Forced labour refers to obliging persons – usually farmers – to spend part of their time working on the construction of public infra-structure (roads, bridges, dams and other projects), on government farms, and for private enterprises. Forced labour thus differed from slavery in that: (1) the persons used were not traded; and (2) usually, only part of their time was used for forced activities (although it could be a large proportion).

The history of coffee cultivation is marked by repeated instances of the use of forced labour. On large plantations, coerced labour was used in a variety of settings. It was used for a long period of time in Central America, and particularly in Guatemala and Soconusco (its neigh-bouring Mexican region) (Williams 1994). In Guatemala, coffee cultivation began around 1860 after the decline in the production of cochineal (a dye material extracted from a bug found on certain species of cactus). To respond to new needs for labour, legislation was implemented to mobilize Indian populations through a decree reviving forced labour drafts (McCreery 2003: 194–5). According to the law, the only alternative to being drafted for indigenous people was to prove that they had a contract with a plantation in the export sector (coffee, sugar, cocoa, banana). Thus, an increasing number of workers became bound by debt contracts with one or more plantations. Some of them, the *colonos*, ended up living permanently on the plantation; others, the *temporalistas*, worked for periods of two to six months. In 1934, the dictator General Jorge Ubico ended labour debts and instituted the *trabajo libre* (*ibid*.: 205). In this system, 'rural men, Indians and ladinos alike, were free to contract their work as they wished, but those who could not prove access to relatively large amounts of land or who did not practise an exempted profession or trade were required to work for wages on export plantations for at least 100 to 150 days a year' (*ibid*.: 205). Legal coerced labour was finally abolished in 1944. Even after this date, however, coercion continued to be used (and still is), with landowners employing armed guards to avoid labour strikes.

Coerced mobilization of indigenous labour on large plantations existed in many other countries, and particularly in European colonies in Africa before the First World War. Forced labour was a widespread practice in the French colonies in sub-Saharan Africa. It was based on the obligation of all taxpayers to provide 15 days' labour per year as a tax. In Côte d'Ivoire, it partially benefited European coffee and cocoa plantations (Losch 1999). Forced labour lasted until 1946 when it was abolished in response to a campaign by the Syndicat Agricole Africain (African Labour Union). The elimination of forced labour was one of the objectives of the League of Nations and of the newly established International Labour Organization (ILO). In fact, at least in colonial Africa, the use of forced labour on large plantations had almost disappeared in the 1920s, to be replaced by forced labour on smaller family farms.

Coffee cultivation in São Paulo was a typical example of a successful transition from slave labour to non-coerced labour within the production model of the large plantation. From the mid-nineteenth century, the *fazendeiros*, like many other planters in the tropical world, had to deal with the interdiction of the slave trade, and were looking for new sources of labour. In a first step, in the 1840s, they experimented with indentured labour. About 60 *fazendas* imported migrants coming first from Germany, and later from Switzerland, Spain and Italy as well. Soon after, this experiment was abandoned. Migrants were supposed to be more or less sharecroppers. However, migrants arrived at the plantations greatly indebted to the *fazendeiros*. They had to reimburse travel expenses from Europe and the living expenses incurred during the first year of residence. For the *fazendeiros*, migrants represented a captive workforce. A few years after their arrival, conflicts broke out between migrants and *fazendeiros* (for a personal account of a migrant, see Davatz 1980). In 1857, governments from Prussia and Switzerland banned this form of migration (Dean 1976), putting an end to the first Brazilian attempt to find a new source of labour. During the following fifteen years, with the exception of migrants coming from Portugal, the *fazendeiros* went back to using slave labour: the number of slaves used on these *fazendas* increased twice as much as the number of free workers.

The invention of the *colono* system took place at the end of the 1880s. *Colono* was the name of a new migrant contracted to work in the *fazenda*. The normal contract provided for a package of wage and other incentives involving three major forms of remuneration: (1) a wage for the care of a fixed number of coffee trees; (2) a payment per unit of volume of coffee picked; and (3) a wage per day worked for unspecified tasks. The *colono* also received free housing and a portion of land on which to grow subsistence crops. In 1887, one year before the abolition of slavery, the *fazendeiros* founded the Sociedade Protetora de Imigração, which, using subsidies provided by the state of São Paulo, covered the transport costs of immigrants. An Immigration Hotel was built in São Paulo to welcome and guide immigrants on their arrival (Holloway 1978). This policy was a remarkable success. The number of immigrants increased from 9,000 in 1886 to 32,000 in 1887, and then to 92,000 in 1888 – almost as many immigrants in a single year as the number of slaves present in the state. São Paulo coffee cultivation thus benefited from a continuous inflow of labour for 20 years, totalling over a million people, most of whom came from Italy. Brazil was thus the only tropical country in Latin America to benefit from part of the wave of European emigration at the end of the nineteenth century.

Coerced cultivation by smallholders was most effective in economic terms in Java under Dutch rule. The cultivation system (*kultuur stelsel*) in Indonesia has been the subject of much research and debate, summarized in recent publications (Clarence-Smith 1994; Fernando 2003). Set up by the governor general of the island, J. van den Bosch, and enforced from 1830 to 1870, it obliged every farmer to devote a fifth of his/her land to growing a tropical export crop (such as indigo, sugar, coffee, tea, tobacco, cotton or pepper). Persons with no land were obliged to work in the administration's fields for a fifth of their time. These products were collected by the colonial administration and sold in Europe for the benefit of the Dutch treasury. There was also an obligation to work on the construction of roads and irrigation systems and the construction of post-harvest processing facilities.

A similar system was used, on a smaller scale, in other colonial territories. In Africa, a general shift took place at the time of the First World War, from using coerced labour on large plantations to coerced cultivation by smallholders. As we explained above, even though some situations of forced labour in large plantations lasted up to 1918 and after, colonial administrators trying to develop African colonial territories became increasingly convinced that it was impossible to create large plantations based on European capital. Therefore, they resorted to mobilizing smallholder farmers. Belgian civil servants, after the transformation of the Congo Free State into a colony, were particularly innovative in looking for the right formula, combining physical constraints with monetary incentives, to promote export crops among smallholders. Many of their institutional innovations were used later in other colonies.

Costa Rica was the first country where independent smallholders started cultivating coffee on a large scale. Coffee cultivation started being developed in the 1840s in the so-called Meseta Central. From the very beginning, the coffee sector in Costa Rica adopted a different organization from other producing countries. First, coffee cultivation was carried out on family farms (Hall 1976). Second, coffee cherries harvested on the farm were sold by smallholders to *benificadores* – the owners of the mills where the cherries were transformed into green coffee using the wet process. Thus, the 'peasantization' of coffee cultivation was accompanied by a vertical disintegration of the value chain. The transformation of coffee cherries into green coffee and the export of green coffee became a business on its own – a prime business for the elite of Costa Rica. According to Hall (1976), the development of smallholder coffee farms can be linked to the shortage of labour in this specific region at that time. The region was quite isolated and characterized by a small number of inhabitants and no slave population. But Hall also points out that there were strong legal limitations on the importation of labour from Africa or China. The employment of such people was prohibited in the Basic Law for Colonization, voted in 1862 and again in 1875. Other authors also highlight that land ownership was not concentrated in this area. Moreover, in Brazil a new agrarian law enacted in 1859 stopped the distribution of land for free. This was done to make the migrants work some years in large plantations before being able to get their own farms. Instead, in Costa Rica, a law limited the size of plots that were authorized to be sold (Kuznesof 1986).

Colombia can be seen as a second and decisive step toward the 'peasantization' of coffee cultivation. The growth of Colombian coffee production in the nineteenth century started in Santander province on the frontier with Venezuela. Coffee growing replaced former slave-based cocoa and cotton production (Palacios 1983). The increase in international prices from 1885 to 1891 favoured the extension of coffee cultivation to Cundimarca-Tolima and Antioquia provinces. Coffee growing in these three regions was developed in large estates (*haciendas*) operating on a sharecropping basis (Santander and Antioquia) or with a semi-servile indigenous wage-earning labour system (Cundimarca-Tolima). The *haciendados* originated in a group of traders that became established during various export booms in Colombia in the nine-teenth century (tobacco, quinine, indigo and gold from Antioquia). However, this first expansion stopped at the end of the nineteenth century. The second period of expansion of coffee cultivation lasted from 1912 until the Second World War and was quite different from the first. Growth shifted towards the South-West and was concentrated in the three departments of Antioquia, Caldas and Tolima. But above all, for the first time in the history of Colombia, small farms – that is to say those employing mainly family labour – did much better than large plantations. Towards the end of this second period of expansion (in the 1930s), farms with less than twelve hectares of land produced more than 60 per cent of the harvest (Machado 1988). At the same time, another organizational change emerged. Smallholders started carrying out the first part of wet processing (pulping, fermenting, washing and drying) in the farm, thanks to a widespread use of small hand pulpers. Thus, they started selling parchment coffee instead of cherry.

The boom of Colombian coffee exports and the tremendous increase of its market share (from 3 per cent in the 1910s to 15 per cent in the 1930s) indicate a major shift in the organization of coffee cultivation at the world level. From then on, smallholder production occupied an increasing and soon dominant place in the world coffee harvest. Most coffee production developed after the Second World War in Africa was smallholder production (with the exception of Kenya). In a similar way, later, Indonesia and Vietnam would build their coffee sectors on small farms.

Even in Brazil, and even in São Paulo, land of the *fazendeiros*, coffee cultivation became increasingly a family farm activity during the interwar period (Font 1990). A large proportion of these independent farmers were previous *colono* families who were able to raise the necessary capital to buy land. *Colono* families employed on the frontier were in a particularly good position to generate savings. New plantations gave them the opportunity to intercrop rows of young coffee trees with corn or beans to be sold in the booming urban markets of the state of São Paulo. Whereas coffee cultivation under slavery had broken families and depended primarily on male workers (far more men than women were imported from Africa), the family was the backbone of the *colono* system (Topik 1998: 49).

In sum, coffee production was profoundly transformed by changes in labour mobilization and the related shift from large plantations to family farms. This resulted in a spectacular decapitalization of coffee cultivation.[7] From the beginning of the twentieth century to the 1970s, coffee production was characterized by an extensive growth model with small gains in productivity. The low use of capital implied that most of the growth of coffee production accrued from mobilizing more labour and land. Pioneer fronts played a central role in this extensive expansion process. Migration and deforestation have accompanied the growth of coffee production in most producing countries. From the 1970s, this process has been partially reversed by the growth in capital- and technology-intensive cultivation in Brazil. More recently, the growth of specialty and sustainable coffees has also led to increased interest in (and competitiveness of) large-scale production units (see Chapter 5). We examine the policy implications of these more recent phenomena in our concluding chapter. In the next section, we examine the history of different organizational systems that characterized coffee trade, with some focus on the role of contracts and quality standards.

Markets, contracts and grades

The commoditization of coffee was a long process and, compared to other tropical products, an incomplete one. Because of the importance of cup characteristics in evaluating the quality of coffee, market operators never really succeeded in collectively defining objective quality criteria and ways of measuring them, although steps have been taken in this direction. These steps were important enough to allow the existence of futures markets and a certain level of interchangeability between producers and between origins. In this section, we discuss the historical construction of coffee as a commodity, its results and its limits. More specific questions regarding quality and new ways of defining and managing it are discussed in Chapters 4 and 5.

In a first historical period, and in a similar way to other tropical products and spices traded in the eighteenth and nineteenth centuries (see Chapter 1), coffee quality was not very well defined because the sale of the product occurred in the consuming country on auction markets. In the first half of the eighteenth century, traded coffees (even Caribbean and Latin American ones) were mainly designated as Mochas (after the name of the Red Sea harbour from which the Yemenite harvest was exported), Bourbons (after the previous name of Réunion) or Javas. According to Topik (2003: 28), these coffees 'were "theoretically" genetically related to those of the first coffee-producing countries'. However, at the beginning of the nineteenth century, a variety of other geographical references started to be used. According to an agronomist,

> [t]he trade does not have fixed rules for the designation of coffees: it sometimes chooses the shipping port (C. Santos), sometimes the name of a district (C. Préanger) and sometimes that of the political nationality (C. Mexico, C. Costa Rica); it sometimes adds the transport port to the provenance (C. Moka Alexandria) or again an agreed name (C. Zanzibar). (Raoul 1897: 124)

Nevertheless, the names of ports appeared to be a major reference.

These names reflected the pre-twentieth-century reality of a mysterious hinterland often off-bounds for international merchants, and the entrepôt ports, which were satellites of the world economy. The ports served as sorts of shock-absorbers that translated domestic grades, measurements and currencies into international standards and distributed foreign revenues, capital and technology to the interior (Topik 2003: 41).

For many years in the eighteenth century, Amsterdam was the centre of the coffee trade. There, a semi-official firm, the Nederlandsche Handel Maatschappij, was exporting and shipping the Javanese small-holder production to be sold at the auction in the Nederlands – on behalf of the state (Fernando 2003). Then, the French auctions became the most important ones, first in Bordeaux and later in Le Havre (Rees 1972). The Napoleonic wars and the continental blockade changed this situation. Subsequently, London emerged as the centre of the coffee trade, thanks to the large availability of warehouses and easy and cheap access to credit. A large part of the coffee traded in the London auction was re-exported towards the continent (Rees 1972). Coffee was mixed and sold in these warehouses under inspection by the buyer, and often also hulled in London.[8]

The creation, in 1881, of the New York Coffee Exchange was a decisive step in the commoditization process. By the end of the century, the US had become the largest coffee-consuming country in the world.[9] For the next sixty years, the New York Coffee Exchange remained the leading market and drove many of the changes occurring in producing countries. Traders made extensive use of its exchange standard.[10]

Transactions in the Coffee Exchange were organized according to rules defining nine grades. No coffees with a grade lower than No. 8 were allowed into the US. Each grade was defined in relation to the number of defects. As presented by Ukers (1935: 359)

> the Exchange ... issues no hard and fast table of imperfections or 'defects' ... The official exchange graders are therefore allowed to use their combined judgment as to relative values of various extraneous matters in addition to damaged or malformed beans in any given sample. The constant changes that would have to be made in an official list to keep pace with changing coffee from each year's crop and changing demand of the trade are therefore eliminated.

Grade No. 7 was used as a basis for the quotation and all other grades were judged in relation to it. The grading system did not make reference to coffee aroma. It did not make reference to the geographical origin of the coffee, either. The Coffee Exchange dealt in all coffees from North, Central and South America and coffee from the West and East Indies. Natural Robusta was not accepted.

Meanwhile, during the second part of the nineteenth century, the US occupied an increasingly important place among the destinations of coffee exports from Brazil. At the beginning of the 1880s, two-thirds of Brazilian coffee was exported to the US (Laerne 1885). With the creation of the New York futures market, the Brazilian coffee sector reorganized profoundly, first in regard to the management of quality, second in regard to the number and kind of activities that marketing operators carried out. These changes occurred more or less simultaneously to the movement of the Brazilian coffee centre of gravity from Rio to Santos.

Around 1880, the Rio coffee trade already presented several important differences compared to the historical organization of trade in tropical products. Some of the activities previously carried out in London were now occurring in Brazil. A first operator intervened on the coffee leaving the plantation: the *commissario*. The *commissario* was for the *fazendeiro* the equivalent of the factor for the West Indies planter: a commission merchant, a banker and even a host for the *fazendeiro* and his family. In relation to the coffee trade, the *commissario* organized the reception of coffee lots in the Rio railway station and their sale (Sweigart 1987). The *commissario* also organized the presentation of samples to potential buyers. In Rio, the buyers were the *ensaccadores*, named this way because they were the ones making the final preparation of coffee lots to be exported. Originally, coffee coming from different plantations was mixed in London by importing commission merchants. In the 1880s, in Rio this activity was carried out by the *ensaccadores*. They mixed coffees according to the wishes of exporters (Laerne 1885) who were usually the agents of European or North American traders (Greenhill 1977: 215).

Twenty years later, in Santos, the *commissario* had absorbed the activity of the *ensaccador*. He was no longer in charge of organizing specific transactions for each *fazenda* but instead focused on preparing lots to be sold to the exporters (Lalière 1909: 321). Each bag coming from a *fazenda* was classified according to type by the *commissario*. The classification was based on six commercial types: *fino, superior, bom, regular, ordinario* and *escolha*. Then the coffee coming from different *fazendas* was gathered and mixed by the commissario to prepare lots homogenous and big enough for the exporters. To prepare these lots, the *commissario* used another classification defined in close relation with the New York Exchange grade. Therefore, the *commissario* was acting as a quality translator between the domestic coffee sector and the world market.

Until 1907, the commercial classification of Santos included eight grades defined in relation to the number of impurities (bad beans and foreign matter). For commercial transactions, each type was subdivided into subtypes defined in relation to the size, the colour and the aroma of the beans. A list of the descriptions used most in Santos in 1907 included 64 types with names like 'superior good bean soft green' or 'prime large bean green'. The exporters and their agents in Europe owned a sample of each grade that was used to organize transactions with buyers in consuming countries. Every year, the exporter agents in Santos and Europe received fairly large quantities of every grade to be distributed to their intermediaries and normal buyers. After 1907, Santos traders and *commissarios* adopted directly the New York standard with nine grades (Lalière 1909). The same year, a regulation voted by the Trading Association of São Paulo confirmed that the coffee sold by the *commissarios* had to be identified by type and not by origin (Lalière 1909: 321).

A further transformation of the coffee trade occurred in the 1920s and the 1930s with the disappearance of the *commissario*. According to Ukers (1935: 333)

> a great change in the merchandising of coffee at Santos in recent years is the disappearance of the *commissario* business which once formed the backbone of the market. Exporters and commission houses are now buying direct from planters in the interiors, and regular markets have sprung up in all important coffee centres like Lins, Rio Preto, Bauru, Araraguara, Ribeirao Preto, etc. As in the case of many other commodities around the world, the tendency of the coffee trade in Brazil is toward the elimination of middlemen.

The elimination of the *commissario* and the emergence of more direct relations between exporters and producers are also related to the changing size of farms and the externalization, for the smallholder, of the hulling operation: 'a typical arrangement was for an operator to set up a small plant for the processing or *beneficiamento* of coffee and other commercial crops. The operator might also serve as buyer and intermediary. He would frequently buy the unprocessed green coffee "benefit", standardize the beans and then sell to a higher-level merchant connected to Santos operatives' (Font 1990: 28).

In 1928, a new contract was created in the New York Exchange. It was based exclusively on deliveries coming from Santos. Grade Santos No. 4 was used as the reference for quotation. This contract remained in use until 1986, when it was replaced by the Mild Arabica 'C' contract. The 'C' contract currently allows delivery of coffee from 18 producing countries. It uses Central American coffee as the reference quality (International Trade Centre 2002). Meanwhile, the New York futures market has become the Coffee, Sugar and Cocoa Market (CSCE), part of the New York Board of Trade (NYBOT).

New York is not the only place where futures markets are dealing in coffee. Other futures markets for coffee were created in Le Havre in 1881, and in Hamburg and London in 1888 (Platt, Latham and Michie 1993: 51). These markets closed down during the two world wars and almost stopped during the interwar period, but have been much more active since the 1950s. The London market has been particularly successful. The Coffee Terminal Market Association of London reopened on 1 July 1958 with a contract based on 'Uganda un-washed, native-grown Robusta coffee'. Some years later, it became the reference market for Robusta coffee. In 1986, the London exchanges for coffee, sugar and cocoa were merged to form the London International Financial Futures and Options Exchange (LIFFE).

Coffee auctions survived the creation of the futures market. After the First World War, East African production was channelled toward London and sold on the London auction market. Later, local auction markets were created in the colonies: for Arabica, in Nairobi in 1935; for Robusta, in Mombasa in 1937 (Laan 1997: 192). The London public auctions disappeared with the Second World War, when the Ministry of Food became the sole buyer of coffee imports. Bulk buying by the Ministry of Food was accompanied by the creation of coffee boards in the British colonies. Sampling and marketing were arranged locally. 'The Ministry of Food sought to re-establish the pre-war system of selling coffee by public sale by itself holding auction on 9 January 1953. However, the discontinuity occasioned by the war proved fatal to the auction system, which never revived when the trade finally returned to private hands' (Rees 1972: 246). Yet, in Kenya and Tanzania, auction systems are still in place (see Chapter 3).

Finally, in a half-complementary, half-competitive way to the establishment of futures markets, governments in producing countries (starting in the 1930s) elaborated national grading systems and tried to implement differentiation policies to get better export prices. Colombia is the most successful example of such a strategy. A presidential decree of 1932 required that all coffee originating in Colombia when exported must be marked 'Café de Colombia' (Ukers 1935). At the same time, eight grades were defined in relation to variety, size, homogeneity and number of imperfections. In parallel, the Colombian coffee agency (Fedecafé) ran an active promotion campaign in consuming countries and succeeded in imposing the name 'Café de Colombia' as a quality sign.

Other producing countries followed the Colombian example. National grading systems were elaborated and public institutions in charge of quality control and classification were created even in colonial territories. In some countries, this process of nationalization occurred quite late. In Mexico, for example, it was not until the end of the 1950s that a national coffee standard was created. However, by the beginning of the 1960s most producing countries had their own quality regulation. In sum, the identity of green coffee being traded on the international market until recently was defined mainly by a national origin and a specific grade.

Retail and consumption: commodity form and the latte revolution

Coffee is consumed mainly in the developed countries of the Northern hemisphere. The only producing countries with sizeable domestic consumption are Brazil and Ethiopia. Until the 1960s, coffee consumption was concentrated in Europe and North America. Afterwards, it increased remarkably in Asia, especially Japan and Korea. Scandinavian countries (which have the highest level of consumption *per capita* in the world) and Germany prefer Mild Arabica coffees in their blends. Robusta and Hard Arabica coffees are key components of espresso blends, and are therefore important in Southern Europe. The

US and UK markets prefer lighter roasts in general, but require a wide spectrum of qualities. Historic trading links are still important in shaping the international coffee trade. A sizeable proportion of East African coffee finds its way to Germany and the UK. France maintains close links with Côte d'Ivoire and other Francophone countries. Dutch trading links with Indonesia remain important as well (McClumpha 1988: 12).

Coffee consumption tends to increase as income rises, but levels off at the highest income levels. For this reason, the coffee market is considered mature due to the relatively stable and low level of growth of consumption – on average, 0.7 per cent per year in the 1980s and 0.4 per cent in the 1990s. The price elasticity of coffee consumption is also low, with coffee demand varying significantly only at times of large variation in coffee prices. The growth of world coffee consumption by volume has slowed down, compared to other commodities, due to low consumption in otherwise dynamic markets such as China and South-East Asia. Low levels of growth of consumption have led roasters and retailers to invest in product innovation and segmentation in order to increase value added and also in efforts to cultivate markets where the

Table 2.5 Coffee consumption in major importing countries (thousands of 60-kg bags and proportion of total, 1980–2 to 2000–2)

Country	1980–2		1990–2		2000–2	
Total importing countries	62,767	100%	73,588	100%	81,003	100%
USA	17,965	29%	18, 417	25%	18,921	23%
EU (15) total	29,866	48%	34,526	47%	33,654	41%
Belgium/ Luxembourg	1,298	2%	910	1%	1,302	2%
France	5,368	9%	5,458	7%	5,378	7%
Germany	8,154	13%	10,109	14%	9,238	11%
Italy	3,841	6%	4,406	6%	5,198	6%
Spain	1,636	3%	2,803	4%	2,945	4%
Sweden	1,667	3%	1,642	2%	1,225	1%
United Kingdom	2,233	4%	2,402	3%	2,238	3%
Japan	3,441	5%	5,515	7%	6,881	8%

Source: ICO database.

potential for growth of consumption is perceived to be most promising – especially Eastern Europe and the traditionally tea-drinking countries of Asia (*ibid.*).

Globally, most coffee for in-home consumption is purchased in supermarkets. The food retail sector is highly concentrated in the US, UK and Northern Europe and plays a dominant role in the food marketing chain (Dijk *et al.* 1998). Yet, through consolidation and with massive investment in advertising their brands, roasters have managed to keep control of the coffee chain (see Chapter 3). This happened in spite of the development of private coffee labels by supermarkets. As a result, supermarkets' retail margins for coffee have remained generally lower than for the average food portfolio. In some countries, such as the US, retailers sell coffee even at a loss in order to 'generate traffic'. Retailers need to stock coffee because consumers expect them to do so. They can attract customers with relatively cheap coffee and entice them to buy other (higher-margin) items during their visit (Dijk *et al.* 1998; Dicum and Luttinger 1999; Pendergrast 2001). Furthermore, recently coffee sales have moved into even lower-margin outlets, such as warehouse and discount stores. In 1997, 10 per cent of total retail coffee purchases in the US were made at Wal-Mart (Dicum and Luttinger 1999: 114, 159).

Recent signals, however, suggest that a fragmentation of the coffee market is also taking place. The emergence of new consumption patterns – with the growing importance of sustainable coffees, single origins, the proliferation of café chains and specialty shops, and increasing out-of-home consumption – poses new challenges to traditional roasters (Dijk *et al.* 1998). The latter are used to selling large quantities of relatively homogeneous and undifferentiated blends of mediocre to poor quality (see Chapter 4). According to coffee industry analysts, these roasters have been slow in changing long-established ways of carrying out business and advertising.

Major coffee roasters lost their regional image and their focus on localized taste preferences a long time ago. In the US, regional roasters such as Folgers, Hills Brothers, and Maxwell House became national in scope and then started being bought by food conglomerates as early as the post-First World War period (Dicum and Luttinger 1999; Pendergrast 2001).[11] When they became part of major industrial empires, coffee roasters moved away from a focus on quality and locality. They started to concentrate on consistency in price, packaging and flavour. As a result, roasters homogenized blends. They started to use cheaper beans and cut down roasting times to reduce weight loss. Overall coffee quality decreased. As brand competition came to the fore in corporate strategies in the US, the product itself became of secondary importance (*ibid.*). Homogenization and mass marketing of coffee further increased with the growing importance of instant coffee after the Second World War. By competing almost exclusively through advertising, the major roasters stripped coffee of most of its charm and appeal, even as *per capita* consumption started to decline after 1962. In Europe, on the contrary, coffee standards remained higher due to different patterns of consumption, even after multinationals moved into the coffee market (Dicum and Luttinger 1999: 116–63).

It is in the background of these changes that the specialty coffee industry emerged as an important player, first in the US and later in Europe (see Chapter 4). One of the characteristics of specialty coffee is that it means different things to different people. Nowadays, the term covers basically all coffees that are not traditional industrial blends, either because of their high quality and/or limited availability on the producing side, or because of flavouring, packaging and/or ambience on the consumption side (ICO, ITC and CFC 2000; see also Lewin, Giovannucci and Varangis 2004).

In 2000, the specialty coffee industry accounted for 17 per cent of total green coffee imports into the US by volume (Giovannucci 2001). Its sales represented approximately 40 per cent of the US coffee market (although some sources think this figure is too high). Estimates indicate that this market is growing by 5–20 per cent per year. These figures, however, mask the fact that the 'coffee content' of these sales is a minor proportion of the total, the rest being added value in flavouring, mixing with milk products, and providing a specific 'consumption experience'.[12]

The evolution of specialty coffee cannot be appreciated without reference to the Starbucks factor. Starbucks was founded in 1971 in Seattle, following the steps of Peet's, another quality roaster based in Berkeley. Like other specialty operators, Starbucks spent most of the 1980s building a loyal customer base and 'educating' consumers on the qualities of fine coffees. The breakthrough that made Starbucks a stunning success was creating a café atmosphere where customers could hang out and consume an 'experience' at a place that was neither home nor work. In the words of Smith (1996, cited in Wrigley and Lowe 2002: 5–6) 'Starbucks outlets are integrally connected to those "landscapes of leisure" where people with disposable income ... go to consume, display themselves and watch others'.

The emergence of Starbucks happened at the same time as other consumer products moved from mass production and marketing to being recast as more authentic, flavourful and healthy (micro-brewed beer, specialty breads, organic vegetables). By combining ambience consumption and the possibility for consumers to choose type, origin, roast, and grind, Starbucks managed to decommoditize coffee. It sold coffee 'pre-packaged with lifestyle signifiers' (Dicum and Luttinger 1999: 153). In a sense, Starbucks discovered what European cafés had done for centuries, but made it palatable to the young by skilful marketing. By 1997, Starbucks was operating 2,000 outlets (mostly directly owned) in six countries. In 1998, it entered the European market through the acquisition of the London-based Seattle Coffee Company. By 2004, it had opened over 7,500 outlets, of which 1,500 were in 31 markets outside North America.[13]

In the US, accompanying the growth in café chains, there has also been an explosive increase in the number of roasters, although the smallest 1,900 roasters still control only 20 per cent of the domestic market. As recently as 1987, the three major roasting companies in the US held almost 90 per cent of the retail market. By 1993 they had lost 12 per cent of the market share to Starbucks, other regional cafés and specialty roasters (Dicum and Luttinger 1999). Specialty coffee consumption is growing rapidly in traditional consuming countries, whereas regular coffee consumption is stagnating. It is estimated that the number of Americans drinking specialty coffees on a daily basis grew from 9 per cent of the adult population in 1999 to 12 per cent in 2003. Occasional consumption was estimated at 51 per cent in 1999 and 54 per cent in 2003 (down from 62 per cent in 2001).[14]

Traditional roasters were slow in responding to this new phenomenon. They put darker roasts on the market and created their own specialty brands, but consumer response had been poor up to the late 1990s (Dicum and Luttinger 1999). Recent acquisitions of specialty brands by mainstream roasters, in addition to their inroads in sustainable coffees (see Chapter 5), indicate that this situation may be changing. One interesting strategy that some industrial suppliers are experimenting with is offering 'high-quality' coffee roasted on the spot by computerized roasters in large discount stores. In this case, it is not the material quality of coffee that makes it better. These coffees are mediocre and are bought in bulk. Their selling point is that they are freshly roasted. They also sell at much cheaper prices than in specialty stores. Another likely future strategy in the mainstream roasters' reconquest of market share will be acquisition of smaller specialty roasters and café chains (*ibid.*).

Starbucks, for its part, has adopted fairly mainstream corporate strategies. It has acquired competing chains, and has opened outlets in neighbourhoods with traditional cafés to drive them out of business (Wal-Mart style). It has also entered into joint marketing programmes with other corporate giants (PepsiCo, Barnes and Noble, Capitol Records, United Airlines). By becoming another large corporation and providing a homogenized retail experience with a consistent but not exceptionally good product, Starbucks has in many ways become the opposite of what independent coffee houses perceive themselves to be (*ibid.*). At the same time, Starbucks officials argue that the company consistently pays higher prices and purchases better quality coffee in producing countries than its competitors. It is also engaged in a preferred supplier system that is supposed to encourage sustainable coffee production (see Chapter 5).

The Starbucks phenomenon may have revitalized interest in coffee in consuming countries and new (higher-value-added) ways of con-suming it. Still, it is unclear whether specialty coffee will be successful in permanently decommoditizing coffee and in breaking the oligopoly held by a few roasting companies. It is not certain whether the specialty coffee industry holds much promise for coffee producers, either. These producers are facing the lowest prices for green coffee in a century in real terms. What difference does it make to a smallholder if a consumer can buy a 'double-tall decaf *latte*' for US$4, or if specialty beans are sold at US$12 per pound in the US if he/she gets less than 50 cents for the same quantity of coffee? Since the coffee content of new coffee consumption experiences is very low (see Fitter and Kaplinsky 2001), the so-called *latte* revolution that specialty coffee has brought to the coffee consumer may have more to do with milk (*latte*) than with coffee.

Conclusion

In this chapter, we have examined the history of changes in the geography of production, systems of labour mobilization, organization of trade and patterns of consumption. A couple of important trends have emerged in this discussion: (1) an increasing fragmentation of the supply base, with the entrance of new coffee-producing countries, most recently Vietnam; (2) the passage from slave and various forms of coerced labour in large farms to smallholder cultivation – and the more recent counter-tendency towards capital-intensive large estate cultivation; (3) the emergence of futures markets and their grades and standards, which led to some degree of commoditization of coffee – partly counteracted by the development of national grades and the survival of auctions; and (4) the recent trend towards differentiated consumption and the challenges it poses for mainstream roasters.

The basic information that we have presented in this chapter on flows and transformations of coffee serves as a background for understanding what one talks about when analysing coffee in its various material forms along the chain – such as cherry, parchment, green bean, blend, roast and ground coffee. However, an exclusive focus on the materiality of coffee can be misleading. As briefly mentioned in the last section, coffee consumption patterns have changed dramatically in the last 25 years. Symbolic and in-person service quality attributes are where new value is generated and appropriated. One of the key questions that we will address in the rest of this book is to what extent the addition of new attributes to coffee consumption is beneficial to producers. A related question is how to make the *latte* revolution work for producers – not only specialty roasters and wealthy consumers. These questions will be examined in Chapter 6 from a theoretical point of view, and in Chapter 7 from a policy perspective. To unpack these issues, however, we first need to examine two broad factors: (1) regulation and governance in the global value chain for coffee (Chapter 3); and (2) what kinds of quality attributes are embedded in the coffee that is sold at different nodes of the value chain (Chapters 4 and 5).

Notes

1   The major exception is Brazil, which is the top producer and also one of the main consuming countries in the world. In Africa, the only country with substantial coffee consumption is Ethiopia.

2   This changed in the 1990s. In 1996/7, coffee ranked only fifth among internationally traded commodities after oil, aluminium, wheat and coal.

3   A 20-foot long container usually holds 300 bags of coffee, or the equivalent weight of 18 tons of coffee plus the weight of bags. If the container is bulk-loaded without bags, it can hold up to 20–21 tons.

4   Some specialty roasters blend the coffee after roasting instead of before. This is done to avoid uneven roasts due to variation in the size and density of coffee beans from different origins, varieties and/or grades.

5   Colombia regained its second position among coffee producers in 2002/3, but in 2003/4 both Vietnam and Colombia produced 11.3 million bags.

6   The deltaic agricultural system was elaborated in the Mekong Delta to produce rice. It is characterized by intensive use of labour, fertilizers and water.

7   Large plantations were (and still are) conceived on the basis of a capital-intensive factory model. Large investments are implemented in cultivation and processing. Machinery is used at different stages of the production process: irrigation canals (and even railways) in the field; separators, washing channels or mechanical washing machines, mechanical dryers, peelers and polishers, and hullers in the factory. In contrast, smallholders produce coffee with limited use of capital other than the trees themselves. They can start production without credit systems – although tree crops require time before they mature for production. Intercropping food crops with the young perennial coffee plants is a regular feature of smallholder management methods. For wet processing, low-cost hand-pulpers and wooden drums or boxes can be used. For dry processing, drying can be done on small concrete racks, drying trays, tarpaulins or even on the surface of a road.

8   According to Ukers (1935), at the beginning of the 1930s, part of the coffee arriving in London was still in parchment form and needed to be hulled and sorted in milling establishments.

9   The US accounted for 40 per cent of world imports at the end of the nineteenth century, and 50 per cent during the interwar period (Rufenacht 1955).

10 The Coffee Exchange charter states that the Exchange purpose 'shall be to provide, regulate and maintain a suitable building, room or rooms for the purchase and sale of coffees and other similar grocery articles in the city of New York, to adjust controversies between members, to inculcate and

establish just and equitable principles in the trade, to establish and maintain uniformity in its rules, regulations and usages, to adopt standards of classification, to acquire, preserve, and disseminate useful and valuable business information' (quoted by Huebner 1911: 296).

11 Maxwell House was bought by General Foods back in 1928. Folgers was taken over by Procter and Gamble in 1963. General Foods was eventually taken over by Philip Morris in 1985 and merged with Kraft in 1995.

12 More recent figures indicate that, in 2003, US retail sales of specialty coffee beans were over US$1.7 billion, while sales of specialty coffee beverages were US$7.2 billion for a total retail market value of almost US$9 billion (Specialty Coffee Association of America (SCAA) (2004) 'Specialty Coffee Retail in the USA 2003', Long Beach, CA: SCAA).

13 Source: www.starbucks.com/aboutus/international.asp, and www.starbucks.com/aboutus/timeline.asp, accessed 6 September 2004.

14 Source: Specialty Coffee Association of America (SCAA) (2004) 'Specialty Coffee Retail in the USA 2003', Long Beach, CA: SCAA.

3
Who calls the shots?
Regulation and governance

Coffee is one of the few commodities for which international agreements aiming to support international prices were in place for several decades in the twentieth century. From the beginning of the century to 1989, producing countries played a substantial role in the global value chain for coffee. They took control of world stocks, held real market power, and influenced international prices. With the end of the International Coffee Agreement (ICA) system, increased concentration in the roasting and international trading segments of the global coffee value chain, and market liberalization in the South, producing country governments lost much of their market power.

In this chapter, we examine these processes through the lens of governance. First, we trace the historical trajectory of governance in two broad historical periods: from the 1900s to the 1980s, when producing countries were influential in the governance of the GVC for coffee; and from the 1990s to the present, a period during which consuming country actors (especially roasters) have driven the chain. Second, we examine the effects of market liberalization in the South, with specific focus on a comparative case study of four East African coffee-producing countries (Ethiopia, Kenya, Tanzania and Uganda). Finally, we analyse supply cycles and the volume and ownership of stocks to better understand fluctuations in international prices. The chapter concludes with a GVC-inspired reflection on governance that prepares the ground for the discussion (pursued later in this book) of producers' prospects for generating and capturing more value out of their coffee.

Producing countries as key actors (1906–89)

The Brazilian monopoly period (1906–37)[1]

Coffee was one of the first commodities for which control of world trade was attempted, starting in 1906 with the valorization process (see below) carried out by the Brazilian state of São Paulo. At the end of the nineteenth century, the international coffee market was dominated by European and US merchant firms. They were then the only macro-units in the coffee business. These firms placed themselves strategically between the numerous growers and middlemen and the small units comprising the roasting industry. In Brazil, which at the turn of the century accounted for three-quarters of global production, the ten leading merchant firms controlled 71 per cent (and the five biggest 53 per cent) of exports (Holloway 1978). These brokerage firms played crucial roles in determining international coffee prices due to their capacity to stockpile reserves (Netto 1979).

The so-called valorization policy implemented by Brazil, later known as the 'permanent defence of coffee' policy, put an end to this situation. Between 1906 and 1927, Brazil (in the first instance, the state of São Paolo) progressively implemented a series of control measures: first, a cooperation agreement with merchant firms; then, unilaterally, a programme of stockpiling large quantities of coffee; and, finally, strict control of export volumes. Brazil consequently became the first producing country to compete successfully with the powerful brokerage firms, eventually emerging as a leading player in the international market. In order to stabilize international prices, the Brazilian authorities implemented a scheme of 'residual supply'. This meant that, to maintain a certain supply–demand balance in the market, each year Brazil planned to export a volume that corresponded to the difference between global imports and the production of its competitors.

By maintaining international prices single-handedly, Brazil was in fact providing all coffee growers in the world with protection, for which it was the only one to pay the price. This policy had dramatic consequences. On the one hand, it encouraged the development of production in Brazil itself, as well as in other countries – Colombia in particular. On the other hand, it predictably resulted in the continuous shrinking of Brazil's market share. The 1929 crisis, which entailed lower international demand for coffee, resulted in a large excess production in Brazil. As a result, the country implemented a vast programme of surplus destruction. Within ten years, the equivalent of two years of world consumption was burnt or dumped into the sea.

Fragmentation of the world market (1930–62)

From the 1930s to the 1950s, the world market became more fragmented as a result of the policies of imperial autarky pursued by European powers and the effects of the Second World War. During the 1930s, the imperial capitals developed these policies in order to stabilize their supply systems. These were carried out through the introduction of discriminatory mechanisms (taxes and quotas, for example) against non-imperial imports, and through direct financial incentives for the development of production capacity in the colonies. France, among the imperial powers, went furthest in the implementation of this strategy. From 1930 onwards, larger taxes were levied on foreign coffees, which were also restricted by quotas. These measures were designed to enable colonial coffees to be sold at twice the price of other coffees. Furthermore, an assistance fund for coffee farming financed production activities and export subsidies.

State control of the market by imperial powers continued in the postwar years. Free international trade in coffee did not start in 1945. It was only towards the end of the 1950s that the world coffee market became reunified and importing countries ceased their controls. In France, the chronic deficit in the balance of payments encouraged the government to maintain or even strengthen the process of imperial integration, and to curtail imports when they were considered super-fluous.

This policy was very successful. In 25 years, coffee production in the colonies increased fifteen-fold. Hardly grown in 1930, except in Madagascar, coffee became an important agricultural export in Franco-phone Africa. French consumers switched from Latin-American Arabica coffee to African Robusta coffee. By 1957, two-thirds of French imports were from African colonies. The other side of the coin was that, after independence, the former colonies had become highly dependent on the French market for the sale of their production: in 1955–7, 70 per cent of Cameroonian exports, 75 per cent of the Central African Republic exports, and 80 per cent of Ivorian and Madagascan exports were directed to France.

Furthermore, the Second World War had changed the conditions of operation of the international coffee market. Since the European market was almost completely closed during the war, North America had become the only buyer of Latin American coffees. Empowered by this situation and wishing to contribute to the economic and political stability of Latin America, the US government energetically encouraged an arrangement with producing countries in the region. In November 1940 the Inter-American Coffee Agreement was signed between the US and all Latin American producing countries. It inaugurated a system of export quotas for the North American market and thus ended the previous fierce competition among producing countries (Di Fulvio 1947). During the six months following the signing of the Agreement, prices soared by 60 per cent. The beginning of the conflict with Japan (in December 1941) led the US administration to freeze import prices. The reins of the coffee market were now securely in the hands of the US. The administrative control of prices was relaxed in 1946 but was soon re-established during the Korean War.

One major outcome of this period of world market fragmentation was the building, in producing countries, of centralized and state-run institutions and procedures to regulate exports and domestic prices. At the end of the 1950s, institutions in charge of the coffee sector – the *instituto* in Latin America, the marketing board in Anglophone Africa, and the *caisse de stabilisation* in Francophone Africa – existed in almost all producing countries.

The International Coffee Agreement regime (1962–89)

In the years 1954–6 the market entered a period of massive over-production, related to the simultaneous rise of coffee production in Brazil (Parana), Africa, Central America and Mexico (Rowe 1963). The slump in international market prices led the Latin American countries, in 1956, to initiate negotiations with a view to stabilizing prices. In 1957, they all signed the Mexico Agreement, renewed a year later as the Latin American Agreement. Both were built upon the need to curtail exports. The expansion of coffee cultivation in Africa, however, strongly limited the chances of success of an agreement that covered only Latin America. African coffees, with the exception of those produced in the French colonies, competed with Latin American coffees in all markets – including the North American one. In 1959

African countries participated in talks that led to the establishment of an International Agreement, which was renewed in 1960 and 1961.

The first ICA was signed in 1962; for the first time, most producing *and* consuming countries were signatories to a common undertaking. Under the ICA regulatory system (1962–89), a target price (or price band) for coffee was set, and export quotas were allocated to each producer. When the indicator price calculated by the International Coffee Organization (ICO) rose over the set price, quotas were relaxed; when it fell below the set price, quotas were tightened. If coffee prices rose particularly sharply (as in 1975–7), quotas were abandoned until prices declined to within the band. Although there were problems with this system, many analysts have shown that it was successful in raising and stabilizing coffee prices (Akiyama and Varangis 1990; Bates 1997; Daviron 1996; Gilbert 1996; Herrmann, Burger and Smit 1993; Ponte 2002b).

The relative success of the regime has been attributed to various factors: (1) the participation of consuming countries in the working of the quota system; (2) the existence of producing countries as 'market units', where governments were in control of decisions concerning exports; (3) Brazil's acceptance of a shrinking market share as a result of successive ICAs; and (4) a common strategy of import substitution in producing countries (Daviron 1996: 86–9).

At the same time, the ICA system was undermined by free-riding and squabbling over quotas. Other problems were the increasing volume of coffee traded with (or through) non-member importing countries (at lower prices) and the continuing fragmentation of the geography of production (Daviron 1993; 1996). Furthermore, quotas were relatively stable because they were costly to negotiate. As a result, the mix of coffee supplied by producers tended to remain stable, while in the 1980s consumers in the US progressively switched from soluble coffees (that employ a high proportion of Robusta) to ground coffees (that use a higher proportion of Arabica). Rigidity on the supply side worried roasters, who feared that competitors could get access to cheaper coffee from non-member countries. This undermined their cooperation within the ICA system. Finally, the Cold War politics of the US in relation to Latin America had changed in the 1980s. The US did not perceive the left in Brazil as a real threat anymore, and the rigidity of quotas meant that the US administration could not punish its (perceived) enemies in Central America (Bates 1997: 172–5). The combined result of these changes was the failed renewal of the ICA in 1989.

The post-ICA regime (1989–present)

The end of international regulation

With the end of the ICA regime, producing country coffee agencies lost almost all influence on the international market. The transfer of stock control from public agencies to private trading companies was one of the major consequences of the breakdown of the agreement. In the months following the suspension of quota regulation, a large part of producer stocks moved from harbours in producing countries to harbours in consuming countries. A brutal drop in international prices resulted from this movement, which later led to a general crisis in the stabilization systems of producing countries and the bankruptcy of state agencies in charge of coffee sectors.

In relation to price levels, we can observe that the average ICO indicator price for the first five years after the breakdown of the ICA (1990–4) was only US$0.77 per pound, as opposed to US$1.34 per pound in the last five years before the breakdown (1984–8). Even accounting for the price rises of 1994/5 and 1997 (due to frost and drought in 1994/5 in Brazil, and a speculative hike in 1997), the average composite price for 1990–2003 amounts to only US$0.62 per pound (source: ICO database). Chronic oversupply, due to technical innovations and new planting, certainly contributed to the generally decreasing level of international coffee prices in the last decade. Global production between 1998 and 2004 exceeded 100 million (60-kg) bags every year. Between 1989 and 1997, oversupply had occurred only twice. Total production in 2002 was a staggering 121 million bags (source: ICO database). Yet, oversupply does not explain the whole story, as we will explain later in this chapter.

In 1993, with the establishment of the Association of Coffee Producer Countries (ACPC),[2] producing countries attempted to re-install some control over supply flows through an export retention scheme. However, the process of liberalization of domestic coffee marketing in producing countries had made it more difficult for them to control stocks and the flow of exports. Also, the scheme lacked proper monitoring and punitive clauses. Some of the major producers did not join the scheme,[3] and other member countries withdrew from it in 1998/9. Finally, during the same season, Brazil exceeded its quota by six million bags. In May 2000, the ACPC adopted a new retention plan operative from 1 October 2000. The plan targeted the retention of 20 per cent of total world production as long as the 15-day moving average of the ICO composite price indicator was below US$0.95 per pound. Major non-member producers provided their support to the plan, but participation by non-members remained largely voluntary. Some of these countries stated that retention had to be cost-free. Mexico, for example, aimed at achieving 'export retention' by increasing consumption in government-controlled institutions. Forecasts also indicated a strong increase in production for 2001/2, which would have implied a further increase in export retention levels.

The retention plan did not include provisions for destroying stocks; therefore, it did not address the fundamental problem of over-production. Even though year-to-year fluctuations of the global production volume are inherent in the world coffee market (see below), the long-term trend is generally perceived to be upward. As a result of these problems, the retention plan did not succeed in raising prices. The average ICO composite price indicator went from US$0.69 per pound in May 2000 (when the retention plan was signed) to US$0.56 in October 2000 (when the plan officially started). By October 2001 (when the plan was abandoned), the average composite price had dropped to US$0.42 per pound (source: ICO). In 2002 and 2003, it hovered in the range of US$0.43–0.54 per pound, with an average for the two years of US$0.5 per pound. In 2004, there were some modest signs of recovery – the average for the year was US$0.62 per pound.

In the 1990s, lower coffee prices were also accompanied by a higher level of price volatility. Price volatility is not a new phenomenon in the coffee market. A major traditional factor in volatility is that coffee yields are vulnerable to changes in temperature and rainfall, as well as disease. Frosts and drought in Brazil have normally led to sudden upward movements in coffee prices. The delay between new planting and production can also contribute to magnifying the price movements in the coffee cycle. However, something qualitatively different took place in the 1990s. The final eight calendar years of ICO activity were characterized by monthly nominal price variability of 14.8 per cent. This indicator almost doubled to 37 per cent in the 1990–7 period (Gilbert 1998) and then further increased to 43 per cent in the 1998–2000 period.[4]

Higher price volatility in the coffee market is linked not only to the end of price stabilization mechanisms that were built into the ICA quota system, but also to increased activity in the coffee futures market. In 1980, the amount of coffee traded in the futures market was only around four times the coffee traded in the physical market. By the early 1990s, the ratio had risen to eleven times (Dijk *et al.* 1998: 45). As explained in Chapter 1, futures markets allow market transactors to fix their prices in advance of delivery so that they can hedge their price volatility risk. However, futures contracts lose much of their hedging function when the price of futures contracts is too volatile. The volatility of futures prices is normally triggered by market 'fundamentals' (demand–supply–stock relationships), but is magnified by speculative activity. In the last decade, investment funds have become increasingly active in commodity markets. Because managed funds operate on the basis of trend-following, 'trigger signals' (which may not necessarily be linked to the actual conditions of supply and demand) tend to cause larger movements in and out of the market than if the market was operated by the coffee industry alone (Crowe 1997).[5] On the one hand, this additional activity increases liquidity in the market. On the other hand, the increased price volatility that ensues affects those actors who do not have access to hedging instruments – farmers and small-scale traders in producing countries (Gilbert 1996).

Corporate strategies

In addition to the regulatory framework, the governance of international coffee trade is linked to the corporate strategies adopted by large international traders, roasters and retailers. In Chapter 2, we have already touched upon the historical changes in the roles played by international traders. In the same chapter, we also examined some of the more recent developments in corporate strategies at the retail level, both in mainstream and specialty markets. Here, we focus on current corporate strategies among major international traders and coffee roasters. In the next section, we will see how international regulation and global corporate strategies 'touch down' in different institutional

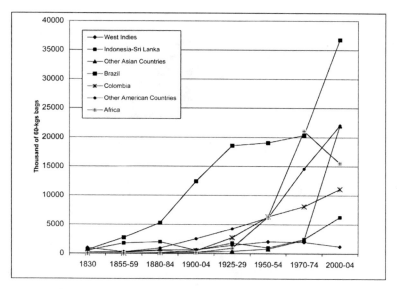

Figure 3.1. Green coffee market share by international trade company, 1998 (%)

settings in coffee-producing countries in the context of market liberalization of the latter. More detailed evidence of how these processes have impacted on the distribution of value added along the value chain will be presented in Chapter 6.

The international trade in coffee (as in other commodities) is a volatile business. International traders get access to green coffee either directly from its origin (if local rules allow) or via the spot markets in the US and Europe. In theory, physical coffee can also be accessed via the futures market, but this happens only rarely. International traders went through considerable restructuring in the last two decades. Mid-sized traders with unhedged positions suffered major losses. They also found themselves too small to compete with larger ones. As a result, they either went bankrupt, merged with others, or were taken over by the majors.[6] Therefore, the market is becoming more concentrated. In 1998, the two largest coffee traders (Neumann and Volcafé) controlled 29 per cent of total market share, and the top six companies 50 per cent (see Figure 3.1). In the early 2000s, with the mergers of Volcafé and ED & F Man, on the one hand, and Esteve and Cargill into Ecom on

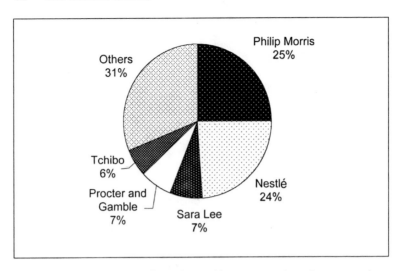

Figure 3.2a Market share of roasting and instant manufacturing companies,
1998 (%)

Holding company	Brands (as of 2004)[7]
Philip Morris (now Altria)	Blendy, Carte Noire, Dadak, Gevalia, Grand' Mère, Jacobs Krönung, Jacobs Monarch, Jacques Vabre, Kaffee HAG, Kenco, Maxim, Maxwell House, Nova Brasilia, ONKO, Saimaza, Splendid
Nestlé	Nescafé, Taster's Choice
Sara Lee/Douwe Egberts	Chock Full o'Nuts, Chase and Sanborn, Café do Ponto, Café Pilão, Cafitesse, Douwe Egberts, Hill Brothers, MJB, Moccona, Maison du Café, Merrild, Piazza D'Oro, Senseo, Superior
P&G (Procter & Gamble)	Folgers, Millstone
Tchibo	Tchibo, Eduscho

Figure 3.2b Holding companies and brands, 2004

the other, the three top groups were likely to account for 45 per cent of the market (but calculated at 1998 levels of market share). At the same time, prospects seem to be good for smaller and specialized companies that trade in the specialty coffee market (high quality and specific origins). With some exceptions, there has been little vertical integration between roasters and international traders (Dijk *et al.* 1998: 34–5).[8]

The level of concentration in the roaster market has reached a level even higher than for international traders. Figure 3.2a shows that the top two groups combined (Nestlé and Philip Morris) control 49 per cent of the world market share for roasted and instant coffees. The top five groups control 69 per cent of the market. Nestlé dominates the soluble market with a market share of 56 per cent (Dijk *et al.* 1998: 34). More recent estimates suggest an even higher level of concentration among roasters (Durevall 2003).

As mentioned in Chapter 2, roasters are still able to maintain a relative position of power *vis-à-vis* retailers due to the special nature of coffee in the retail business and the fact that in many markets coffee is offered to consumers at a low margin for retailers, or even at a loss. This applies to mainstream coffee. Specialty coffees exhibit higher margins at the retail level (see details in Chapter 6). Yet, supermarkets' own brands have not been able to enter the specialty segment in meaningful ways. More likely, one finds high-quality brands such as Starbucks or Illy dominating the high-end market in retail chains. Greater changes in the balance of power in the coffee value chain have actually occurred at the roaster–international trader node. In this case, roasters have actually increased their influence on international traders as a result of oversupply, increased flexibility in blending, market concentration, and especially through the implementation of the supplier-managed inventory (SMI) system.[9]

The precise motivations behind the adoption of SMI systems by roasters are unclear. One interpretation is that SMI allows roasters to minimize costs by transferring the working capital costs of inventory holding to trading houses. However, successful management of SMI requires at least two key conditions: (1) a close balance between supply and demand, or a supply surplus; and (2) supply conditions of various types and origins of coffee that do not force roasters to change blends in ways that would not satisfy their consumers.[10] According to Lodder (1997), these factors were not present when roasters started to apply

SMI in 1997. Therefore, they found themselves short of Arabica and scrambled for coffee purchases, triggering a panic-buying situation that led to a major price hike. However, in later years, roasters seem to have been able to implement a more cautious SMI system successfully.

A second interpretation of the adoption of SMI is that roasting companies quoted in stock markets need to contain the size of inventories and of circulating capital within optimal parameters set by financial analysts – large inventories and a high ratio of circulating capital being normally interpreted as indicators of inefficiency (see Gibbon and Ponte 2005). When roasters started carrying out SMI, the futures market was in 'backwardation'.[11] In that situation, carrying stocks was costly because forward future contracts were valued less than nearby positions. Therefore, applying SMI also made sense for roasters in terms of financial returns. However, the coffee market has been 'carrying' in more recent years, which means that contracts with distant delivery months are valued more than contracts with nearby delivery months. In this situation, if the costs of stocking (warehousing, finance, and insurance) are lower than the spread between positions, the holder of stocks can make a profit just by holding inventory.

In sum, outsourcing stock management during a period of backwardation could be interpreted as an effect of the increasing power of roasters over international traders. However, sticking to an SMI system in a carrying market indicates the effect of the logic of financial markets on quoted roasting companies, rather than a rise of traders' power over roasters. In any case, as a result of the adoption of SMI by roasters – and in combination with market liberalization in producing countries – international traders had to strengthen their supply networks. This has taken place through coordination (mostly financing) or vertical integration with local exporters. In some countries, international traders have moved upstream[12] all the way to domestic trade and in some cases to estate production (Akiyama 2001; Losch 1999; Ponte 2002a). International traders are likely to continue investing in operations in origin countries so that they can cater to the needs of major roasters.

Roasters seem to have little interest in vertical integration upstream in the current market conditions. They are better off concentrating on marketing and branding, while leaving supply to a network of independent traders – even if, in periods of carrying markets, this means forgoing a source of profit. Some roasters (such as Nestlé) are said to source not only from a variety of international traders, but also directly from some local exporters. The aim is to allow these exporters to compete with international traders in strategic origins. This allows the roaster to be less dependent on any actor, and especially on major traders. Furthermore, more flexibility in developing blending formulas has made roasters less vulnerable to shortages of particular types of coffee in recent years. Shortages of Colombian coffee have been offset by greater use of Central American Milds. Another example of substitution is the greater use of Mexican beans in place of Brazilian. The new technique of steam-cleaning Robusta and Hard Arabica allows roasters to improve their quality and to substitute premium-grade Robustas and Hard Arabicas for poorer Mild Arabicas.

Another trend emerging in the industry is towards the creation of a system of first-line and second-line suppliers, subject to price premiums and discounts. Major roasters tend not to accept coffee for their blends from countries that cannot guarantee a reliable minimum supply. As a result, on the one hand, minor producers may become increasingly marginalized in the future – without necessarily increasing the bargaining power of major producers *vis-à-vis* roasters. On the other hand, this has pushed some international traders to be (directly or indirectly) involved in domestic trade in major producing countries (Uganda, for example) even though these operations may not be profitable, as long as they can satisfy their major roaster clients (Ponte 2002a).

As a result of these factors, no vertical integration between international traders and roasters has emerged so far. The traditional market, as long as there is oversupply and roasters can manage SMI effectively, is likely to remain governed by a mixture of spot market transactions, forward contracts of short duration (under 12 months), and/or SMI agreements. However, where brand development in relation to a particular origin or estate requires security of supply, roasters may be pushed towards tighter forms of coordination with international traders and exporters in the near future.[13]

Regulation in producing countries

Domestic regulation of coffee markets

The last leg of our discussion of governance in coffee value chains concerns the organization of domestic markets in producing countries, which encompasses transactions and transformations between the farm gate and the export point. In Latin America, *institutos do/del café* existed in almost every producing country until the 1980s. The most famous and powerful were the Instituto Brasileiro do Café (IBC) and the Federación Nacional de Cafeteros de Colombia (Fedecafé). Most of them controlled exports that were carried out by private traders; sometimes (as in Colombia and Mexico), they bought and exported coffee directly to stabilize domestic prices and influence international prices. Some of these *institutos* were also providing extension, inputs and credit.

Mexico was the first country where the liberalization of domestic coffee trade occurred. It began in 1982. At the end of the 1970s, the Instituto Mexicano del Café was buying, processing and selling half of the coffee harvest. In a few years, it had been dismantled and the involvement of the Mexican state had become limited to agronomic research. Many Latin American countries imitated Mexico in the following two decades. In Brazil, the IBC was suppressed overnight by a presidential decree in 1990. For the first time since 1906, the Brazilian state was no longer intervening in the management of the domestic coffee market and could no longer control the quantity exported. This is still the case. At the time of writing, Colombia was the last country where a national agency was still trying to support domestic prices by buying (through a cooperative) and storing coffee – in spite of strong pressure against this from within the government and from outside.

In Africa, coffee marketing between independence and the start of the liberalization process in the 1980s was monopolized by the public sector through two main systems: the marketing board system common throughout the continent, and the *caisse de stabilisation* (stabilization fund) system typical of export crop marketing in Francophone West Africa. The marketing board system was characterized by pan-territorial and pan-seasonal pricing, monopoly of domestic and export markets, and control of transport and processing functions. Private sector involvement was formally limited or non-existent, although parallel markets were fairly active in many countries.

In the stabilization fund system of Francophone West Africa, private sector actors were contracted to handle crops, but prices and margins at all levels of marketing and processing were administered by the fund.

This system was meant to stabilize prices so that when international prices were above a set level – calculated against a long-term trend – the difference could be used for financing the fund to cover losses incurred when international prices fell below the set price. In practice, at times of high commodity prices, stabilization funds were used to finance government budgets. Yet, at times of low commodity prices, the funds failed to revise prices downward, leading to the accumulation of increasing debt.

In the rest of this section, we carry out a comparative case study of domestic market liberalization in four East African countries. This allows us to compare the dynamics of restructuring of the coffee marketing chain in locations with different degrees and trajectories of liberalization. Kenya and Ethiopia still run tightly regulated export auction systems; Kenya has only recently and partially liberalized its domestic market; Ethiopia's domestic market liberalization has gone further, but foreign companies are not allowed to trade. Tanzania liberalized its domestic coffee market in the mid-1990s, has retained some regulatory powers through its coffee board, and runs a mandatory auction system that works as a true auction only to a limited extent. Uganda swiftly liberalized its domestic coffee market in the early 1990s, and has a coffee regulatory body that steers the market with a relatively light hand. These differences have to some extent mediated the impact of global changes on the functioning and organization of domestic markets, competition, pricing systems, incentive structures, and contractual relations among actors.

East African coffees: an introduction[14]

In the 2000s, East African exports represented on average 60 per cent of total African exports of green coffee and 7 to 8 per cent of total world exports (USDA database). In 2002/3 and 2003/4, cumulative exports from East Africa were on average 6.5 million bags (see Table 3.1). Ethiopia is the first African coffee producer and, because of the importance of domestic consumption, the second exporter. Ethiopian harvests have been quite stable during the last 10 years at around 3.8 million bags (see Figure 3.3). Kenya and Tanzania, even with a low proportion of global coffee exports, play an important role in the category of Colombian Milds. Coffee production in Kenya has declined from an average of 1.5 million bags in the 1990s and 2 million

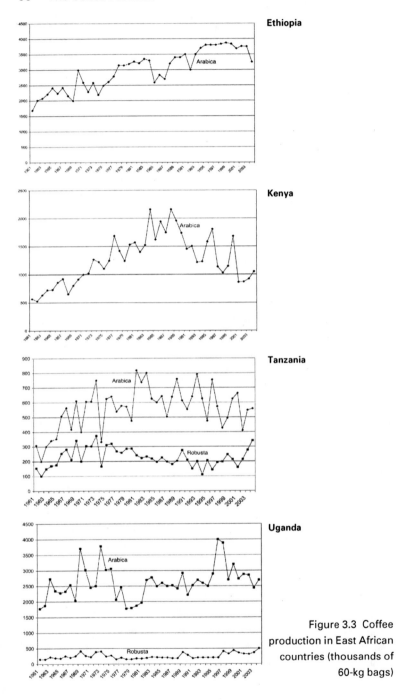

Figure 3.3 Coffee production in East African countries (thousands of 60-kg bags)

Box 3.1 Basic characteristics of East African coffees

The bulk of coffee production in *Kenya* is Mild Arabica, approximately 60 per cent coming from smallholders and 40 per cent from estates. Almost all coffee is processed at the primary level in central pulperies run by cooperatives or estates. Small amounts of top Kenyan coffee find their way into many coffee blends and give a specific flavour to them. Good Kenyan coffee is also sought after by the specialty industry and sold as 'single origin' coffee.

Tanzania produces all three types of internationally traded coffee: Mild Arabica, Hard Arabica and Robusta. Mild Arabica is the most important in terms of volume and value, followed by Robusta and smaller amounts of Hard Arabica. Most Tanzanian coffee (95 per cent) is produced by smallholders, although estate production is set to increase in the near future. Almost all smallholder coffee is processed at the primary level by farmers – by hand pulpers for Mild Arabica, and by simply drying the coffee in the case of Hard Arabica and Robusta.

Ethiopia is the primary centre of origin and genetic diversity of Arabica coffee. It is the home of unique and world-renowned coffees such as Harrar and Yrgacheffe. Unlike the other East African countries analysed here, Ethiopia has a strong coffee-drinking culture. Between 30 and 35 per cent of total production is consumed locally. In the last decade, exports have ranged between 670,000 and 2 million bags, of which 18 to 27 per cent is Mild Arabica and the rest Hard Arabica.[15] As in Kenya, top Ethiopian coffees are sold at high premiums over the New York market price and are essential to give 'character' to blends. They are also sold as single origins in the specialty market. In contrast to Kenya, however, coffees from different areas are kept separate from each other and sold with their regional name (Sidamo, Harrar, Limu, Yrgacheffe).

Uganda exports primarily Robusta, but also some Mild Arabica and a little Hard Arabica. Ugandan Robusta is important in the global market for its volume and because of its neutral flavour. These characteristics make it of higher quality than the harsher West African and most Asian Robustas. Ugandan coffee is considered one of the best Robusta coffees in the world. There are Robustas of similar quality available (Brazilian and Indian/Bangalore) but not with the volume available in Uganda (most Brazilian Robusta is consumed domestically). As a result, it commands a considerable premium over the London futures price.

Table 3.1 Ethiopia, Kenya, Tanzania and Uganda: green coffee exports by type, 2002/3, 2003/4 (thousands of 60-kg bags)

	2002/03	2003/04	Average
Ethiopia			
Arabica	2,277	2,374	2,325
Kenya			
Arabica	878	831	854
Tanzania			
Arabica	559	445	502
Robusta	282	102	192
Uganda			
Arabica	297	346	321
Robusta	2,515	2,177	2,346
East Africa			
Arabica	4,011	3,996	4,003
Robusta	2,797	2,279	2,538

Source: ICO database.

in the mid-1980s to about 0.8 million in 2001/2 and 2002/3. Tanzanian coffee production has fluctuated between 600,000 and 950,000 bags but with a decreasing share of Arabica. In 2004, Uganda was the first African coffee exporter and the fourth world producer of Robusta coffee (after Vietnam, Brazil, Indonesia and India; see Tables 2.3 and 2.4). Ugandan production increased during the first half of the 1990s from 2.5 to 4 million bags, but declined substantially after 1997 due to the impact of wilt.

Although the total share of coffee exports from the four East African countries examined here is marginal relative to world supply, some of these countries play an important role in the global value chain for coffee: Uganda for the volume and special quality of its Robusta; Kenya and Ethiopia for their fine quality coffees. Generally, Tanzanian coffee is used as a substitute for Colombian, and Ethiopian coffee as a substitute for Brazilian.

The organization of East African coffee value chains prior to liberalization

In East Africa, the organization of exports followed two different models before liberalization. Kenya, Tanzania and Ethiopia had auction systems for exports. In Uganda, exports were arranged by the marketing board. In Kenya, until the mid-1980s, the majority of shares of export companies could not formally be owned by non-Kenyans. Therefore, full vertical integration in the export sector was impossible for international traders and roasters, who had to resort to joint ventures or contractual relationships with local companies. In later years, because of the easing of these restrictions and increasing difficulties in getting finance from local banks, many independent exporters were taken over by international trading houses or resorted to them for financing. Still, monopolization of domestic trade and the auction system ensured that even smaller exporters could survive as long as they could manage to obtain finance from international traders or banks. This meant that competitive bidding continued to characterize the auction, especially for top-quality coffees. A similar process took place in Tanzania. The difference was that most exporters attending the auction in Tanzania were either based in Kenya or operated as subsidiaries of Kenyan export companies. In Uganda before liberalization, private buyers and hullers were local companies of small size. There was no formal involvement of foreign companies even at the export level, since the Coffee Marketing Board (CMB) was the sole exporter.[16]

Previous to market liberalization, the domestic coffee trade in East Africa was mostly under the control of cooperatives and state-controlled marketing boards. In Kenya and Tanzania, Mild Arabica coffee was owned by smallholders (through cooperatives) and estates until it was sold at the export auctions. There was no private sector participation in domestic trade and processing. The only private sector actors allowed in the marketing chain were private exporters who bought coffee at the auction. Although farmers bore the price fluctuation risk until they sold their coffee at the auction, the payment system allowed the smoothing out of price variations within the marketing year. Farmers were paid the same price irrespective of when they delivered the coffee to the cooperative or to the auction, and when that particular coffee was sold (this is also known as the 'pool system'). Furthermore, in both countries, farmers received payments in relation to the quality of coffee they delivered to the cooperative (see details in Ponte 2002a). The marketing system also provided agro-chemical inputs on credit to farmers, which cost was deducted from the payment for the coffee they sold. A similar system operated for the Mild Arabica trade in Uganda, although coffee was sold by the marketing board directly to importers, rather than at the export auction.

The handling and payment systems were fairly laborious and slowed down the flow of coffee from the farmer to the importer. Overhead costs associated with these procedures were high, meaning that farmers received a lower proportion of the export price than they would have in a more efficient system (quality considerations being equal). Payments to farmers were often late and resources were siphoned off the system at various levels. However, price stabilization was ensured within one season. Most important, the system provided quality incentives to cooperative societies and (less directly) to farmers (see Chapter 4).

In Tanzania, the Hard Arabica and Robusta trade was organized in the same way as the Mild Arabica trade. In Uganda, the domestic Robusta trade was carried out by cooperative societies in competition with licensed private buyers. Both cooperatives and private operators operated under fixed producer prices and fixed margins (as in the West African *caisse* system). All hulled coffee was sold to the Coffee Marketing Board, the sole exporter (Akiyama 2001: 96). The price stabilization mechanism was facilitated by the practice of forward sales arranged by CMB with importers.

Ethiopia went through two different marketing systems before 1991. Previous to the revolution of 1974, both the domestic and export markets were open to the private sector and the level of regulation was minimal. Coffee could be exported directly or could be sold at voluntary auctions in Addis Ababa and Dire Dawa. The government simply regulated the auction and enforced quality standards for export (Love 2001; 2002). After 1974, coffee marketing was heavily controlled by the state. Two layers of private traders (*sebsabies*, buying coffee from farmers, and *akrabies*, buying from *sebsabies* and selling at the auction) were allowed to operate, but only for Hard Arabica coffee. All Mild Arabica was delivered by farmers to washing stations owned by cooperatives or a state-owned company. Service cooperatives also provided farmers with short-term crop finance and fertilizer (used on food crops, rather than on coffee). A few private exporters were permitted to continue operating, but the bulk of the crop was handled by a state-owned company. Subsequently, the

Table 3.2 Kenya: market share of coffee exports by type of company, 1998/9
and 1999/2000

	1998/9	1999/2000
Number of registered export companies (n)*	51	51
Market share of top 5 companies (%)	46.2	44.1
of which MNCs	17.5	17.9
of which local	28.7	26.2
Market share of top 10 companies (%)	75.6	75.2
of which MNCs	28.7	24.3
of which local	46.9	50.9
Market share of companies ranked 11th to 20th (%)	19.0	19.4
Market share of other companies (%)	5.4	5.5
MNC share of total exports (%)	30.5	28.4

* Sister companies are counted as one company.
Source: Elaboration from Coffee Board of Kenya (CBK) data.

auction became mandatory and (in 1977) a price fixing and quota
system was established. Private exporters were not allowed to compete
for coffee at the auction until the state-owned company had filled its
quota.

The effects of liberalization on value chain structure

In the following discussion, we examine the main features that
emerged from different paths of liberalization of domestic coffee value
chains in East Africa. Here, we focus on the changing organizational
structure of these value chains, and the typology of actors involved in
domestic procurement, processing and export. Specific changes in
coffee quality will be dealt with in Chapter 4.

In Kenya, the process of liberalization of the coffee value chain
started in the early 1990s, but has progressed very slowly. The basic
structure of the chain has remained almost the same.[17] Coffee is
marketed through cooperative societies and the marketing board and
does not change hands until sold at the auction to exporters.[18] An
increasing number of local exporters have been seeking alliances with
MNCs through ownership or finance contracts. In this way, they can
get easier and cheaper access to working capital (in view of the credit
crunch in the domestic banking sector) and easier access to the more

Table 3.3 Market share of Tanzania coffee auction purchases by type of
company, 1994/5–1999/2000*

	1994/5	1995/6	1996/7	1997/8	1998/9	1999/00
Active export companies (n)	23	26	24	–	27	22
Market share of top 5 companies (%)	59.5	63.8	62.1	–	62.2	63.7
of which foreign	41.0	55.7	52.3	–	53.7	63.7
of which local	18.5	8.2	9.8	–	8.5	0.0
Market share of top 10 companies	83.6	87.0	87.7	–	87.3	84.7
of which foreign	49.5	60.4	62.0	–	58.5	67.4
of which local	34.2	26.6	25.6	–	28.7	17.3
Market share of companies ranked 11th to 20th (%)	15.9	11.3	11.5	–	11.4	15.2
Market share of other companies (%)	0.5	1.7	0.8	–	1.3	0.2
Foreign share of total auction purchases (%)	51.0	60.4	62.0	–	59.9	67.4

* Sister companies are counted as one company.
Source: Elaboration from Tanzania Coffee Board (as in Ponte 2004).

sophisticated risk management and marketing tools needed in an increasingly unstable global coffee market. Yet the export market is still fairly fragmented because the capital requirements for buying coffee at the auction are much smaller than those required to buy parchment in domestic markets, where these markets are liberalized. MNCs control only about one third of the export market through direct subsidiaries (see Table 3.2). Because preserving high quality is critical to the marketability of Kenyan coffee in the global market, some MNCs have been against the liberalization of domestic marketing and insisted on the maintenance of the auction system. The auction was still characterized by competitive buying in the early 2000s. Yet the sector as a whole has been marred by corruption and mismanagement at various levels. As a result, farmers receive a relatively low proportion of the export price, and production levels have generally decreased in the 1990s.

In Tanzania, the process of coffee marketing reform started in 1994/5, and has resulted in the liberalization of domestic trade and processing. Yet regulatory requirements have remained quite demanding at all levels of the marketing chain. The auction system has been maintained and domestic traders can buy parchment/dry cherry coffee only at authorized buying posts. High barriers to entry (due to licensing requirements) have facilitated consolidation. Some exporters (subsidiaries of major international trading and/or roasting companies) have vertically integrated into curing and domestic procurement, in some cases even into estate production and primary processing. This has yielded mixed results. On the one hand, farmers are paid cash on delivery and receive a higher proportion of the export price than in the pre-liberalization period (Temu 2001; Winter-Nelson and Temu 2002; Baffes 2005). On the other hand, input-credit schemes have collapsed, the volume of coffee exports has not improved[19] and there are strong indications that coffee quality has decreased because farmers are paid one price for all coffee – irrespective of quality (see Chapter 4).[20] Most important, liberalization saw the dramatic 'capturing' of the Tanzanian coffee market by foreign companies at all levels (domestic trade, processing and export) except for farming – where 95 per cent of coffee is still produced by smallholders. At the same time, foreign investors have recently come to dominate the estate production sector.

Tanzania still runs a mandatory export auction, but the majority of coffee going through the auction is simply re-acquired by the same company that bought it domestically. Thus, there is little or no competitive bidding for this so-called 'captive' coffee. The market share of cooperative unions in both domestic marketing and processing has decreased substantially to the benefit of the private sector. MNCs are now dominating domestic procurement, processing and export markets (see Table 3.3). They control more than half of the export market through direct subsidiaries and another substantial proportion through finance agreements with local companies. As the domestic market has matured in the years following liberalization, and as international prices have tumbled in the late 1990s, MNCs have started outsourcing some of the functions they previously performed (transport, primary buying, input distribution).

These changes have triggered a series of reactions attempting to re-empower local interests – such as manipulating licensing rules, encouraging direct selling of coffee at the auction by independent cooperatives and farmer groups, auction haggling, threats of tightening

Table 3.4 Uganda: market share of coffee exports by type of company,
1996/7–2000/1

	1996/7	1997/8	1998/9	1999/00	2000/1	2001/2
Number of registered export companies (n)	60	46	40	35	29	33
Market share of top 5 companies (%)	52.2	50.3	53.0	46.1	54.7	53.1
of which MNCs	24.0	23.7	38.4	24.9	32.4	23.1
of which local	28.2	26.6	14.7	21.2	22.2	30.0
Market share of top 10 companies (%)	72.8	70.9	77.1	75.1	80.8	80.5
of which MNCs	28.2	31.9	46.7	38.8	42.5	37.4
of which local	44.5	39.0	30.4	36.3	38.3	43.1
Market share of companies ranked 11th to 20th (%)	17.8	21.5	19.7	22.5	17.7	17.6
Market share of other companies (%)	9.5	7.6	3.3	2.5	1.5	1.9
MNC share of total exports (%)	32.6	33.8	46.7	42.6	42.5	38.6

Source: Elaboration from Uganda Coffee Development Authority (UCDA) data.

regulation and a period of re-monopolization of domestic coffee marketing in some regions of the country (Ponte 2004). The objective of these actions was finally embedded in the 2001 Coffee Act, as a result of which export companies have been banned from concurrently holding domestic trade licences.

In Uganda, the process of liberalization and deregulation has reached the most advanced degree in East Africa, although it is still more regulated than in other coffee-producing countries where there are no formal export certification procedures. Uganda started to liberalize its coffee sector in 1990/1. The process was carried out quickly and efficiently. Licensing requirements for private sector actors are minimal, coffee can be bought anywhere, in any form, and can be sold anywhere else within the country. Regulatory powers were transferred to the newly created Uganda Coffee Development Authority (UCDA), which is in charge of testing export consignments for minimum quality standards and releasing export certificates. The CMB has closed down and the cooperative sector has almost disappeared.

Table 3.5 Ethiopia: market share of coffee exports by type of company,
2000/1

	2000/1
Number of registered export companies (n)*	72
Market share of top 5 companies (%)	29.7
of which MNCs	0.0
of which local	29.7
Market share of top 10 companies (%)	52.9
of which MNCs	0.0
of which local	52.9
Market share of companies ranked 11th to 20th (%)	26.2
Market share of other companies (%)	20.8
MNC share of total exports (%)	0.0

Source: Elaboration from Ethiopian Coffee Exporters Association (ECEA) data.

Full liberalization at all levels of the value chain has prompted a proliferation of private export companies, primary-level buyers, hulling plants and export processing plants. The cooperative sector has almost disappeared in Uganda. Following liberalization, and because of favourable trade margins in the mid-1990s, the number of active exporters increased dramatically while MNCs attempted a process of vertical integration to establish market share and internalize profits. Since 1996/7, however, exporters have been buying at a loss.[21] Because Ugandan Robusta plays a key role in major blends, international traders need to be present in Uganda even if they do not make profits, just to keep their major clients happy. This has led to consolidation of the industry. In 1994/5, there were 117 registered exporters; in 2001/2 only 33 (see Table 3.4).

Exporters have restructured their operations dramatically since 1997. They have retreated from buying in the field and now buy only hulled coffee – mostly in Kampala and a few other major towns. The level of industry consolidation at the export level remained fairly constant between 1996/7 and 2001/2. As international prices fell in the late 1990s, the number of exporters decreased substantially and MNCs consolidated their presence. However, low entry barriers in the domestic trade and hulling segments of the chain meant that MNCs eventually gave up (or chose to abandon) attempts to control them. These sectors are now mostly in the hands of a large numbers of small-to medium-scale local enterprises. At the same time, one of the MNCs (Neumann) made a large investment at the production level, and in 2001 inaugurated a Robusta farm measuring 2,524 hectares (Kaweri Coffee Plantation). The company plans to establish an out-grower scheme as well.

In Ethiopia, the process of liberalization of the coffee value chain started in 1991. It has been only partial and was carried out in phases. With the end of the Derg regime, the state-owned company that used to handle most coffee in the country was split into two companies – one operating in domestic procurement and one in exports. Both had to compete with private sector traders, exporters and cooperatives. At the time of writing, both companies had closed down and domestic coffee procurement was in the hands of *sebsabies*, *akrabies* and a small number of cooperatives. The mandatory auction has been maintained. All coffee is now exported by private sector companies. An exception has been made for two newly established cooperative unions, which can export directly without going through the auction. In contrast to the other three East African countries, Ethiopia does not allow MNCs to register as exporters. There are only a handful of foreign companies operating at the auction, and all were established before the advent of the Derg in 1974. As a result of the absence of MNC competition at the auction level, the industry is much more locally controlled than elsewhere in East Africa. Both the domestic and export markets are extremely fragmented (see Table 3.5).

The Ethiopian coffee marketing chain is still highly regulated. In addition to maintaining the auction, the Coffee and Tea Authority (CTA) enforces an artificial vertical segmentation of the market through licensing rules. As we have seen above, coffee flows from farmers to *sebsabies*, then to *akrabies* and then to exporters. A company can only hold one of these three different licences; at least on paper, therefore, it cannot operate in other segments of the market. This situation, however, has recently changed. In 2000, *akrabies* were allowed to buy directly from farmers. This is supposed to ensure more competition at the local level and a better flow of quality information from farmer to auction. Also, some exporters have registered sister companies as *akrabies*, so they are able to control coffee from the farm level to export. This is still a limited phenomenon, but if it increases the auction would become as non-competitive as the Tanzanian one. For the time being, the level of vertical integration is still limited. Only an estimated 20 per cent of coffee sold at the auction is considered 'captive'. Also, most *akrabies* are still using *sebsabies* for their primary-level purchasing.

Coffee pricing has also been liberalized only partially. Domestic pricing is now free, although floor-level farm-gate prices were maintained until 1996/7 for fresh cherry purchases and, more recently, for dry cherry. At the export level, the Coffee Price Differential Setting Committee sets minimum export differentials for various types of regional coffees. This is creating some problems as some exporters have complained of not being able to sell their coffee owing to differences between what international traders and roasters deem acceptable prices and the minimum differentials set by the committee. Other exporters actually make the opposite claim. Setting a minimum differential makes it difficult to sell higher-quality coffees at higher prices.

The lessons of liberalization

The East African experience in the liberalization of domestic coffee sectors suggests that market power of MNCs at the export level is positively correlated to the level of entry barriers. The total market share of MNC exporters is highest in Tanzania, where establishing export market share means controlling the domestic market. In Tanzania, formal entry barriers at the export level are not demanding; however, entering the domestic trade is more difficult owing to complex licensing procedures and high fees. The proportion of exports controlled by MNCs is lowest in Kenya, where an exporter just needs to have a price-competitive order from an importer and access to finance in order to participate in the auction. In Uganda, low entry barriers in the domestic trade mean that MNCs find it difficult to control primary buying. Therefore, they have to compete on procurement price. Entry barriers are not quite as high as in Tanzania, but are higher than in Kenya. As a result, the share of exports controlled by MNCs in Uganda stands in between the other two countries. Not unexpectedly, the share of MNC exports generally increases over time in liberalized markets (Tanzania and Uganda), but not in more regulated ones (Kenya). Ethiopia is an exceptional case, in that MNCs are banned from the auction and the domestic market.

The East African case studies also indicate that the effects of changes in the governance and organizational structures of the global coffee value chain are to some extent mediated by national-level policy. MNCs involved in the coffee chains examined here adapted their behaviour to local market conditions and the limitations imposed (although sometimes only formally) by remaining regulatory systems. Although liberalization of domestic coffee markets has taken place in most producing countries, its dynamics have not been uniform. There has been no single liberalization/deregulation path. Different degrees and trajectories of reform (or lack thereof) have had different consequences. Overall, the East African case studies suggest that appropriate regulation at the domestic level is essential if a more active role for producing countries in the governance of the global value chain for coffee is envisioned. In the absence of this, they will remain at the receiving end of decisions and strategies taken elsewhere. As we show in the next section, overproduction on its own does not explain the current coffee crisis. Ownership of stocks is essential to influence prices, and currently ownership is firmly in the hands of actors based in consuming countries.

Coffee blues: international prices in historical perspective

The international coffee market is characterized by relatively low price elasticities of supply and demand (McClumpha 1988; Daviron 1993). This leads to a dynamics of world coffee production that, for decades, followed cycles determined by the alternation of long periods of overproduction and lower prices, and short periods of shortage and higher prices. A classical interpretation of these cycles relies on constraint factors. Traditional coffee trees need five to six years before they yield a first regular harvest. Once they reach this stage, they can then produce coffee for more than forty years. With such character-istics, the price elasticity of coffee supply is low in the short term. This means that an increase in prices determines a low increase of production in the short term. The main way to increase coffee production is to plant new coffee trees, which entails waiting for five years. Another way is to improve farm practices and/or input use. However, this approach can have a significant impact on overall production only where: (1) there is a high-input production system in

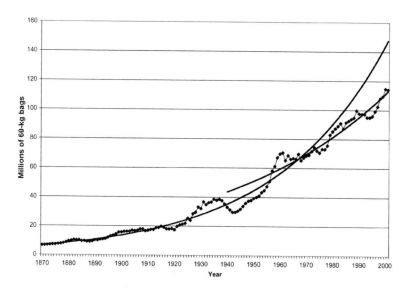

Figure 3.4 World coffee production, 1870–2000 (based on five-year averages)

place (see below); (2) it is possible to switch from a low-input system to a high-input system; or (3) trees have been neglected or semi-abandoned for an extended period owing to low prices or lack of market access. In the long run, a supply response based on the planting of new trees usually leads to a higher than necessary supply response. Once planted, coffee trees will continue producing for many years, even after a sharp price decline. A usually brief situation of supply shortage and high prices will then be followed by a longer period of oversupply and low prices.

A statistical analysis of long-term production data (see Figures 3.4 and 3.5) shows that, until 1970, coffee production followed repeated cycles around an average growth rate of 2.3 per cent per year. From 1880 to 1972, four cycles of boom and bust can be identified: 1889–1921, 1922–45, and 1945–72. But the behaviour of world coffee production started to change in the 1970s. First, in the 1970–2004 period the average growth rate decreased to 1.6 per cent. More important, the differences between actual values and the trend are much more limited – less than 10 per cent as opposed to 20 per cent

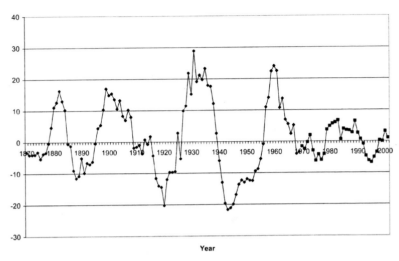

Figure 3.5 World coffee production: trend difference, 1970–2000

during the previous cycles.[22] The boom and bust cycle has almost disappeared. This change can be interpreted in relation to new technologies used in coffee production. With the introduction of new varieties, it takes only two years for new trees to be productive. Furthermore, input-intensive production systems provide better capacity to adjust the level of production to the level of price through changing the quantity of inputs employed.

What it is important to underline here is that the current crisis of the coffee market is not a classical overproduction crisis similar to that of the 1930s, when Brazil was burning coffee to run locomotives. It is not similar to that of the 1960s, either – when world production increased dramatically with the expansion of coffee cultivation in the Brazilian state of Parana and in Africa. The reason for the current crisis must be found somewhere else. In this chapter, we discussed how roasters have been driving the value chain since the early 1990s. This has an influence on price transmission between import and retail (as we will see in Chapter 6). We have also discussed how producing countries lost their ability to control export flows and stocks, which has weakened their position. In the rest of this section, we continue the analysis of the influence of stocks (and stock ownership) on international prices.

First, we need to measure the extent and the specificity of this crisis in historical terms. Figure 3.6 presents the evolution of international coffee prices from 1880 to 2002.[23] It indicates that the international price for green coffee in the early 2000s was at its lowest level for more than a century, a level even lower than that reached in the worst previous conjuncture (after the First and before the Second World War). Figure 3.6 also shows the long-term evolution of world coffee stocks.[24] This evolution is itself the result of a succession of disequilibria between world production and consumption. Figure 3.6 clearly shows the inverse relation between world stocks and international prices. It also shows that this relation has not been stable in the course of history. The huge stocks of the 1950s and 1960s did not cause a price fall in proportion to their scale, and the disproportion is even clearer when comparison is made with the beginning of the twentieth century or the 1930s. On the contrary, the dramatic price fall after 1989 appears totally disproportionate compared with the evolution of stocks. Although several years of production surplus accumulated in the 1980s, the level of stocks was much lower than during the previous crisis and well below the level in the 1960s (the equivalent of eight months of world imports against twenty-two). Furthermore, it has almost stabilized after 1982. Since the mid-1990s, stocks have been decreasing from an average of eight months of world imports to an average of four. In a first period, between 1994 and 1998, prices reacted by attaining relatively high levels, but then fell again after 1999 in spite of minor changes in the level of stocks. Since 1999, the market has been characterized by historically low levels of prices and of stocks – a radically new situation.

Stocks and prices are related because stocks represent, *a priori*, the availability of the most immediately mobilizable coffee on the market to respond to a demand increase. However, understanding the relation between prices and stocks necessitates the ability to distinguish, within world stocks, the part that is truly available and mobilizable. We argue that the impact of world stocks on prices depends on the identity of the operator owning or controlling them. Historically, one of the main objectives of producing-country coffee policies, and particularly of Brazilian coffee policy, was precisely to control world stocks by 'neutralizing' them – taking them out of the market. Thus, when stocks are owned by producing-country governments, they are absent from the market, or at least there is strong uncertainty about their

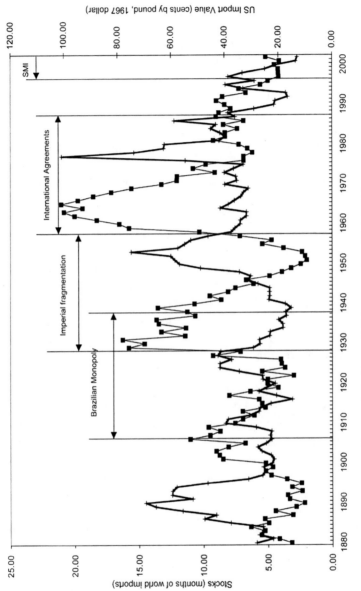

Figure 3.6 Stocks and US import value, 1880–2002[25]

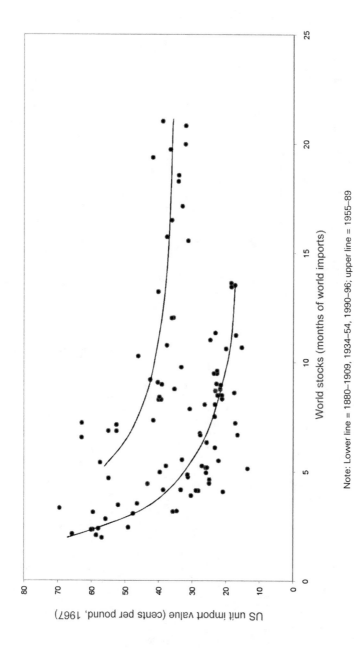

Note: Lower line = 1880–1909, 1934–54, 1990–96; upper line = 1955–89

Figure 3.7 Stocks and US import value

Table 3.6 Characteristics of coffee value chain restructuring
(input–output structure and geographies of production and consumption)

	ICA regime (1957–89)	Post-ICA regime (1989–present)
Geography of production (see Chapter 2)	At first concentrated in a few large producing countries (Brazil, Colombia); later, increasingly dispersed with the emergence of new producers	Fragmentation continues
Entry barriers to production (see Chapter 3)	Low, due to government intervention (input and credit supply, extension, coffee cultivation campaigns, price stabilization)	Increased, due to government withdrawal from the provision of services to farmers (end of input supply schemes, breakdown of research and extension networks, end of price stabilization mechanisms)
Characteristics of Internationally traded product (see Chapters 2 and 4)	Relatively homogeneous, but distinguished by physical qualities, some times taste qualities (the latter especially for Mild Arabica) and national origin	Bifurcated trend: increased homogenization of lower quality coffees, especially Robusta (bulk export in containers without bags); at the same time, increased trade of small quantities of specific high-end quality beans (Mild Arabica)
Entry barriers to trade (see Chapters 2, 3 and 4)	*Domestic trade and export*: high barriers due to monopoly of marketing or politically set domestic trade quotas but risk limited by domestic price stabilization policies *International trade*: Increasing due to consolidation	*Domestic trade and export*: First, decreased entry barriers due to liberalization; later, increased barriers following the strengthening of international trader operations in producing countries, the lack of domestic credit and the limited access to futures markets; *International trade*: Increasing entry barriers in mainstream market due to further consolidation and requirements set by roasters through SMI; decreasing in the specialty market due to fragmentation and the growing importance of e-commerce sales

Distribution of total income generated along the chain (see Chapter 6)	Relatively stable, with farmers getting around 20 per cent of the total, and consuming country operators around 50 per cent	Shifted to the advantage of consuming country operators
Geography of consumption (see Chapter 2)	Concentrated in North America, Western Europe and Japan	Quite stable with the slow emergence of new markets (Eastern Europe, China, East Asia)
Typology of consumption (see Chapters 2, 4 and 5)	Segmented by group of countries (different coffee types and blends catering for the US/UK markets, Southern Europe, Scandinavia, Central Europe, Japan), but relatively homogeneous consumption within these geographical areas	Increased fragmentation: multiplication of types of product and blurring of distinctive lines of preference between different groups of countries; increasing importance of single-origin coffees and sustainability initiatives.

Table 3.7 Characteristics of coffee chain restructuring (governance structure and institutional framework)

	ICA regime (1957–89)	Post-ICA regime (1989–present)
Governance structure of the chain (see Chapter 3)	Producing countries have influence in governing the coffee GVC; increasing concentration in roasting and trading segments raises entry barriers, but roasters are neither in the position to dictate the terms of the trade to international traders, nor to set inclusion/exclusion thresholds; control over the chain by any actor is limited	Buyer-driven (specifically, roaster-driven); further consolidation in roasting; oversupply; adoption of SMI by roasters forces traders to integrate upstream; vertical integration by traders made easier by market liberalization in producing countries
Vertical integration (see Chapter 3)	Not common; sometimes occurring in export/international trade links; more rarely in domestic trade and processing	Increasing: international traders integrate into export, processing, domestic trade and sometimes even estate production; vertical integration much more limited in the roaster-international trader link
Producer–consumer country relations (see Chapter 3)	In relative equilibrium; mediated through the ICAs	Absence of formalized relations; consuming country domination
Institutional framework (international) (see Chapter 3)	Strong: international trade regulated by ICAs	Weak: end of ICA; producing country cartels fail to set up effective quota or retention schemes; futures market increasingly de-linked from market fundamentals

Institutional framework (domestic) (see Chapter 3)	Strong: markets monopolized by marketing boards, or regulated by stabilization funds and quasi-governmental producer associations	Weak: government and quasi-governmental institutions retreat into oversight functions or are eliminated altogether; trade associations fill only part of the formal institutional vacuum
Control and ownership of stocks (see Chapter 3)	Producing country marketing boards, stabilization funds and *institutos* are in control of a large proportion of stocks	Stocks move from producing to consuming countries; stocks still in producing countries are controlled increasingly by private sector, often consuming-country-based actors; from the late 1990s, roasters outsource stock management to international traders; proportion of readily available stocks increases
Quality evaluation (see Chapters 4 and 5)	*International level:* product-based; set in negotiation with producing-country sellers (and/or marketing boards) and maintained via instrument-based testing and inspection, cup testing, and certification of the product; in general, quality assessed by the buyer ex-post; *Domestic level:* set by a regulatory agency; includes specific quality control procedures along the chain	*International level:* increasing importance of quality attributes defined by buyers; process monitoring (in addition to product testing) becomes important for fair trade, organic, shade-grown coffees; quality increasingly assessed by buyers ex-ante; *Domestic level:* increasingly set by buyers; formal rules of quality control remain but are increasingly disregarded
Upgrading possibilities (see Chapters 5, 6 and 7)	Limited; undifferentiated trade; however, producing countries achieve product valorization through higher international prices provided by the ICA	Potentially increasing through marketing of sustainable coffee and direct e-commerce sales; openings in specialty markets more suitable to estates than smallholders

availability. In a different way, but with a similar impact on prices, stocks owned by roasters are stocks taken out of the market. They are not available anymore. Only stocks owned by traders or producers represent permanent availability and exert a full influence on prices.

By taking into account the diverse identity of stock owners or controllers and their different behaviour, we can better understand the changing impact of stocks on prices, particularly in the last few decades. After the Second World War, by means of the interventions of state coffee agencies, producing countries were able to master the main part of world stocks. Because of the international coffee agreements, they could maintain world prices at quite high levels. The impact of international coffee agreements can be better visualized in Figure 3.7, where each year is represented with the level of stocks on the x axis and the level of prices on the y axis. This figure suggests that, for a given level of worlds stocks, the international price during the ICA period was equal to the price that would be determined on the free market, plus a fixed amount (US$0.21/lb in 1967 terms).[26]

Thus, on average, from the end of the 1950s to the end of the 1980s, the international price was more or less double what it would have been on the free market. Including the post-Second World War price boom, the coffee market generated a rent for more than forty years. Producing-country coffee policies, the organization of national coffee value chains, and the behaviour of operators were structured by the existence of this rent. During these years, the international coffee market did not impose any notable price-competitive constraint on producing countries. Its working authorized the coexistence of coffee sectors with very diverse costs and productivities.

With the breakdown of the international coffee agreement in 1989, the relation between stock and price altered again, now working much in the way it had at the beginning of the century. Stocks were no longer controlled by producing countries. This loss of control was provoked by a physical displacement of the stocks from producing countries to consuming countries, following the suspension of export quotas. It was also reinforced, confirmed and made permanent by liberalization policies in producing countries and the dismantling of coffee state agencies. Even in producing countries, stocks are now neither owned nor controlled by governments, but by producers and above all by traders.

Finally, since 1998, the relation between stocks and prices seems to have changed again. The impact of stocks on prices appears stronger than before. This can be interpreted in relation to the implementation of SMI strategies by roasters. SMI means, for the roaster, a reduction of working stocks – achieved through the outsourcing of stock management. For the market, this means an increase in the volume of stocks that are immediately available (mobilizable stocks). Previous to 1997, the measurement of world stocks included an important volume of stocks owned by roasters – non-mobilizable stocks. By the early 2000s, a bigger part of world stocks had become mobilizable. This is part of the reason why the same volume of stock generates an international price much lower than in the previous decade.

Conclusion

The last quarter of a century has witnessed at least four major transformations in the global value chain for coffee: (1) the ICA regime collapsed; (2) roasters and international traders went through a period of consolidation that has led to a situation of oligopoly; (3) producing countries, via domestic market liberalization, lost their ability to control export flows and stocks; and (4) a larger proportion of coffee stocks have become more readily available, leading to a previously unknown situation of low levels of stocks *and* low international prices.

The governance implications of these changes have been dramatic (see Tables 3.6 and 3.7 for a summary). During the ICA regime, producing countries had some influence in the governance of the global value chain for coffee. Entry barriers in farming and in domestic trade were often mediated by governments. The international coffee trade was regulated by the commodity agreement. The establishment of quotas and their periodic negotiation entailed that entry barriers for countries as producer units were politically negotiated within the ICA mechanisms – although the rise of the power of roasters over international traders had already started to occur. The inherently stabilizing force of the ICAs and regulated markets in producing countries created a relatively stable institutional environment where rules were relatively clear, change was politically negotiated, and proportions of generated income were relatively fairly distributed between consuming and producing countries (but not necessarily within producing countries).

The relatively homogeneous form of trade limited the possibilities of product upgrading, but producing countries ensured product valorization through higher prices generated by the ICA.

Contrary to what was claimed in another analysis of the global value chain for coffee (see Fitter and Kaplinsky 2001: 78), we would argue that the post-ICA regime exhibits many of the characteristics of what in GVC parlance is a 'buyer-driven' chain. Strategic choices made by roasters in the last ten years have shaped entry barriers not only in the roaster segment of the chain, but also in other segments upstream. Several indicators suggest an increase in the level of 'roaster power':

- New requirements set by roasters on minimum quantities needed from any particular origin to be included in a major blend can be interpreted as setting entry barriers to producing countries. These barriers used to be set by governments on the basis of political negotiation under the ICA regime. Now, private firms set them on the basis of market requirements.

- Roasters have been able to devise new technological solutions to be less dependent on any type or origin of coffee. It is not clear yet how roasters have combined the minimum supply quantity strategy with more flexibility in product substitution, and which one of the two has relatively more weight in their global sourcing strategy. In any case, they both indicate a potential increase in roasters' ability to drive the global value chain for coffee.

- Roasters have been able to set the terms of coffee supply with the implementation of SMI. The adoption of SMI has added new requirements for international traders to be part of the game. Guaranteeing a constant supply of a variety of origins and coffee types has prompted international traders to get even more involved in producing countries than they would have anyway as a result of market liberalization. In addition to this, SMI increases the levels of stocks that are readily available, which means that supply shortages have a lower impact on prices than before. This explains the situation of low prices and low levels of stocks that characterizes the early 2000s.

- The persistent ability of roasters to keep retailer margins at low levels suggests that they are still the driving force in the chain even downstream. Countervailing tendencies are arising in the specialty market. However, these may not be as threatening to main roasters as they seem, because these large corporations are always able to buy out significant specialty players. Also, as specialty coffee actors grow, they tend to streamline operations and homogenize products; therefore, they adopt some of the same supply strategies used by giant conglomerates.

In the post-ICA regime, market relations have replaced political negotiation over quotas. Producing countries have disappeared as actors in these interactions, with the exception of not-so-successful retention attempts under the ACPC umbrella. Domestic regulation of coffee markets plays an increasingly weaker role. Product upgrading possibilities have increased through the fragmentation of consumption patterns, the marketing of specialty/sustainable coffees and e-commerce sales. However, as Chapters 4 and 5 will show, openings in specialty markets so far have been more suitable to estates than smallholders. Is the solution to this situation going back to ICAs and full-blown market re-regulation in producing countries? In the next chapters, we suggest that although regulation has a role to play, an exclusive focus on material quality attributes of coffee and control of physical flows is not enough to unravel the coffee paradox.

Notes

1   The dates provided to characterize different 'periods' in this section and following ones are only indicative. These periods did not start or end exactly at the dates provided, and different periods overlapped significantly.

2   At the time of its demise in 2001, the ACPC had 14 ratified members: Angola, Brazil, Colombia, Costa Rica, Côte d'Ivoire, Democratic Republic of Congo, El Salvador, India, Indonesia, Kenya, Tanzania, Togo, Uganda and Venezuela. At that time, these countries produced nearly 85 per cent of world coffee supply.

3   Vietnam (No. 2 world producer, ranked by volume of 1999/2000 crop), Mexico (No. 4), and Guatemala (No. 8) had not joined the retention scheme.

4   Calculated from CSCE data. Fitter and Kaplinsky (2001: 77) show a similar trend using a different data set.

5   However, see also Mitchell and Gilbert (1997), who contest the argument

that non-industry players affect commodity prices.

6 In the 1990s, takeover instances included Rothfos by Neumann, SICAFE by Bolloré, and ACLII by Cargill (Daviron 1996).

7 Hill Brothers, MJB, and Chase and Sanborn were still owned by Nestlé in 1998. They were subsequently sold to Sara Lee. Therefore, the current proportional allocation among major roaster groups is likely to be different to the one presented in Figure 3.2 for 1998. A more recent breakdown was not available at the time of writing.

8 Exceptions are represented by Decotrade, the trading arm of Sara Lee/Douwe Egberts, and Taloca, which is owned by the Jacobs Suchard/Kraft group (Philip Morris). Tchibo has a trading arm that is very active in Kenya and Tanzania. Roasters/traders, however, do not rely on their trading arms alone for their supply needs. They source from a variety of other international traders as well.

9 SMI is the mirror image of a just-in-time stock management system, and has been adopted in many global value chains (see Gibbon and Ponte 2005). In the case of coffee, the roaster holds a minimum quantity of stock linked to projected sales of roasted coffee and adjusted to actual sales; the international trader manages the procurement and stock of green coffee from various origins that will match a supply schedule – which is subject to some flexibility. As a result of the adoption of SMI, a proportion of the stock (and its ownership) has moved from roasters to traders.

10 Roasters producing high-quality blends need to have greater cover (store a larger number of varieties and origins) than roasters that produce traditional blends. The latter are able to substitute coffee types more readily than the former.

11 'Backwardation' is a market condition in which a futures price is lower in the distant delivery months than in the near delivery months. The opposite condition characterizes a market when it is 'carrying'.

12 'Upstream' means movement towards producers. 'Downstream' means movement towards consumers.

13 Vertical integration issues are more complex in the case of instant coffee, where a number of manufacturers have installed plants in coffee-producing countries. For an exhaustive treatment of this subsector of the coffee industry, see Talbot (1997b).

14 The material presented here is based on a total of ten months of fieldwork carried out in East Africa in 2000 and 2002 by one of the authors.

15 These figures do not accurately reflect total exports, as a substantial proportion of coffee that is registered for domestic consumption is actually smuggled to Eritrea, Somalia and Sudan.

16 However, international traders had their agents in Uganda to check con-

signments, monitor the crop, and facilitate the export logistics.

17   The only meaningful changes implemented in the liberalization process have been: (1) farmers are being paid in dollars; in this way their exchange rate risk is reduced; (2) an 'out-of-pool' payment system has been created; (3) private curing plants have been allowed to provide commercial services in competition with the main plant owned by the Kenya Planters Cooperative Union (KPCU); (4) cooperative societies and estates can choose their 'payment agent'; the agency service was previously provided by KPCU only; and (5) more auctioneers have been allowed to operate.

18   In practice, there have been reports of private pulperies buying cherry coffee from smallholders instead of just providing a fee-based service. There are also reports of traders buying cherry from farmers and selling it to the central pulperies (Nyangito 2000).

19   According to ICO export data, in the last eight years before liberalization (1987–94), Tanzania exported an annual average of 49,600 tons of coffee. In the eight years after liberalization (1995-2002), this average fell to 45,600 tons (Ponte 2002a).

20   For a more general discussion of agricultural market liberalization in Tanzania and its effects on rural livelihoods, see Ponte (2002d).

21   Because Ugandan Robusta still plays a key role in major coffee blends, international traders need to be present in the country even though they may not make profits, just to keep their major clients (roasters) happy. MNC exporters are also undercut by the practices of some major roasters (such as Nestlé), who often buy an origin from more than one source – including directly financed local exporters.

22   The objective in this calculation is to eliminate the long-term trend in order to compare different cycles from one 'boom' to the next.

23   The price indicator used in this figure is the unit import value of green coffee in the US. This indicator gives the possibility to measure a synthetic green coffee price taking into account the diversity of geographical origins and the diversity of coffee varieties. The unit import value is given in constant US dollars. This means that current values, the ones we can calculate dividing the value of the US imports by the volume of imports, have been deflated by a wholesale price index (now a production price index) provided by the US administration. This indicator provides an evaluation of the long-term evolution of the purchasing power of one unit of green coffee.

24   To take into account the growth of the coffee market, stocks here are measured in months of world coffee imports.

25   Sources for Figures 3.6 and 3.7:
Unit import value of green coffee:

1860–1950: Hopp (1954)
1950–60: Netto (1979)
1960–2002: FAO (2004)
Wholesale price index:
1869–1970: United States Department of Commerce (1973)
1970–2002: IMF (2003)
World stocks:
1880–1929: Rufenacht (1955)
1929–48: Hopp (1954)
1949–60: Delaporte (1976)
1961–2002: USDA (2004) and ICO database.

26 The relation between stocks and prices is roughly represented by the following function: Price = $\alpha.1/\text{Stocks} + \beta$. Using a simple linear regression method we calculated two different functions depending on the period – with or without international agreements – with the same factor and differing only in the factor β. The function relating international prices to stocks has taken two different forms during the last century: $P = 10/S + 8$, during the periods 1880–1909, 1934–54 and 1990–6 (lower line in Figure 3.7); and $P = 10/S + 29$, during 1955–89 (upper line in Figure 3.7).

4
Is this any good?
Material and symbolic production
of coffee quality

From material to symbolic and in-person service attributes: quality along coffee value chains

Much of the economics literature on quality points out that the transaction costs of evaluating quality at various points of a value chain depend on the ease with which quality can be measured. While this is the case, quality does not pertain to physical characteristics alone. Furthermore, evaluators have different capacities for assessing quality attributes. These capacities vary between actors, in time and in space, and in practice also depend on the behaviour of others. In this chapter, we apply the analytical framework based on the distinction between *material, symbolic* and *in-person service* attributes laid out in Chapter 1 to the specific case study of coffee.

To recapitulate, *material* attributes of a product are usually seen as objective, existing independently of the identity of sellers and buyers. The ability to measure these attributes depends on the existence of measurement operations and devices, and on the accuracy of these measurements. Measurement can be made by human senses or more or less sophisticated technological devices. Indirect measurement through the use of proxies supposes a previous building of equivalences. The setting of measurement devices, indicators, units and intervals is a source of power.

Symbolic quality attributes are based on reputation. Often, reputation is signalled through trademarks, geographical indications and sustainability labels. Symbolic quality, although not directly measurable, is increasingly subject to evaluation through metrics of different kinds. Trademarks and geographical indications are protected by a legal framework based on intellectual property rights against misleading use and dilution of meaning. The main difference between brands and indications lies in the collective nature of property for the latter. Labels are awarded to products provided by enterprises or organizations that meet specific criteria. They are also protected, to some degree as intellectual property, but are in principle open to all actors who can match their criteria.

In-person service quality attributes are first of all the product of interpersonal relations between producers/providers and consumers. In-person services can only take place through direct contact between the consumer and the producer and cannot exist independently of them. Most in-person services imply some physical transformation of a good (preparing a drink, for example) or, directly, of the consumer (hairdressing, for example). All in-person services include affective work. Some in-person services are exclusively or mainly constituted by affective work (psychotherapy is the extreme case). In-person service quality attributes include the quality of the physical transformation but also, and importantly, the quality of the affective work. Moreover, because of the necessary direct contact between the provider and the consumer, in-person services often imply some grouping of consumers in a specific place (a bar, a restaurant, a school, a hospital, a barber shop). A further attribute is therefore associated with in-person services: the behaviour of other consumers and the interactions between them.

In this chapter, we map out how the material, symbolic and in-person service attributes of coffee quality are created, discovered and/or evaluated along the value chain. We start from producing countries, where material quality attributes are paramount in shaping transactions. We discuss general features of quality evaluation in coffee-producing countries and then draw on our East African case studies for a more detailed examination of how evaluation systems have changed as a result of domestic market liberalization.

In the following section, we move to consuming countries, examining quality in international trade, roasting and retailing. As we move up the value chain, symbolic and in-person quality attributes become increasingly important. Case studies of the mainstream Italian market (in its home consumption and bar segments) and the US specialty market will shed light on some of the intricacies of coffee quality in consuming countries and highlight some perhaps unexpected features.

Quality in producing countries

General criteria

Quality standards and quality control procedures are key aspects of the domestic coffee trade in producing countries. At this level, quality is mainly assessed in its material attributes, including sometimes aroma and taste. Except for Brazil and Ethiopia, producing countries do not have substantial populations of coffee consumers. Thus, symbolic attributes generated through branding, packaging, retailing and consumption do not play an important role. Coffee is simply an export crop to be consumed elsewhere. A major exception is when quality is embedded in a geographical origin (national, regional, local, or single-estate). When this is the case, producers and their cooperatives, associations or governments create symbolic attributes. It is not only the material coffee that is sold, but also a place, a story, sometimes a sense of exoticism. The same applies when the content of quality refers to production and processing that follow sound environmental guidelines, or when a minimum price is guaranteed to smallholder farmers (see Chapter 5 on sustainable coffees). Due to the distance between the sites of production and consumption, in-person services do not play a role in the creation of value in producing countries, with the possible exception of local coffee served in the tourist industry (in Kenya and Tanzania, for example), and the 'cultural performance' aspect of the coffee ceremony in Ethiopia.

Mainstream coffees are normally evaluated in producing countries on the basis of material quality through what the industry calls 'objective' physical parameters (colour, size, defects, etcetera). These are measurable by means of sensory inspection and more or less sophisticated mechanical and optical processes of separation and sorting. Some types of coffee (especially higher-quality Mild Arabicas) are also assessed for aroma and taste before export. This is a much more subjective evaluation, although it is surrounded by an aura of scientificity. Professional tasters (also called liquorers or cuppers) in white laboratory gowns slurp and spit from long lines of white coffee cups, and annotate their scoring on pre-made evaluation forms. In reality, the taster performs art, craft and science at the same time.

Cup testing in the country of origin is not sufficient for the complete disclosure of quality that is sometimes demanded by importers and roasters. As a result, especially for higher-end coffees, cuppers based in the consuming country may carry out their own evaluation on pre-purchased samples. In the past, aroma and taste were based on rough description. Sensory analysis, however, is now becoming more of a science. It was born in the wine industry, but is spreading to other products. One of the problems in the coffee industry is that cuppers operating in one producing country have only limited comparative knowledge of coffees with other origins. Also, coffee cupping in producing countries focuses on defects. But a complete sensorial profile includes a detailed description of positive aspects. In the process of developing these, a language of description is being invented in consuming countries. Therefore, coffee is not simply described as 'AA grade, low acidity, medium body, earthy' (as it may be at the export point), but rather as 'coffee with floral notes and deep, lush fruit; blackberry, strawberry, raspberry, currant, sometimes grape-fruit; with a very corporal quality, a muscular quality, with an undeniable sensuality to be found in its musky scent'.

The material quality of coffee is generated by inherent and external factors. So-called 'inherent' factors include: (1) the genetic type of the coffee tree (Arabica, Robusta); (2) the cultivar (Bourbon, Blue Mountain, Kent, etcetera); and (3) agro-climatic conditions (soil type, rainfall, altitude). So-called 'external' factors include: (1) farm practices (input application, pruning, weeding, mulching, irrigation when available, sun- or shade-growing); (2) harvesting procedures (picking only ripe cherries); (3) primary processing (wet or dry methods); (4) export preparation; and (5) handling and storage during the passages from one stage to the next in the marketing chain (Brown 1991).

Primary processing of coffee does not improve material quality. Its aim is to maintain the original quality of the bean and this is possible only when the bean is dry. Therefore, quality control at every stage of processing and trading is critical to the final level of quality of coffee. Poor handling, pulping, fermentation, drying, storage or shipping result in deterioration of the appearance of the bean and the flavour of the liquor extracted from it. Inadequate sorting, grading or cleaning increases the proportion of defects in the sample and reduces price and acceptability for export of a coffee consignment (Brown 1991).

Smallholder coffee producers relate to quality mostly through farm practices rather than their own consumption experiences. Therefore, quality is seen as the outcome of what they do on the farm. The main indicator of quality is the appearance of the coffee beans at the first change of hands between farmer and primary-level trader or processor. At this point, both actors have only limited information on the material properties of coffee quality. If dry cherry is sold (Hard Arabica, Robusta), quality is assessed by making sure that the coffee is properly dried and that there is no foreign matter mixed up with it. If the consignment is larger, the buyer may hull a small sample to assess the quality of the bean inside. If fresh cherry is sold (Mild Arabica processed at centralized pulperies), quality checks are also limited to discarding unripe cherries (of green colour) and foreign matter. Sometimes, a rough grading procedure can be carried out by floating a consignment in a water tank (lighter cherries will float). If parchment coffee is sold (Mild Arabica processed by individual farmers with small pulpers), more attributes can be evaluated in addition to moisture and absence of foreign matter, such as the size of coffee beans, their colour and their smell.

In no cases, however, can taste characteristics be assessed. The primary buyer relies on the reputation of the seller or the area where the coffee is bought to minimize the quality risk. The higher the quality risk, the higher the price discount that will be applied to all coffee bought from a specific farmer or area. The amount of quality information accessible to the primary buyer usually depends on the degree of vertical integration in the value chain. The more fragmented the chain, the more difficult the flow of quality information is. However, there are exceptions to this rule (see next section), as quality management depends heavily on the regulatory framework of the coffee trade in producing countries.

In most coffee-producing countries, the analytical valuation of coffee at the export point is achieved through official grade standards (see Chapter 2). These standards vary from country to country, but generally describe the size of the bean, its density, colour, shape, moisture content, and the number of defects in a standard weight sample. In the Robusta and Hard Arabica trade, this information, sometimes together with a report of 'clean cup' (absence of spoiled or foreign flavours assessed through cup testing), is generally sufficient for export. The coffee is then sold 'on description', using the vocabulary defined in a specific national grade.

In the Mild Arabica trade, and especially where quality variation within an origin is high (as in East Africa), additional information is needed. After grading, coffee is evaluated on the basis of a points system that combines scores for the raw appearance of the beans, its roast qualities and its liquor. By looking at a roasted coffee sample, a seller or buyer can check the evenness of the roast and assess whether the coffee was overdried (in which case, the beans will break). By looking at the colour of the roast, sellers and buyers can detect whether coffee was over-fermented or poorly washed. Cup testing consists in brewing a sample of coffee and in evaluating its body, acidity, aroma, and the presence of foreign flavours in descriptive terms (in a similar way to what happens in wine tasting). These qualifications are then combined in a matrix that takes into consideration the grade of the coffee as well. The final result is the coffee 'class', which is the overall indicator of coffee quality in Mild Arabica (at least in East Africa). These classes achieve a fairly complete analytical valuation from the point of view of the exporter. To what extent these are sufficient for the importer will depend on the kind of coffee, the relationship between exporter and importer, and whether the importer has the opportunity to assess pre-shipment samples. In the next section, we go back to our East African case studies to examine in more detail how domestic market regulation, together with commercial strategies adopted by traders and exporters, affects quality evaluation procedures and quality incentives in domestic coffee markets. This analysis will shed light on why oversupply of commodity coffee can coexist with shortages of high-quality coffee.

Coffee payment systems and quality control in East Africa

Quality control systems before liberalization

Previous to market liberalization (which took place in the 1990s; see Chapter 3), farmers in Kenya and Tanzania received payments that were linked to the quality of coffee they delivered to a cooperative or the auction (see details in Ponte 2002a). Cooperatives paid a fixed advance payment per unit of weight of coffee delivered, and then paid another one or two instalments after having delivered the coffee to a curing plant or having exported it. Usually, the last payment was proportional to the quality of coffee delivered by the farmer to the cooperative and to the overall quality of coffee sold by the cooperative to the marketing board. The marketing system also provided agro-chemical inputs on credit to farmers, whose cost was deducted from the payment for the coffee they sold. A similar system operated for the Mild Arabica trade in Uganda, although coffee was sold by the marketing board directly to importers, rather than at the export auction. In all three countries, coffee quality was evaluated before export (and/or before the auction) and needed to match minimum standards set by the regulatory agency.

In Tanzania, the Hard Arabica and Robusta trade was organized in the same way as the Mild Arabica trade. However, quality considerations are generally less important in the Robusta and Hard Arabica trade. It is difficult to determine the quality of the bean inside the dry cherry when is delivered, unless a sample is hulled. Therefore, quality control at the primary level was normally limited to removing foreign matter and under-dried cherries. Yet, at least in Tanzania, a quality incentive governed the output delivered by cooperative societies. Societies that delivered bigger beans with a lower defect count were paid more. Their farmers were paid more as well. In Uganda, the domestic Robusta trade was carried out by cooperative societies in competition with licensed private buyers. Coffee prices were fixed at all stages and determined by the marketing board.

In Ethiopia, quality control of Mild Arabica was carried out when fresh cherry was delivered to washing stations (where only ripe and newly harvested cherries would be purchased). A further control was carried out after processing. Coffee that failed this second test was sold in the domestic market. Quality control of Hard Arabica was less strict, but is said to have been more effectively carried out during the imperial regime (pre-1974), when extension officers were entitled to burn the coffee that they saw being dried directly on the earth instead of on mats. For both types of coffee, the moisture level was checked at over 50 market centres before the coffee was allowed to be transported to the auctions. Further quality assessments were carried out before the auction and before export (Love 2002).

Impact of market liberalization on quality in Tanzania and Uganda
In Tanzania, at least on paper, quality control procedures at the primary buying level have not changed with liberalization. In reality, one price

is paid for any kind of parchment/dry cherry bought at the primary level. Buying of wet coffee to beat the competition has also been a major problem. The one-price-for-all buying practice means that there is no direct incentive for farmers to deliver better-quality coffee. Cooperatives, which in the past offered differentiated prices in relation to quality, had to adapt to the new market situation and now operate in a way very similar to private traders in terms of pricing. They have also discontinued the provision of inputs on credit to their farmers. However, quality control procedures at cooperative societies are still stricter than in private buying posts.[1]

Contrary to the case of domestic trade, quality control procedures at the auction and export levels have been maintained. Also, liberalization of the curing sector has increased the speed of coffee turnaround. The new plants also have superior technology, which allows for better grading and lower losses. More efficient marketing and curing operations have led to lower overheads, with a higher proportion of the export price being paid to farmers. At the same time, lower international prices and lack of price competition in domestic trade have led to lower farm-gate prices. The maintenance of the auction system could have ensured that the exported coffee fetched the highest price possible. However, due to vertical integration of exporters into domestic buying, most of the coffee sold at the auction does not actually change hands but is simply re-purchased by the same company (Temu 2001; Winter-Nelson and Temu 2002; Ponte 2004; Baffes 2005). With the passage of a new coffee act, however, things may be changing (see Chapter 3). The general outcome of these transformations has been a

Table 4.1 Tanzania: quality performance by class for Mild Arabica coffee, 1968/9–1999/2000

Percentage of total volume traded at the auction (average)	Classes			
	1–5	6–10	11–13	14–17
1968/9–1972/3	13.1	74.3	8.7	4.0
1979/80–1993/4	2.1	73.3	19.6	5.1
1988/9–1993/4	2.3	75.6	16.9	5.2
1994/5–1999/2000	1.6	69.0	24.5	5.1

Sources: Elaboration from Tanzania Coffee Board and Marketing Development Bureau data.

serious quality decline of green coffee, reflected in the decreasing proportion of top-quality coffees sold at the auction after liberalization (see Table 4.1). This has further affected the reputation and the premium paid for Tanzanian coffee in the international market.

Uganda is a major world producer of Robusta coffee. As mentioned above, quality considerations for Robusta and Hard Arabica coffees are much less stringent than for Mild Arabica. Proper differentiation of the product at the primary buying stage is not simple unless large deliveries of dry cherry are made. The most pressing factors at this level are the separation of extraneous matter and the moisture content of the hulled coffee. The maximum level of moisture in hulled coffee suitable for trade is set by the Uganda Coffee Development Authority (UCDA) but rarely enforced. Robusta coffee is grown mostly without agro-chemicals, so the breakdown of input provision on credit by cooperatives has had only a minor effect on coffee yields and quality in Uganda.

As seen in Chapter 3, after liberalization export companies opted for maximal vertical integration, even to the point of buying dry cherry instead of hulled coffee. As in Tanzania, this created incentives to 'buy fast' without proper quality monitoring. According to industry actors, this led to a massive decrease of quality because of increased trade and hulling of cherry coffee that was not dry enough. However, the following process of de-verticalization (local-level trade and hulling are now almost completely in the hands of independent local operators) led to improvements in quality control. Some of the major exporters have started to apply quality-related pricing conventions in their buying posts, where they purchase large amounts of green coffee. Because buying is now more centralized, quality control is easier to carry out and its incentive effects are more likely to reach actors upstream.

Table 4.2 Uganda: quality performance by proportion of 'clean cup' and distribution of defects for Robusta coffee, 1992/3–2001/2 (% of total lots tested)

1992/3	1993/4	1995/6	1996/7	1997/8	1998/9	1999/2000	2000/1	2001/2
66.0	79.0	91.2	93.5	92.6	89.2	85.0	89.6	87.0

Source: Elaboration from Uganda Coffee Development Authority data.

In sum, liberalization of domestic marketing in Uganda led to a period of quality deterioration and a later recovery and relative stabilization (see Table 4.2). This did not lead to a loss of reputation for Ugandan Robusta because export quality was maintained through UCDA monitoring. If coffee does not reach 'clean cup' quality[2] or does not pass screen, humidity and defect count tests it cannot be exported and needs to be resorted. The special characteristics of Ugandan Robusta lie in the fact that it is grown at higher altitudes than most other Robustas. Therefore, the most important quality trait is embedded in the product and is less easy to spoil than in the case of Mild Arabicas. From this point of view, liberalization did not affect the reputation of Ugandan Robusta and, at the same time, benefited farmers, who are paid a higher share of the export price than in the pre-liberalization period.

Gradual/partial liberalization and premium preservation: Kenya and Ethiopia
As mentioned in Chapter 3, the basic structure of the marketing chain in Kenya has remained almost the same throughout the 1990s and early 2000s. The basic quality control and payment procedures have been maintained. As a result of the maintenance of the old quality control system – and contrary to other Mild Arabica producing countries in Africa where the process of liberalization has been faster and more pronounced (such as Tanzania, Cameroon and Madagascar) – the overall class performance of Kenyan coffee actually improved from 1990/1 to 1996/7 (see Table 4.3). This happened even though the coffee marketing system in the country was marred by financial mismanagement and production volumes were decreasing. Quality performance substantially improved in the top coffee classes (the ones that drive export prices), although the proportion of *mbuni* (unwashed coffee of the lowest quality) also increased. It is also clear from Table 4.3 that smallholders and their cooperatives achieve a higher proportion of top-end coffees than estates. Owing to a lack of quality data for following years, the impact of lower international prices since 1999 and political turmoil in the coffee industry cannot yet be assessed. In late 2001, a new Coffee Act was passed, which provides for a more extensive liberalization of the industry. If this means that the domestic market is liberalized, Kenyan coffee quality is bound to decline. As in Tanzania, liberalization would lead to more homogenous mixtures with the result that

Table 4.3 Kenya: quality performance by class and sector for Mild Arabica coffee, 1990/1–1996/7 (% of total volume traded at the auction)

Sector	Class	1990/1	1991/2	1992/3	1993/4	1994/5	1995/6	1996/7
Coops	1 to 3	16.5	15.6	17.8	18.9	20.5	25.3	23.3
	4 to 6	58.1	53.8	57.3	56.3	47.8	54.5	48.2
	7 to 10	7.6	12.4	8.3	10.7	3.7	6.1	7.9
	mbuni	17.7	18.3	16.7	14.1	28.0	17.2	18.6
Estate	1 to 3	3.5	4.3	5.0	1.4	7.3	4.0	5.2
	4 to 6	80.5	74.5	78.2	77.7	68.0	78.0	75.5
	7 to 10	8.5	14.5	10.2	12.9	5.7	9.7	9.5
	mbuni	7.5	6.7	6.7	8.0	19.0	8.3	9.9
Total	1 to 3	11.1	10.8	12.1	10.1	13.9	16.5	16.5
	4 to 6	67.1	62.2	66.2	67.0	57.9	62.4	60.2
	7 to 10	8.2	13.6	9.5	11.8	4.7	7.6	8.6
	mbuni	13.6	13.4	12.3	11.0	23.5	13.5	14.7

Source: Elaboration from Coffee Board of Kenya data.

the average quality of bad coffees would improve, but also that the quality of top coffees would deteriorate. This is likely to lead to lower differentials for Kenyan coffees in general.

In Ethiopia, the domestic market is substantially less regulated than before 1991. At the farm level, coffee is bought all at one price, irrespectively of quality – although there are wide price differences between different areas. Because coffee is delivered un-hulled (as fresh or dry cherry), quality screening at the delivery point is usually limited to discarding under-ripe cherries and foreign matter. Yet governmental quality controls have been maintained, both at the local level and at the auction. Coffee needs to be sealed by government officers in provincial towns before being sent to the auctions in Addis Ababa and Dire Dawa. Moisture level is strictly checked and enforced at these control points, avoiding transport- and humidity-related quality deterioration.

In other words, contrary to what happened in Tanzania and Uganda, liberalization has not been followed by quality control relaxation at the local level. Coffee is tested by the Coffee and Tea Authority (CTA) before going to the auction and again before export. From 1998/9, the CTA has also started to cup test all Hard Arabica

Table 4.4 Ethiopia: quality performance by cup quality for Mild and Hard Arabica coffees, 1991/2–2000/1 (% of total arrivals at the auction)

	Mild Arabica Grade					Hard Arabica Grade				
	1	2	3	4	Reject	1	2	3	4	Reject
2000/1	2.9	35.5	48.0	6.6	7.1	2.3	19.9	40.9	20.2	16.6
Average 1991/2– 1995/6	2.0	32.1	51.2	9.6	5.1					
Average 1996/7– 2000/1	2.0	34.0	48.6	8.9	6.5	0.8	7.9	49.6	31.6	10.2

Source: Elaboration from Coffee and Tea Authority of Ethiopia data.

(only Mild Arabica was cup tested previously). This allows exporters to have better information about the quality of coffee. One of the main remaining problems with quality information is that exporters are not allowed to cup test coffee before buying it at the auction; therefore, they have to rely solely on CTA quality reports. This means that, if they do not trust the CTA's assessments, they may pay a lower price than they would have if they had cup tested the coffee themselves, as happens in Tanzania and Kenya.

The overall quality performance of Ethiopian coffee in the liberalization period has been fairly stable. As we can see in Table 4.4, the proportion of top cup quality grades in Mild Arabica slightly improved on average from 1992–6 to 1997–2001, although the proportion of rejects also increased slightly. Cup quality for Hard Arabica has been introduced only in the late 1990s, so not much can be said except that the 2000/1 season has seen a marked increase in the proportion of top-quality coffee, coupled with an increase in rejects. Such a large variation could be linked to the change in regulation that has allowed *akrabies* to buy directly from farmers. *Sebsabies* have long been accused of tampering with the coffee to increase its weight (by mixing it with water and foreign matter). According to some exporters, it may be more difficult for *sebsabies* to get away with this practice now that *akrabies* have the alternative of buying coffee from farmers themselves. Still, this does not explain the increase in the proportion of rejects.

In sum, partial liberalization does not seem to have had a negative effect on coffee quality in Ethiopia. The breakdown in input provision on credit from cooperatives has had a greater effect on food crops than on coffee, as most Ethiopian coffee is grown without agro-chemicals. Coffee is bought at one price from farmers irrespectively of quality. However, no direct price incentives on quality were paid to farmers even before market liberalization. Therefore, quality preservation can be linked to the maintenance of strict governmental quality controls at the local level, together with restrictions on the movement of coffee between coffee-growing regions and the auction centres. The separation of coffee from different regions has avoided mixing of coffee with peculiar characteristics, therefore avoiding homogenization. Selected Ethiopian coffees are bought for their unique cup taste. The preservation of this uniqueness via appropriate regulation has proved to be a winning strategy even in a partially liberalized market. Finally, the setting of minimum differentials has allowed the government to still have a say in the valuation of its coffee, if not in absolute terms, at least in comparison to other origins.

The quality lessons of liberalization

Although liberalization of domestic coffee markets has taken place in most coffee-producing countries worldwide, the dynamics have differed from place to place. Quality preservation may not be an important feature in countries of origin where volume rather than quality represents the insertion point in the global value chain for coffee, or where quality deterioration is less vulnerable to changes in marketing systems. However, where quality is more important, it has become clearer that preserving quality and reputation is more difficult, if not impossible, in deregulated markets. The experiences of partly liberalized markets suggest that appropriate regulation can maintain quality levels and reputation, and can also ensure that local actors have more control over the meaning and valuation of their coffee. At the same time, lack of appropriate checks and balances in the running of regulated systems can also play against producers (when they receive a very low proportion of the export price) and can lead to declining volumes of production in the long term.

Quality in consuming countries

As coffee moves from producing to consuming countries, the content of quality and its evaluation become more complex. Quality gets manipulated in various ways – in relation to material, symbolic and in-person service attributes. It is embedded in the reputations of actors, brands and origins. Quality may refer to the material attributes of coffee itself, or it may be linked to the preparation method. It may be generated by consumption ambience and serve as a lifestyle signifier. It may be created through in-person service provision, such as an exchange with the *barista* (*espresso* coffee bartender). It may arise from conscious or unconscious interaction with other consumers. Depending on what market segment and what country is analysed, some actors have more influence than others on specific aspects of quality content. In the mainstream market, roasters through their global brands are key players in the manipulation of quality attributes. In specialty markets, quality is created in complex dynamics between small roasters and retailers, café chains and consumers. In both markets, consumers may play more or less active roles depending on the country, market outlet and preparation type.

The agro-food literature on consumption and retail suggests that retailers decisively shape the way consumers approach quality. At the same time, it is recognized that different actors along agro-food chains hold different quality perspectives and adopt different measurement approaches, and that quality, as a social construction, is shaped by socio-cultural, political and economic contexts (Marsden and Arce 1995; see also our discussion on agents of change in Chapter 6).

In the next sections, we unpack some of these issues through the analysis of coffee quality in different market segments and countries. Specifically, we look at the role of various actors in generating quality attributes, including consumers. First, we start with mainstream coffee markets in general, and Italy in particular. Second, we analyse quality issues in the specialty market, with some focus on the US.

Mainstream markets

In the mainstream market, international traders and roasters award quality through the payment of prices for Arabica coffees as differentials in relation to the futures price of Colombian Milds (C contract) quoted on the New York Coffee, Sugar and Cocoa Exchange (CSCE). The reference price for Robusta is set at the London International Financial Futures and Options Exchange (LIFFE). Price differentials for a particular coffee are set in relation to demand/supply/stock conditions, analytical quality and reputation. At this level, the evaluation of the material attributes of coffee is still important. Roasters need coffees with specific characteristics to fit in their blends. Coffees still have an identity, depending on their processing method and origin. Roasters try to minimize costs by sourcing the cheapest combination of coffees possible to maintain a certain flavour profile.

Once coffee is roasted and blended, the most important quality issue for mainstream roasters is homogeneity. Any one blend needs to taste the same every day and in all outlets. Although roasters have been increasing the number of products they offer to the public, homogeneity of each product in time and space is still a key issue. Most roasted coffee is branded. The composition of branded blends is a tightly kept industrial secret. In the mainstream market, consumers do not have the skills to identify the subtle differences from one blend or brand to another. As a result, they use brand reputation as a proxy for variance in quality. This does not mean that a higher price necessarily buys a better coffee. Packaging, shelf placement and advertisement also play a major role in establishing consumers' ideas of quality.

Although most coffee for in-home consumption is currently pur-chased in supermarket chains, large branded roasters are to some extent still the movers and shakers of the mainstream market. These roasters sell large quantities of relatively homogeneous and undifferentiated blends of varying quality. As a rule of thumb, better quality blends are found in Northern Europe than in the US. Yet what is considered good coffee by the average consumer differs widely from country to country (see Chapter 2). In most countries, branded roasters compete almost exclusively on advertising, pricing, product differentiation and shelf placement.

Roasters have complete information on quality when they buy coffee and release next to no information to their clients. This factor, together with increasing market concentration, has allowed them to gain a driving seat in the global value chain for coffee. While super-market chains have a predominant power position in other agro-food chains such as fresh fruit and vegetables – and dictate quality and logistics standards to other actors upstream – coffee roasters have been able to use the asymmetry of quality information on coffee to their advantage. They have downgraded the quality of their product to increase their margins.[3] The results of poor quality offerings in the US in the post-Second World War period were two-fold: first, a reduction in *per capita* consumption; second, a switch to specialty coffee. Thus, consumers did not influence the quality offering of mainstream brands. It was only recently that mainstream roasters started to enter the specialty market, and often by purchasing specialty brands rather than improving the quality of mainstream brands. In this sense, the mainstream market has remained stuck in its relatively poor quality offering.

To further examine quality issues in consuming countries, in the next section we examine the Italian coffee industry.[4] This case study is particularly informative because it compares quality in the very concentrated mainstream market (roasted and ground coffee sold in supermarket chains) and in the large but fragmented coffee bar sector. Therefore, it provides comparative evidence on different ways of creating value through the production of symbolic and in-person service attributes in markets characterized by different levels of concentration.

A case study: coffee quality in the Italian coffee market

Overview
Coffee consumption is part of everyday life for most Italians. It is a daily routine marked by regular events: *cappuccino* for breakfast, *espresso macchiato* in the mid-morning, a straight shot after lunch, and maybe *espresso corretto* (with *grappa*) after dinner. Italian coffee is obviously not Italian as far as the origin of the raw material is concerned. It is the *espresso* preparation that makes it such. Yet, with the boom of cafés in North America and Europe, *espresso* and its derivative preparations have spread around the world. At the same time, there is often little resemblance between the short *espresso* drunk as a 'pit stop' in a family-owned bar in Italy and some of the sophisticated *espresso*-based drinks consumed leisurely at a Starbucks, sitting on a retro-looking sofa with a laptop computer.

Italians pride themselves on their coffee consumption culture, and often take it for granted that their coffee is of good quality. However, their idea of quality has more to do with how strong the coffee blend/brew is (darker roasts, heavier body) and how good the *barista* is in delivering a foam with perfect texture, than on other material quality attributes. Delivering quality in these terms depends on the dexterity of the *barista*, the quality and maintenance of the *espresso* machine, the quality of the water used, and the specific composition of the *espresso* blend. Only Hard Arabica and Robusta coffees can generate the foam on top of the *espresso*. Contrary to other consumption cultures (the North American specialty market, Scandinavian and German markets), acidity is not necessarily sought out in *espresso* blends. Smoothness is.

Italy is the fifth coffee importer in the world in terms of volume. It is the third in Europe after Germany and France. Consumption *per capita* increased from under 1 kilogram per year in the 1940s to 2.5 kilograms in the mid-1960s. It stabilized at around 4.5–5 kilograms in the late 1980s and 1990s (ICO 2000). Until the end of the 1950s, most consumers purchased coffee in loose form from small roasters. 'When vacuum packing was introduced, roasted coffee became a stored good that could be transported everywhere' (ICO 2000: 5). In the 1990s, imports ranged between 5 and 6 million bags a year, mostly in green form. Starting in the 1980s, a substantial proportion of this coffee has been re-exported, normally as a roasted *espresso* blend. In the second half of the 1990s, almost one million bags of green coffee equivalent were exported on average per year, largely to France, Germany, Eastern Europe and the US (ICO 2000). Sustainable coffees (see Chapter 5) accounted for only 0.3 per cent of the Italian market in 2001 (Giovannucci and Koekoek 2003: 125).

In the early 1970s, Robusta coffee accounted for just under one-third of total imports by volume (half of which was sourced from what was then Zaïre, with most of the rest coming from other Francophone African producers); 60 per cent of imports was Hard Arabica, mostly from Brazil; the remaining 11 per cent was Mild Arabica from a variety of origins. In contrast, in the second half of the 1990s Robusta made up 44 per cent of imports (mostly from Côte d'Ivoire, Vietnam, Cameroon and Uganda); Hard Arabica (still sourced mainly from Brazil) and Mild Arabica (with larger shares from Colombia and India) followed with 27 per cent each (ICO 2000). Thus there has been a significant reconfiguration of blends, with cheap Robusta used in place of Hard Arabica. In partial compensation, increasing use is made of Mild Arabica to improve the taste profile. The increase in Robusta imports took on a new dimension in the mid-1990s. Roasters had to absorb a large increase in coffee prices in 1994–5 and 1997. In Italy, the sale price of a cup of *espresso* remained fairly stable. Thus, roasters had to downgrade their blends. Yet when coffee prices plummeted, blends were not upgraded again, as consumer response had not been adverse.

In Italy, about two-thirds of coffee consumption by volume takes place in the household, largely in the form of roast and ground blends prepared with the traditional stove-top coffee maker (*caffettiera*). Home consumption, however, corresponds to only 30 per cent of the total value of sales. About one-third of coffee consumption by volume takes place in bars, restaurants and institutional settings (representing almost 70 per cent of total sales). Vending machines represent a small but fast-growing proportion of sales. The most notable of recent innovations in the Italian coffee market has been the introduction of the single serving pod (coffee is packaged between two layers of filter paper for use with 'easy-serving *espresso* machines'). This system was pioneered by Illy in the early 1990s, but is now marketed by Lavazza and other brands as well. Illy has also introduced a new can that ensures a good con-servation of aroma after it is opened – in almost air-tight conditions. Other roasters have attempted the introduction of flavoured coffees and coffees in a can, without much success. Lavazza has started to promote 'American-style' preparation, which remains a small niche. There have also been increased sales of whole beans at supermarkets. Finally, Segafredo Zanetti has started franchising cafés both in Italy and elsewhere (the first of these was opened in Paris in 1988).

The home consumption market
Distribution for home consumption coffee takes place mostly through modern retail chains. In the North of Italy, this channel controls up to 70 per cent of sales. If compared to other retail markets such as the UK, Holland and Scandinavia, traditional shops still account for a substantial proportion of sales, especially in the South of the country. In 2000, supermarkets accounted for about 60 per cent of sales in the modern retail channel, followed by hypermarkets (23 per cent) and superettes (10 per cent). A few branded roasters dominate the home consumption market. In 2001, four main groups (Lavazza, Splendid/Kraft, Café do

Brasil/Kimbo and Segafredo Zanetti) controlled 75 per cent of sales. Lavazza alone controlled almost 50 per cent. Private labels have expanded in the 1990s, but only in the low price range. Consumers consider them to be of lower quality than major brands, although the coffee blend is often the same. In 2001, private labels accounted for about 6 per cent of sales.

Large mainstream roasters buy approximately 80 per cent of their coffee directly from origins, and the rest from importers. This means that importers work mostly with smaller roasters that serve the bar market. Mainstream roasters buy coffee mostly on description, on the basis of a reference quality profile determined at the beginning of the supply season (for an exception, see our discussion of the Illy phenomenon, p. 148 below). Focus is on reliability and homogeneity of supply and coverage throughout the year. Large buyers such as Lavazza purchase from all the top ten coffee-producing countries. They purchase from smaller suppliers only for particular blends.

There are three main price categories in the home consumption market in Italy: (1) blends made with a high percentage of Robusta coffee (up to 90–100 per cent) for the heavy-discount market; (2) middle-range blends (typically, 30 per cent Hard Arabica, 20 per cent Mild Arabica and 50 per cent Robusta); and (3) 100 per cent Arabica blends (60–70 per cent Hard and 30–40 per cent Mild). Yet, quality does not necessarily follows the proportion of Arabica in the blend. There are good Arabicas and bad Arabicas. It is also not clear how consumers relate to '100 per cent Arabica' as an indicator of quality – a small roaster in Piedmont recently launched its proudly labelled '100 per cent Robusta coffee'.

National-level advertising of main brands is extremely important in the home consumption market. Lavazza is said to be spending up to 10 per cent of turnover on advertising. Price competition, promotional sales and shelf space are keys to successful sales. Promotional sales account for almost 40 per cent of sale volumes in supermarkets and hypermarkets. These usually take place in the form of 'buy three, pay for two' promotions. This means that good relationships with retailers (and a hedge over them) are essential to roasters. Supermarket chain margins vary from 12 to 15 per cent for lower-quality to 20 per cent for higher-quality blends. In comparison to other food items, these are fairly low margins. They are justified by the fact that coffee (especially leading brands such as Lavazza) is an item that brings consumers to the supermarket. According to industry actors, leader brands with a solid market share can actually impose some conditions on supermarket chains (visibility, placement at easy eye reach). Competition for shelf space and visibility has led to an increase in the number of blends that are offered to the public by the major brands. Major roasters are trying to offer more blends so that they can take more space on the supermarket shelf and cut out the small roasters. As a small roaster put it to one of the authors,[5]

> on the one hand, they [large roasters] fragment the supply. On the other hand, they homogenize taste because they do not want to be short in any type of coffee. In theory, one could also sell different coffees for different times of the day (morning coffee that goes well with lots of milk, etcetera). This has not been used as a marketing strategy in Italy because homogenization is paramount. The final consumer at the supermarket buys on the basis of price and wants a taste that is constant in time. Consumers are not attentive to the quality of the product. There are small companies that focus on quality, but the consumer does not understand what they are offering. Also, coffee prepared with the *caffettiera* at home does not translate all the qualities of the blend in the brew. It is easier to appreciate these qualities in an *espresso*.

The general picture emerging in the Italian home consumption market is one of a highly concentrated brand offering of average-to-poor quality (high percentage of Robusta, bitter taste), and of down-grading of blends without adverse consumer response. Quality is embedded in the brand name and roasters do not talk about quality in advertising. This not-so-flattering picture is similar to the one characterizing the US mainstream market. The difference is that Italians think that they drink excellent coffee. Increased exports of Italian *espresso* blends in the last 20 years indicate that this view is shared by consumers abroad as well. Mainstream US consumers, on the other hand, are to some extent aware that their coffee is poor (hence the growth of the specialty industry). The material presented in the next section suggests that quality in the Italian bar market is not much better either.

The bar market
There are an estimated 750–1,000 roasters in Italy (down from over 3,000 in the 1980s) and 187,000 independently owned bars. The bar

market (which also includes consumption in restaurants and hotels) is extremely fragmented. The market leader (Illy) controls only about 6 per cent of sales by volume. The top three players (Illy, Segafredo Zanetti and Lavazza) together control less than 15 per cent of sales and are active in the home consumption market as well. Other roasters focus on regional and local markets and specialize in bar sales and roast-to-order. Most roasters working in the bar segment provide a whole range of services, from coffee machines and grinders on loan, to technical assistance, serving cups and financing for refurbishing – in exchange for long-term contracts. Brand recognition (and thus media advertising) does not seem to be as important in this market segment as it is in the home consumption segment. According to a number of market studies 'over 75 per cent of the consumers interviewed coming out of a bar could not remember what brand of coffee the bar sold' (ICO 2000: 28).

If quality in the home consumption market is about brand and not blend, in the bar market it is about the services provided, many of which are in-person services. Competition among roasters takes place on the basis of personal interaction, delivery on time (normally weekly consignments), client assistance and financial support. Provision of in-person services is the essence of Italian bars as well. These bars are often family-owned, rarely franchised, and rely on a core group of clients visiting the establishment daily. Rather than the provision of ambience (as in US bar chains), Italian bars' *modus vivendi* is in-person services based on repeated interactions with clients that have elements of affective service provision. These services are also based on the facilitation of implicit and explicit exchange between consumers. In short, both roasters and bar-owners depend to a large extent on in-person service attributes of coffee quality for value creation.

One material quality attribute that is important in the bar sector is the appearance of the beans, since coffee is displayed in whole bean form in the container above the grinder. As for taste, good quality is obtained only by using 100 per cent Arabica blends. Even 20–30 per cent of Robusta yields a much inferior product. However, 100 per cent Arabica coffees are delicate and difficult to handle. If the *espresso* machine is not perfectly tuned, the coffee tends to acquire a burnt taste. Thus, most price-conscious roasters who still want to deliver a decent product seek the most neutral Robusta coffees (such as Ugandan Robusta).

Perhaps, the most telling description of the bar market in Italy was provided by a regional roaster who operates in it:

> The bar market is not sensitive to quality; *espresso* is consumed in a rush, it does not get tasted, just ingested.... The best coffees are all sold in Northern Europe. In Italy, even in some of the best restaurants, you drink coffee that is truly disgusting.[6]

According to a coffee importer who deals with bar-oriented roasters,

> In Italy roasters working in the bar segment offer especially services (financing) that tie bar owners to them; in this way, the quality of the product is of secondary importance. A majority of roasters do not even have cuppers or cupping experience and make decisions on the basis of tradition. If they change anything, it is to decrease the cost of the blend.[7]

The Illy phenomenon

So is all Italian coffee 'bad' in its material attributes? In Italy, specialty coffees – single-origin, specially prepared, limited-release coffees – have not as yet taken hold. If an American definition for specialty coffee (that includes all *espresso*-based preparations) was applied to Italy, the whole market would qualify. Obviously, this makes no sense, since most Italian coffees are run-of-the-mill mainstream blends. The closest one gets to specialty coffee in Italy is Illy coffee – a high-quality but homogenized branded *espresso* blend, accompanied by symbolic and stylistic references to art and collectionism.

If Starbucks is the key to understanding changing ideas and valuation of quality in the US market, Illycaffé (the company) and Illy (the brand) are the key to understanding the high-quality segment of the Italian market and perceptions of the quality of Italian coffee abroad. A family company with a turnover of €55 million in 1992, in 2002 it had grown to over €190 million. In Italy, Illy sells 60 per cent of its coffee (by volume) through bars and restaurants and 40 per cent through retailers. Exports represent almost 50 per cent of total sales volume, and target mainly hotel, restaurant and catering channels. Illy coffee is exported to over 70 countries, and is now the top *espresso* brand in the US.

Illy was founded in 1933 by Francesco Illy in Trieste. At that time, roasted coffee sales took place only locally because of the limited preservation technologies available for roasted coffee. But Francesco was on a mission. He wanted to sell his coffee all over Italy, not only in the north-east, so he invented a pressurization system that took air out of the can and inserted neutral gases. He was able to maintain roast and ground coffee relatively fresh in this way. After the Second World War, Francesco's son, Ernesto, started running the company. Ernesto, a scientist and researcher, was the one who developed the current quality profile of Illy. He discovered that pressurization enables the formation of oils on the surface of cells, and that these oils transmit olfactory sensations and capture aromas. This is the reason why Illy leaves the coffee to rest for 15 days under pressure, so that the oils are well fixed on the surface of the coffee particles. In this way, when consumers open the can, they can enjoy the aroma.

Not surprisingly, freshness is not an attribute used for quality at Illy. Illy coffee is 'aged' and has a shelf life that can reach three years. Illy's personnel insist that freshness is more of an issue in filter coffee, but is not too important for *espresso*. The Illy approach to quality is then quite different from the US specialty coffee industry, where the rule of thumb is that freshly roasted coffee should be consumed within 15 days. The US industry is based on product differentiation, both at the roasted bean and brew levels. Illy's approach is the opposite. It provides only one blend (from 9–12 origins, only Arabicas) and three roast profiles. Illy does not offer organic or fair trade coffee.

Until the early 1980s, Illy prepared eight different degrees of roasting (six for Italy and two for foreign markets). Now it offers only three different roasts: *chiaro* (light) for Northern Europe; *medio* (medium) for Northern Italy, France and Germany; and *scuro* (dark) for the US, Brazil, Greece, Spain and Southern Italy. The Illy blend is subject to micro-adjustments in relation to the supply situation in the origins and the time of the year. The key point is that the roasted product needs to have a constant quality profile. Thus, there are strict limitations on substituting one coffee for another in the blend.

Quality control on incoming green coffees is serious business at Illy. In the Trieste coffee quality lab, samples of green coffee beans are analysed through an instrument called Mappadora, which sorts each bean and generates a chromatic map that indicates various kinds of defects. Roast and brew analysis is done by five different cuppers for each sample. Three methods are conducted for cup testing: the traditional 'Brazilian method' of simply pouring hot water on coarsely ground coffee and letting it brew; a double *espresso* preparation diluted with water; and a straight *espresso* preparation.

Having the 'perfect blend', however, is not all it takes to deliver a high-quality *espresso*. The main challenge is to make sure that the coffee is brewed correctly. This is a major problem, especially abroad. In Italy, the *barista* is a proper profession. Abroad, cafés have a high turnover of personnel – brewing coffee is just a job in between others. This is one of the reasons Illy has developed automatic *espresso* machines working with single serving pods. This solves dosage and cleanliness problems. However, it does nothing to address the fact that *espresso* is often brewed too long – thus transferring all the bitter elements of the coffee into the cup. Training and technical assistance, in an environment of high labour turnover, can only go so far.

Illy, like almost all other roasters in Italy, is still a family-owned business. This does not mean that it is a 'traditional' company. As Ernesto's children took over the running of the company, they developed its image, both in Italy and abroad, in connection to design and art. The company has invested heavily in patronizing art exhibitions (most notably, the Venice Biennale) and has developed a successful series of limited-release cup collections. Ernesto, however, is still the chief quality controller and shows up in the cupping lab every day to test pre-shipment consignments. Illy's quality image is firmly embedded in symbolic quality offerings – a brand, science, design and art.

Some interim reflections
According a well-respected actor in the Italian coffee market,

> the clientele is ignorant [about coffee quality]. If consumers understood more about coffee, like they do about wine, then roasters would have to provide a better product. The big industrial roasters do not want that to happen.[8]

This view is echoed by another key figure in the industry, who stated that 'roasters have no interest in spreading the culture of origins because they want to defend their brands. They do not want consumers to identify coffee as Kenyan, but as Lavazza.'[9] Given this situation, attempts by developing countries to add value to their coffees through higher-quality offerings and geographical appellations have limited prospects of success.

Yet the Illy story demonstrates that high-quality supply can turn markets around and that consumers are available to pay for quality. At the same time, the quality message of Illy to its consumers is related to a brand, not to coffee origins. Its product is homogeneous and mass-marketed. It is also not clear to what extent consumers appreciate quality in terms of the purported excellence of material coffee attributes and to what extent they like the limited-release cups and shining silver cans.

From a development perspective, a couple of questions come to mind. What kind of in-person services, styles, designs and stories can be sold by producing-country actors? How can value-added be transferred to them without excessive appropriation by other actors along the value chain? Do higher-quality roasters pay higher prices for the coffee they buy? From whom do they source coffee?

Coffee exporters in East Africa consider Illy one of the toughest buyers in terms of quality, but one that pays up to twice the market rate for high-quality coffee. The problem is that most smallholder suppliers cannot match Illy's standards. In 2000 in Tanzania, for example, Illy was purchasing from only one estate in Kilimanjaro – owned by an Italian. In Brazil and other countries of origin, with the exception of Ethiopia, Illy buys most of its coffee from estates. What does this mean for smallholders, producing countries' development strategies, and future prospects for coffee farmers in general? How much of the value added in high-quality coffee markets is credited to the producer? What kind of producer? In the rest of this section, we will ask a similar set of questions in relation to the North American specialty industry. Chapter 5 will extend the analysis to sustainable coffees. In Chapter 6, we will provide some examples of the distribution of the value added in mainstream and specialty markets.

Quality and the North American specialty coffee industry

Specialty coffee was born in North America as a reaction to the post-Second World War decline in the quality of coffee offered by mainstream roasters (see Chapter 2). When the Specialty Coffee Association of America (SCAA) was created in 1982, its founding members defined specialty coffee as 'good preparation from unique origin and distinctive taste'.[10] An alternative take on the definition of specialty coffee is to describe what it is not. As an SCAA member stated, commercial buyers want the cheapest price possible and perhaps a certain bean size and crop date. Cup quality only enters the picture commercially if the coffee is unmistakably tainted.... The vast majority of coffee buyers believe that coffee is for selling, not for drinking.[11]

According to SCAA, the specialty coffee industry has facilitated a change in ideas of quality among consumers.

Coffee consumers have been moving away from price-based purchasing to a purchasing trend that focuses on product variety and quality.... [This] has evolved coffee from a beverage of pseudo-commodity characteristics to one with cultural and sensory ties. (SCAA 1999: 4)

In its literature, SCAA tends to portray changes in consumption patterns in the US in the last 25 years as driven by the industry (smaller roasters, retailers, coffee bars). The dynamics of consumption, however, are more complex than that. Some pioneer roasters and roaster/retailers, such as Peet's, have definitely led the taste revolution, but this took place in a context of day-to-day interactions with an initially small (but rapidly growing) pool of customers-cum-connoisseurs. Thus the development of the early specialty coffee industry was the result of a two-way exchange of information on taste, roasting styles and origins of coffee that allowed roasters to experiment with new roasting methods, packaging and previously unknown origins.

It is in this milieu that new attributes started to be embedded in coffee quality profiles, especially in relation to organic and shade production processes.[12] Even cosy roaster–consumer relationships, however, do not alone account for the sweeping changes in consumption patterns and quality perceptions that took place in the US in the last 20 years. In her work on the spread of the organic salad mix in California, Guthman (2002; 2003) sees the new aesthetic sensibilities of the emerging yuppie class in the 1980s and the high-tech boom of the late 1990s as two factors that reshaped personal identities through food and beverage consumption. The same factors probably played a role in the development of what is known as the *latte* revolution in coffee markets (see Dicum and Luttinger 1999; Ponte 2002a).

In parallel with what happened in organic agriculture (Allen and Kovach 2000; Guthman 2002; 2003; Raynolds 2004), as the specialty coffee industry expanded, it lost much of its original spirit – although there are still small roasters whose economy is based on day-to-day interaction with their customers. As a result, the original link between the term 'specialty' and perceived excellence in material quality is under increased pressure. Some mainstream suppliers have started to offer 'high-quality' or 'specialty' coffee roasted on the spot by computerized roasters in large discount stores. In this case, it is not the material quality of the bean that makes the coffee better. These coffees are mediocre and are bought in bulk. Their selling point is that they are freshly roasted. They also sell at much cheaper prices than in specialty stores (ICO, ITC and CFC 2000: 7).

Parts of the specialty industry are also drifting from a strict insistence on the material quality of coffee itself towards the supply of more manipulated products in which the quality of the underlying coffee sometimes takes second place. Increasing sales of *espresso*-based drinks (which according to industry actors have higher profit margins) entail a relatively more important presence of cheaper Hard Arabica and Robusta at the expense of more expensive Mild Arabica coffees (*ibid.*: 6). The coffee content of specialty sales is also decreasing as value is added through flavouring, mixing with milk products and providing a specific consumption ambience. Furthermore, as café chains (such as Starbucks) consolidate and expand, material quality *per se* may not be as important in the future in some segments of the specialty industry in the US. When chains get bigger, they tend to simplify sourcing practices. Higher sales entail more centralized buying requirements and more difficult relations with smaller suppliers. They are usually accompanied by more prominence for blends rather than single origins (ICO, ITC and CFC 2000). Therefore, more consumption of specialty coffee may not entail increased use of coffee of high material quality.

A different kind of crisis

As seen earlier in this chapter, before market liberalization many coffee-producing countries had single-channel marketing systems that allowed pricing on the basis of quality. Cooperatives paid a fixed advance payment per volume of coffee delivered, and then paid another one or two instalments after having delivered the coffee to a curing plant or exported it. Usually, the last payment was proportional to the overall quality of coffee sold by the cooperative to the marketing board, and sometimes also to the quality of coffee delivered by the farmer to the cooperative.

One of the results of market liberalization in producing countries has been high levels of buyer competition. This means that the proportion of the export price going to the farmer has generally increased and that farmers are paid promptly. On the other hand, domestic traders have to move coffee quickly to minimize capital costs. They cannot afford to spend too much time evaluating small batches of coffee, nor can they preserve the identity of these batches for a future payment in relation to quality. Therefore, they buy all coffee at one price, performing only perfunctory checks to ensure that the coffee is not too wet or full of stones and sticks. As a result, farmers have no direct incentive to produce high-quality coffee. This has led to deteriorating export crop quality in several countries and, in some cases, to price discounting in international markets and loss of reputation for certain origins.[13] Another way of interpreting this in relation to international, and not only domestic, deregulation is that the ICA system provided enough rents in producing countries to effectively subsidize the costs of sorting out coffee quality, while the liberalized system is much more hand-to-mouth.[14]

Another result of market liberalization has been the weakening of cooperatives. Cooperatives now have to compete with private traders on the basis of their first payment. If they pay a lower price than traders, they fail to get coffee from farmers. If they pay a high price, they risk losing money if the market price goes down, and also fail to make a second or third payment in relation to quality. As a result, they have either gone bankrupt, or have competed on the same basis as commercial traders – but without their speed and flexibility. The combined result is that good and bad coffee is all mixed together and exporters can only perform a partial selection process to re-separate high quality for specialty exports. In any case, exporters pocket the value added, while the farmer gets no premium. In the long term, the supply of high-quality coffee dwindles, and traders/exporters tend to source high-quality coffee increasingly from estates, with whom they can do business based on more suitable quality checks and contractual forms (Ponte 2002c). The deterioration of the coffee quality control system has also compromised donor-led efforts to implement integrated pest management systems among smallholders, because no reward is there for farmers to deliver better beans, and thus to control coffee cherry borer damage (Duque and Baker 2003).

The failure to pay higher prices for quality at the farm level is threatening the supply base of the specialty coffee industry. The industry is also under threat from the appropriation of the specialty concept by mainstream roasters and/or specialty free riders. These are the two constitutive elements of a quality crisis in the specialty industry.

> There is a shortage of high-quality coffee in the specialty market. The New York price [the main futures market reference price for Arabica coffee] has no relation to the specialty sector now. Most traders do not even consider it as a benchmark. My clients want specific coffees, and they would pay anything to have it. Sometimes, price is not even discussed. Specialty roasters are so desperate for good quality that they are now buying coffee at fair trade prices without the certification.[15]

Because the specialty industry is as diverse as it is difficult to define, a variety of different strategies (including neglect) have being adopted to address the quality crisis. Some actors are less concerned with material quality, as symbolic and in-person service quality production is their focus. Others are not concerned because their coffee is drowned in so much milk, cream and syrups that it does not matter what it actually tastes like. Others, especially smaller-scale specialty roasters–retailers, do have a problem with material quality. Some are mainly worried about the watering down of the term 'specialty' and have pushed the SCAA board to develop an industry-wide product quality standard with an SCAA-certified mark of integrity. A green Arabica coffee classification system and a cupping procedure and description have been developed, but not yet adopted due to internal disagreements on the whole scheme. The original idea was that discrete single lots from an origin would be certified individually by local and/or international certifying judges. SCAA would administer the movement and storage of samples, and lots would be tracked all the way to the roaster. In this way, the roaster would be able to apply the SCAA label to the final product.[16]

Other actors, both in and out of SCAA, are trying to tackle the supply crisis mainly through three kinds of approaches: (1) the development of 'relationship coffees'; (2) the staging of 'competition–auction events'; and (3) the establishment of geographical appellation systems. In this chapter, we will cover the first two. Geographical appellation is examined in Chapter 6.

Relationship coffees

Single-origin coffees have been one of the fundamental elements of the specialty coffee industry, whether they come from a large region or from a single farm. Yet any of these coffees can be bought through a maze of intermediaries, or directly at the source. The increased tendency in the specialty industry to sell a story together with the coffee has prompted a number of operators to get involved in direct relationships with producers. The marketing literature in companies that do so is rich with references to travelling and the exotic. This has led to the formulation of a sourcing system called 'relationship coffees', of which there are various kinds. One kind is based on a direct connection between the end buyer and the primary supplier – a very small niche. Others are based on long-term relationships with varying degrees of involvement from roasters.

An increasingly common view in the specialty industry is that prices should be based on considerations of quality and costs of production, and therefore completely de-linked from the New York futures market price. This is accompanied by the idea that specialty buyers (be they importers, wholesalers or roasters) should formulate multi-year fixed price contracts with their suppliers. These contracts allow small roasters to know the price at the beginning of the year, so that they can concentrate on roasting instead of dedicating too much time and energy to sourcing. They have obvious advantages for producers as well: they can minimize risk, upgrade their production and processing methods, and invest in achieving supply reliability. Finally, bankers on both sides are more likely to provide finance.[17]

Only a small number of companies in the specialty industry are currently involved in relationship coffees. However, this form of coordination is slowly spreading. For example, San Francisco Bay Gourmet Coffee is estimated to buy approximately 100,000 bags of high-quality coffee each year, and to source directly for about 70 per cent of the total. Green Mountain Coffee Roasters, a Vermont-based company, buys about 35 per cent of its approximate need of 100,000 bags of green coffee a year through relationship coffees on the basis of long-term fixed-price contracts. The company pays above the market price, sometimes close to fair trade levels. One estate owner said he had been paid US$1.3 per pound (free on board) when the market price for Other Milds in the NY futures market hovered at US$0.55–0.65.[18]

The relationship coffee purchases of these two companies alone are the equivalent of 8 per cent of total exports from a high-quality producing country like Kenya. It is a small proportion, but not exactly a drop in the ocean either.

Competition-auction processes

A second way of rewarding quality is through 'competition-auction processes'. These are exemplified by the Cup of Excellence programme, which is organized by the Alliance of Coffee Excellence (ACE). The Cup of Excellence is based on country-level competitions to select the highest-quality coffees, which are then sold through Internet auctions. The goal is to find the best coffees of a harvest season and reward the farmers who produced them, not only with a trophy but also with a higher premium. Competitions started in 1999, and have taken place in Brazil, Bolivia, Guatemala, Nicaragua, El Salvador and Honduras. Any coffee farmer in one of the countries where the competition takes place can submit samples, although politically connected and financially able farmers are more likely to submit samples than poorer and more isolated ones.

A similar initiative, the Q auction, was launched in 2004 by the Coffee Quality Institute (CQI) – the research and education arm of SCAA. In 2004, Q auctions facilitated the sale of a small amount (24 containers) of high-quality coffee (defined as 80 points or above the SCAA cupping standard), with an average sale price 50 per cent above New York C market prices. In this scheme, farmers should receive at least 75 per cent of the auction gross sales. In addition, 2 per cent of the proceeds are supposed to be reinvested in local community projects. Again, the programme focuses on Latin American producers (Costa Rica, El Salvador, Guatemala and Nicaragua).

Both these programmes have provided high premiums directly to producers for quality coffee, and recognition in the marketplace for coffee regions and origins that were not necessarily known as 'specialty'. For buyers in search of top-quality coffees, they provide a bridge to producers that saves time and expense. It is costly for small roasters to find the right quality of coffee, year after year. The greater the difficulty, the larger the cost, and the lower the price paid to the producer. The more information is available on quality (through pre-auction samples), the lower the degree of quality-related risk a buyer incurs, and the higher the price that will be paid for a certain level of quality. Producers who win awards gain market recognition that can be followed by the building of long-term relationships with buyers. In the case of Q auctions, producers are also assured of receiving a minimum proportion of the auction price. Buyers winning coffee lots at the auction gain image and an additional marketing tool. Through the auctions, quality information and prices are transmitted directly between producer and roaster. This may lead to future direct contacts and two-way feedback on quality. Most of these aspects, as we have seen above, are missing in the mainstream coffee market and even in the lower-end specialty coffee market. In these markets, quality is not recognized in higher prices at the farm level, there are many intermediaries between producer and roaster, and little or no information on quality is fed back to producers.[19]

Paying for quality?

Although many, if not all, of the specialty coffee initiatives addressing the quality crisis described above are viewed in the industry as positive, when the impact on farmers (and especially smallholders) is included in the framework, things look a bit different. For a start, any minimum standard on quality raises entry barriers and therefore has distributional effects. For example, the 'SCAA-certified' approach to specialty coffee sets strict standards on cup quality for the use of its mark of integrity. The problem is that if a producer does not meet the standard, he/she will find no mechanism within the system itself to get access to capital, financial aid and/or technical assistance needed to make further investment and upgrade. In general, estates have better access to finance, markets and infrastructure. They are therefore more likely to find the resources to meet the increasing demands of new standards than smallholders and cooperatives. Also, many estates have cupping skills and facilities, while most smallholders (and many of their cooperatives) do not. Estates are better equipped to forge direct links with specialty importers and roasters, can better internalize feedback information about quality, and are thus better placed in the quality learning curve.

The Cup of Excellence programme can help forge direct contacts between producers and specialty coffee operators. Yet competitions are costly and can be carried out only when donors fund them. In El Salvador, the 2004 competition cost US$180,000 to set up and handled only small amounts of coffee. According to a stakeholder analysis carried out in relation to this event, the only real winners were roasters.[20] It is somewhat ironic that Northern country taxpayers are helping to improve the quality choice for roasters. In its current configuration, the programme covers only a tiny minority of producing countries (all in Latin America) and, within these countries, of good-quality coffee. Initially, a majority of coffees participating in these competitions (and of those awarded) came from estates, rather than cooperatives and smallholders. An important exception has been Nicaragua, where co-operatives (and, recently, a fair trade cooperative) have been able to place well in the competitions, and even to win them. These cooperatives own cupping laboratories, provided through a project funded by the US Agency for International Development (USAID). The Cup of Excellence programme envisions an increase in the number of origins and an expansion of the competition-auction system from top-quality coffees into a larger segment of specialty coffees. This could have a positive impact on cooperatives and smallholders. A more direct and favourable measure would be to organize special competition-auction processes exclusively dedicated to smallholder coffees. Some of the same problems apply to the Q auctions, which have moved small amounts of coffee so far. However, some of the provisions in these auctions seem to be more favourable to producers.

Even relationship coffees raise equity concerns because they are easier to establish with estates than with smallholders or cooperatives. The key issue in this case is not increasing entry barriers (relationship coffees actually lower them), but who gets involved and who does not. As one estate owner put it: 'It is easier to work with estates than with cooperatives. You just have to deal with one person and one mind; you get homogeneous farming practices, consistent quality and faster decision making.'[21] As argued above, estates are much better equipped to meet the quality demands of the specialty market than smallholders and cooperatives. In other words, they are more likely to deliver high enough quality and uniformity year after year. Yet not everyone agrees with this assessment. Some specialty industry actors claim that working with cooperatives is not much more difficult than working with estates. The key aspect is that many buyers 'prefer soft toilet paper in their hotel rooms rather than an outhouse in the woods without running water'.[22]

On the positive side, these initiatives facilitate farmers' generation and control of symbolic elements of coffee quality, especially through direct contacts and competition-auction processes, even though the explicit focus is usually on discovering coffees with the best material attributes. Also, farmers may gain a good reputation from winning or even participating in competitions. In establishing direct contacts with small roasters in relationship coffees, they are involved in more explicitly reciprocal ways of communicating information on quality and have better opportunities to provide individualized services. However, their degree of control in the generation of symbolic quality attributes is still limited. As we will see in following chapters, geographical appellation systems may provide a more legally effective option for farmers. At the end of the day, the extra effort in delivering material and symbolic quality has to have a pay-off for coffee farmers and their organizations.

Conclusion

Ideas and content of quality change dramatically not only along coffee value chains, but also in relation to different subsectors. In producing countries, coffee is traded and priced mainly in relation to its material quality attributes. The evaluation of some of these attributes can only be carried out in a rough manner at the farm level. One of the most valuable (taste) is usually evaluated only at the export point. Market liberalization has made it more difficult to provide incentives and information feedback to farmers on the material quality of the coffee they produce. It is even more difficult for them to generate and control symbolic and in-person service attributes, given their lack of resources and the distance from final consumption markets. This partly explains the existence of a coffee paradox in the global value chain for coffee. Farmers and other producer-country actors sell material coffee. In consuming countries, coffee is sold packaged with symbolic and in-person service components, which value is firmly controlled by roasters, retailers and coffee bar owners. This is perhaps best exemplified by the text of a Starbucks advertisement placed in an American magazine in 2004:

> Sometimes the coffee stirs you. A completed sentence ends with a small black dot, but that's how epiphanies begin. A coffee bean. A tiny, good

thing from the earth. But the best ones have something special locked inside: an exotic destination, a spirited conversation, a divine inspiration. We search the world to find those beans and bring them to you.

In mainstream coffee markets, roasters tend to release as little information on quality as possible to consumers. They buy in bulk and try to minimize costs. Their main preoccupation is to maintain a constant profile of their blends. Branding is supposed to provide a guarantee of quality to consumers. Yet mainstream roasters continued to downgrade their blends in the post-Second World War period, until the specialty coffee industry emerged. The specialty coffee industry was based (at least in its original configuration) on a more transparent system, where consumers and roasters engaged in a mutual definition and redefinition of what quality is. Growth-related pressures and imitation by mainstream players, however, are pushing parts of the specialty industry towards representations of quality and coordination systems that are more similar to the one used by mainstream coffee players (including the coupling of brand and origin that Starbucks carries out). The distinction between the two industries is becoming increasingly difficult to identify.

As underlined in much of the literature on agro-food studies, local and trust-based mutual interactions in so-called alternative agro-food networks suffer when these networks are extended. The imitation strategies of larger mainstream players place a strain on the financial viability of smaller players. Smaller players who become bigger need to embed trust in a label or brand (when, for example, roasted coffee travels further away); they thus apply a different logic in their operations and have more difficulty in guaranteeing quality. This results in two over-lapping phenomena. The first is that quality content is reconceptualized (quality related to ambience of consumption; identity formation; references to exotic places; freshness). The second is that some of the original players try to preserve a higher (or different) standard of material quality by resorting to quality assurance schemes, such as the SCAA-certified mark of integrity. Yet if this standard is able to defend the idea of specialty at all, it will do so in different ways from the original trust-based, interactive and locally grounded construction of quality ideas in the early specialty coffee business. Also, there is nothing in this scheme that guarantees that higher quality is awarded with higher prices at the producer level. Competition-auction processes, relationship coffees and other direct sourcing efforts offer better, but limited, prospects for this to happen.

One key outcome of the dialectical relation between mainstream and specialty coffees is an increasing pressure in mainstream markets to provide more information on coffee to consumers. This started with the development of new quality attributes and related preoccupations with the socio-economic and environmental conditions of production – leading to the emergence of a sustainable coffee subsector of the specialty coffee industry. This is heralded in NGO and progressive policy circles as a win–win development: consumers gain a 'feel good factor' and at the same time help to protect the environment and to foster better socio-economic conditions of production. In the end, however, the underlying structure of the industry is being reasserted, and large roasters have become heavily involved in new mainstream sustainability initiatives. In the next chapter, we critically assess whether sustainable coffees deliver better conditions to farmers or not.

Notes

1 Coffee value chain actors, regulators and farmers give several general explanations for this evolution: (1) some buyers and their agents were not familiar with quality control procedures at the beginning of the liberalization process; (2) in the first years after liberalization, there was a rush to establish market share; therefore, buyers were not very selective in their purchases for fear that farmers would go somewhere else to sell their coffee; (3) buyers cannot lose time sorting through the coffee at the buying post because they need to move it fast to maximize the velocity of capital turnaround; therefore, they buy all their coffee at one time and one price.

2 'Clean cup' quality in Robusta derives from a rough taste examination and means that there are no major taints in the cup quality.

3 Source: various interviews with Italian and US roasters.

4 For a case study on Denmark, see Christensen (2005).

5 Interview IT01/01, 03/10/2001 – translated by the author.

6 Interview IT01/02, 09/10/2001 – translated by the author.

7 Interview IT01/04, 03/10/2001 – translated by the author.

8 Interview IT01/03, 04/10/2001 – translated by the author.

9 Interview IT01/04, 03/10/2001 – translated by the author.

10 Specialty coffee in Europe is more difficult to define, as consumption practices and quality profiles vary enormously from country to country.

The Specialty Coffee Association of Europe (SCAE), broadly inspired by the SCAA, was founded only in 1998 and is a much smaller organization. North American definitions of specialty cannot apply across the board in Europe. While the North American specialty industry was born as a reaction to the supply of large quantities of relatively homogeneous and undifferentiated blends of mediocre-to-poor quality by mainstream roasters, much good coffee has always been available in Europe. An exception is the UK, which historically has had a high proportion of soluble coffee consumption, and where the specialty industry closely resembles the US specialty industry.

11 Interview UG02/24, 15 February 2002.

12 In contrast, social content was developed first in Europe by fair trade orga-nizations and other NGOs – rather than by small-scale roasters (see Chapter 5).

13 For recent contributions to market liberalization in the coffee sector (with specific focus on selected African producing countries), see Akiyama (2001), Baffes (2005), Common Fund for Commodities (2000), Losch (1999), Love (2001; 2002), Ndjieunde *et al.* (2002), Pelupessy (1999), Ponte (2002b), Temu (2001) and Winter-Nelson and Temu (2002).

14 We owe this observation to Peter Baker.

15 Interview UG02/24, 15 February 2002.

16 In our discussion, we focus on SCAA product quality certification. However, the SCAA has also initiated a coffee brewer certification programme, which is designed to evaluate coffee-brewing devices on the basis of technical parameters. It also certifies brewing operators through its Golden Cup Award Standards. Source: presentations and hand-out at the SCAA 14th Annual Conference and Exhibition, panel 'Certified quality – an industry-wide initiative', Anaheim, California, 6 May 2002.

17 Presentations and hand-out at the SCAA 14th Annual Conference and Exhibition, panel 'Economic viability for farmers: the roaster/retailer role', Anaheim, California, 3 May 2002.

18 *Ibid.*

19 Presentations at the SCAA 14th Annual Conference and Exhibition, panel 'Search and reward for quality: competition-auction process', Anaheim, California, 4 May 2002; see also http://www.cupofexcellence.org/

20 Peter Baker, personal communication, December 2004.

21 Comment from the floor at the SCAA 14th Annual Conference and Exhibition, panel 'Economic viability for farmers: the roaster/retailer role', Anaheim, California, 3 May 2002.

22 Personal communication with SCAA member, 24 October 2002.

5

For whose benefit?
'Sustainable' coffee initiatives

Consuming sustainability

Sustainability has become a hot topic in the coffee industry. The broad notion of sustainable coffee was developed within the North American specialty industry – although the first forms of sustainable certified coffee were developed in Europe by the fair trade movement. The concept of sustainability in the realm of specialty coffee includes aspects variously referred to as 'economic viability for farmers', 'environmental conservation' and 'social responsibility'. Some of these coffees are sold as certified coffee, such as organic, fair trade, bird-friendly, Rainforest Alliance-certified, and Utz Kapeh. Others are sold under sustainability initiatives that are designed by private companies, with or without third party monitoring (Green Mountain Coffee Roasters' Stewardship Programme; Thanksgiving Coffee Company's Song Bird and Bat Magic coffees; Starbucks' CAFE programme, and Rapunzel Pure Organics' E-Blend and E-Espresso).

Organic coffee is produced with methods that aim at promoting a viable and sustainable agro-ecosystem. Fair trade coffee is based on a trading relationship between stakeholders that has both market-based and ethical elements and aims to be sustainable in the long term. Shade-grown coffee is grown under forest cover, thus preserving biodiversity and providing an appropriate habitat for migratory birds. The Rainforest Alliance's certification and the Utz Kapeh code of conduct attempt to combine some elements of the other three sustainability traditions.

The estimated size of certified organic, fair trade, and shade-grown coffee sales in North America was almost 85,000 60-kilogram bags in 2000, with a value of US$152 million at the retail level (see Table 5.1). By value, this represented less than 1 per cent of the US$20.7 billion

Table 5.1 Size and value of specialty and sustainable coffee markets in North America (US and Canada), 2000

	Volume		Retail value	
	(thousand 60-kg bags)	% of total coffee market	(million US$)	% of total coffee market
Total coffee market	23,800		20,700	
Total specialty coffee market	4,046	17.0	8,280	40.0
Total sustainable coffee (including non-certified)	114	0.5	188	0.9
Certified sustainable coffee	85	0.4	152	0.7
Total organic coffee (including non-certified)	90	0.4	146	0.7
Certified organic coffee	68	0.3	122	0.6
Certified fair trade	36	0.1	64	0.3
Total shade-grown (incl. non-certified)	16	0.1	28	0.1
Certified shade-grown	8	0.0	15	0.1

Source: Total coffee market volume = total imports into the US in 2000 (ICO database); for all other figures, Giovannucci (2001).

Table 5.2 Size and value of global sustainable coffee markets, 2000

	(Thousand 60-kg bags)	% of total coffee market	(million US$)	% of total coffee market
Total coffee market	111,546		49,257	
Total sustainable coffee (including non-certified)	318	0.3	565	1.2
Certified sustainable coffee	273	0.2	490	1.0
Total organic coffee (including non-certified)	161	0.1	286	0.6
Certified organic coffee	125	0.1	223	0.5
Certified fair trade	221	0.2	393	0.8
Total shade-grown (including non-certified)	17	0.0	31	0.1
Certified shade-grown	9	0.0	16	0.0

Sources: for sustainable coffee, Giovannucci (2001); Total coffee market volume = global production in 2000 (ICO database); Total coffee market value = average retail prices in top nine importing countries times their import volumes + 11.7 per cent for rest of import value for other countries + estimated value of domestic consumption in Brazil and Ethiopia (from ICO database).[1]

Table 5.3 Average premiums paid for organic, fair trade and shade-grown
coffees in North America, 2000 (US$/lb)

	Organic	Fair trade	Shade-grown
Importers	0.36	0.74	0.35
Distributors	0.47	0.48	0.44
Wholesalers	0.50	0.58	0.49
Roasters	0.46	0.51	0.41
Retailers	0.64	0.65	0.60
Industry average	0.59	0.62	0.53
Average across categories	0.49	0.59	0.46

Source: Adapted from Giovannucci (2001: 11).

North American coffee market and less than 2 per cent of the specialty coffee market. Even accounting for non-certified coffees that are marketed as sustainable, the total market value of sustainable coffee in North America was about US$188 million in 2000 (for a volume of 113,600 bags).

Globally, the volume of certified sustainable coffee was estimated to be around 272,000 bags for a retail value of US$490 million in 2000; if we include non-certified coffee sold as sustainable, the figures rise to 318,000 bags and US$565 million, around 1.2 per cent of the global coffee market (see Table 5.2). According to a survey of 2,098 North American coffee firms (importers, distributors, wholesalers, roasters and retailers) carried out in 2001 (see Giovannucci 2001), there is a relatively high level of awareness of sustainable coffees in the industry (98.7 per cent for organic, 76.4 per cent for shade-grown, and 82.5 per cent for fair trade), although the proportion of operators offering them is lower (78.6 per cent offer organic, 51.8 per cent shade-grown, and 54 per cent fair trade). Even more problematic is the fact that many firms sell sustainable coffee without an independent certification or verification (*ibid.*).

Sustainable coffees provide positive returns for operators based in consumer countries. They fetch average premiums of 0.49 US$/lb for organic, 0.59 US$/lb for fair trade, and 0.46 US$/lb for shade-grown. These are average premiums paid by various operators to their suppliers (see Table 5.3). It does not necessarily mean that these premiums are transferred all the way to producers in their entirety – or at all. The survey also suggests that sustainability and the material quality of coffee cannot be kept in isolation. The most important factor in making sustainable coffee valued to businesses was the 'specialty quality of taste' (indicated in almost 92 per cent of cases), followed by personal ethics and beliefs about fair trade and the environment. Interestingly, sustainable coffees do not seem to be customer-driven. Customer demand was rated as an important factor by only 51 per cent of coffee firms (*ibid.*).

A more recent study covering 11 European countries and Japan (Giovannucci and Koekoek 2003) estimates the volume of sustainable coffee in these countries in 2001 to have been about 354,400 bags – equivalent to 1.1 per cent of the total volume of coffee consumed. This is a much higher estimate than the one provided for the global market for certified coffees in 2000 – 272,700 bags (Giovannucci 2001). Estimated annual average growth of sustainable coffee for the 1999–2004 period in these countries is about 10 per cent (Giovannucci and Koekoek 2003).

Table 5.4 Estimated size of certified coffee markets, 2003

	Utz Kapeh	Organic	Fair trade	Shade-grown	Total[2]
Total volume (thousand 60-kg bags)	233	440	298	11	851

Sources: Utz Kapeh: Utz Kapeh data; organic: 15 per cent annual growth over figure cited in Lewin, Giovannucci and Varangis (2004) for 2001; fair trade: Giovannucci and Koekoek (2003); shade-grown: 10 per cent annual growth over figure cited in Giovannucci (2001) for 2001.

Table 5.4 estimates the market size of sustainable coffee for 2003. Organic and fair trade are the largest by volume. It should also be noted that there is extensive overlap between the two: over 40 per cent of the fair trade market is now also certified organic. The total volume estimated (851,000 bags) is much higher than in previous estimations presented above. This is explained on the basis of much higher estimates on organic and the recent growth of a new sustainability initiative – Utz Kapeh (see details below).

The sustainable coffee market is still a small niche – about 1 per cent of the 85.7 million bags exported by International Coffee Organization

(ICO) member countries in 2003. Yet it is growing fairly rapidly and attracting increased interest in the industry. Three major coffee buyers made substantial commitments in 2004: Sara Lee said that it would be buying 41,000 bags (or 2,500 tons) of Utz Kapeh coffee in 2004. Kraft committed to buying more or less the same amount of Rainforest Alliance-certified coffee. Procter and Gamble started buying fair trade coffee through its specialty division Millstone and said it would purchase up to 15,000 bags in the following years. But the main concern of large mainstream operators in the last few years has been to establish internal sourcing guidelines: individual and/or industry-level codes of conduct to achieve one form or another of sustainability. In the next section, we provide an in-depth analysis of the main third-party certification systems that address issues of sustainability in the coffee sector. This will be followed by a brief discussion of private and public–private initiatives.

Analysis of selected sustainable coffee certification systems

Organic

Organic agriculture is a production management system that seeks to promote and enhance biodiversity and soil activity. It is based on minimal use of off-farm inputs and on management practices that restore, maintain and enhance ecological harmony. Organic standards are devised by government authorities, international organizations (FAO/WHO Codex Alimentarius) and the International Federation of Organic Agriculture Movements (IFOAM). Accredited certification agencies monitor organic standards on production, processing and handling.

In general, a grower or processer of organic coffee may be certified by a public or private certification company if the following standards and procedures, among others, are met: (1) coffee is grown without the use of synthetic agro-chemicals for three years prior to certification; (2) farmers and processers keep detailed records of methods and materials used in coffee production and management plans; and (3) a third-party certifier annually inspects all methods and materials.

Organic standards have been developed through government regulation and the efforts of international organizations, and within private organizations. Government regulation of imports of organic products started in the 1980s in France, Denmark and selected states in the US. This often happened under pressure from organic growers wanting to

Box 5.1 Organic standards and regulations

In the European Union, regulation of organic products started in 1991 with the approval of council regulation (EEC) 2092/91. 'This regulation covers the marketing of all products labelled as "organic". It covers production standards and inspection measures that should be implemented to ensure the integrity of production. The regulation lists all the inputs that may be used in organic agriculture and identifies the production methods that are allowed and those that are prohibited. Some issues may be decided [by member states]' (Rundgren and Lustig 2002: 7). The import rules are complex and constantly changing and will not be covered in detail here. In general, there are three different systems for approval of imports: approval of country, importer derogation, and approval of a certification organization (following the proposal of a member state). In practice, the importer derogation system is by far the most common. Its implementation is not harmonized, so one product may be accepted when imported to one of the EU member states and rejected when imported to another. Yet, once within the EU border, it may be freely circulated. Even though this rule is based on the approval of individual lots, the emphasis for this approval is tightly linked to which certification organization approves a lot. Certification organizations are assessed by 'competent authorities' in EU member states (*ibid.*).

The United States regulations on organic production are included in the Organic Foods Production Act (OFPA) of 1990 and the National Organic Program (NOP). The Final Rule of the NOP (implemented in October 2002) states that foreign products exported as 'organic' in the US need to follow US certification and labelling rules. Three systems can be followed for importing organic products into the US: direct accreditation by USDA, accreditation by a foreign government, and equivalency. In practice, only direct accreditation by USDA is operational (Rundgren and Lustig 2002: 8–9).

'The Codex Alimentarius Commission, a joint FAO/WHO Food Standards Programme, the body that sets international food standards, started to develop guidelines for the production, processing, labelling and marketing of organically produced food in 1991' (Schmid 2002: 41). The requirements in these Codex Guidelines are generally in line with IFOAM Basic Standards (see below) and the EU regulation for organic food (2092/91 and amendments, ⇨

1804/99), but there are differences in some of the details and the areas covered by these standards (*ibid.*).

Over the years, the International Federation of Organic Agriculture Movements (IFOAM) has developed a set of standards for organic agriculture (commonly known as Basic Standards). These standards are under constant revision and development. They are not usually employed for certification on their own. They provide a framework for certification programmes to develop their own national or regional standards. In 1992, IFOAM also established an accreditation programme to provide international equivalency of organic quality claims on the basis of the Basic Standards. 'In theory, the International Organic Accreditation Service of IFOAM ... could provide a mechanism for regulatory acceptance of certification organizations in exporting countries. However, so far the efforts of IFOAM to get a formal recognition for this service have not been so successful' (Rundgren and Lustig 2002: 10). For the time being, IFOAM accreditation is most helpful for imports to the EU under the 'importer derogation' system and to achieve market recognition.

Table 5.5 Organic coffee sales in selected European countries, 2001

Country	Volume (thousands of 60-kg bags)	Average annual growth % (1999–2001)
Germany	56.7	17
Sweden	24.6	28
Denmark	24.1	4
Netherlands	16.3	15
UK	11.5	18
Italy	10.7	60
France	10.0	18
Belgium	7.6	15
Switzerland	7.2	15
Norway	3.8	2
Finland	1.7	18
Total	174.3	

Source: Giovannucci and Koekoek (2003).

avoid marketing of 'organic' products that had not been cultivated according to organic principles and/or as a result of political efforts to support or subsidize organic farming (Rundgren and Lustig 2002: 7).

According to industry operators, the organic coffee market has experienced substantial growth rates in the last decade in many high-income countries. Increased consumer interest in the conditions under which coffee is grown has been accompanied by cut-throat competition among supermarket chains to attract consumers through a differentiated offer of customized products. Organic coffee has been used as a marketing tool to attract new consumers. Because organic products are sold at a premium at the retail level, higher margins have been generated for all those involved in the marketing chain (but not on an equal basis – see Table 5.3). In most European countries, organic coffee is still mainly sold in natural food stores and Third World Shops. In Germany, Switzerland, the Netherlands and Denmark, however, organic coffee is also sold in mainstream supermarkets.

Estimates of organic coffee consumption vary enormously, implying that they are not very reliable.[3] According to a first source, certified organic coffee exports in 1999/2000 were approximately 125,000 bags, with an estimated retail value of US$223 million. Of these, more than half (55 per cent) was imported by North America (Giovannucci 2001). If we include non-certified organic coffee sales (a substantial proportion in the US before the enactment of new organic regulations in 2002), the global market is estimated by one source to have been in the region of 160,000 bags for a market value of US$286 million (*ibid.*). Another estimate of organic coffee sales in selected European countries for the 2001 season shows a market of 174,000 bags (see Table 5.5).

Added to North American demand, the total market size of organic coffee in 2001 should have been about 330,000 bags. Estimated growth projections for 1999–2004 are about 15 per cent on average (Giovannucci and Koekoek 2003). Assuming this average rate of growth, the organic coffee market in 2003 should have been around 440,000 bags. A positive factor for the organic coffee market is that quality has improved dramatically in the last few years. At the same time, increased supply has led to reduced premiums.

On the supply side, most organic coffee imported in North America originates from Latin America, especially Mexico.[4] There are no precise figures for the total area of certified organic coffee in the world,

Table 5.6 Prices and premiums for organic coffee in Uganda, 2002/3
(US$/lb)

Export level	Robusta	Mild Arabica (Bugisu)
Fob price	0.34	0.63
Organic export price	0.45	0.79
Premium	0.10	0.16
Premium (%)	30	25

Farm level	Robusta (dry cherry)	Mild Arabica Bugisu (parchment)
Regular price	0.11	0.26
Organic price	0.14	0.31
Premium	0.04	0.05
Premium (%)	35	17

Source: Ponte and Kawuma (2003).

but industry observers estimate it at over 205,000 hectares. Latin America accounts for more than 85 per cent of this area, and Mexico alone accounts for 45 per cent (Rice and McLean 1999).

A case study on coffee certification in Uganda (Ponte and Kawuma 2003) shows that premiums at the export level are in the range of 25–30 per cent depending on the type of coffee (at the time of writing, this translated into US$0.1/lb for Robusta and US$0.16–0.2/lb for washed Arabica). At the farm level, premiums were in the range of 17–35 per cent. This translated into a premium of US$0.04/lb of *kiboko* (dry cherry Robusta) and US$0.05/lb of washed Arabica parchment. In general, these data suggest that premiums range between 17 and 35 per cent over regular coffee in producing countries (see Table 5.6). However, it should be noted that all organic projects in Uganda have led to quality improvements. This means that the organic premium itself is a combination of a premium for organic practices and a premium for improved quality. The quality component is estimated to be at least half of the total premium.

Other comparable studies have reported premiums at the farm level for organic Mild Arabica in 2001 in the range of US$0.08/lb in Guatemala (18 per cent over the farm-gate price of conventional coffee) and US$0.26/lb in Mexico (63 per cent premium) (Damiani 2001; 2002). Other sources give organic premiums averaging US$0.15–0.2/lb at the farm level. Export-level premiums for Mild Arabica from Latin America are estimated at US$0.15–0.3/lb (a standard US$0.15/lb if sold in the fair trade channel). The average consumer-level premium is reported to be US$1/lb, with a range of US$0.2–2/lb. Organic coffee premiums have fallen dramatically over the last 20 years even as quality has increased, mainly because supply has grown. With lower premiums, some of the larger roasters may move into organics. At the same time, the motivation and commitment of organic farmers and exporters may falter (Rice and McLean 1999).

Fair trade

Fair trade is defined as 'an alternative approach to conventional trade that aims to improve the livelihoods and well-being of small producers by improving their market access, strengthening their organizations, paying them a fair price with a fixed minimum, and providing continuity in trading relationships' (Giovannucci and Koekoek 2003: 38). Fair trade is based on partnerships between so-called alternative trade organizations (ATOs) – such as Twin Trading, Oxfam Trading, Equal Exchange – and producers. ATOs started to operate in the 1950s and 1960s, purchasing products in developing countries directly from producers and selling them through networks of so-called Third World shops. In the late 1980s, ATOs began labelling fair trade products through fair trade labelling organizations (such as the Max Havelaar Foundation and the Fairtrade Foundation), and started a push to make them available in mainstream retail spaces, especially supermarkets (Murray, Raynolds and Taylor 2003; Tallontire 1999; 2000; 2001). Fair trade in the coffee sector was pioneered by the Max Havelaar Foundation in the Netherlands in the late 1980s, with the establishment of fair trade labelling.

Labelling organizations are national-level initiatives that issue fair trade labels to importers and verify that fair trade standards for specific products are met. They certify products, select, verify and monitor fair trade coffee producers, and promote fair trade products to retailers and consumers. They are not involved in trading products. Fair trade labels are now used both by conventional companies and by ATOs that are registered with one of the national initiatives. Labelling is meant to guarantee that the product has been produced and traded according to pre-defined social, contractual and sometimes environmental standards, including the payment of the agreed FLO-determined minimum price (see below). This price is not only intended to provide a better return to the producer, but includes a social premium to be used by producer groups for social development activities (Tallontire 2001).

Recently, umbrella organizations have also been set up to coordinate the activities of labelling organizations and to draft general guidelines. The most important of these is the Fair Trade Labelling Organizations International (FLO). FLO has established detailed standards for ten products that are currently labelled: coffee, cocoa, tea, orange juice, honey, sugar, rice, bananas, sports balls and wine. At least two of these (coffee and bananas) are also being traded with double certification (fair trade and organic). FLO maintains a producer register, which has over 350 producer groups. At present, coffee producers are the largest group in the register. These ten fair trade products are sourced from over 50 developing countries and marketed through national initiatives. FLO monitors producers and traders and de-certifies those that fail to match the required standards.

In relation to coffee, a group of producers (such as a cooperative or farmers' association) can be registered with FLO if: (1) its members are smallholders; and (2) the group is democratically run and politically independent. The first condition is strictly enforced by FLO. The track record in relation to the second condition could be questioned in some countries where fair trade importers buy coffee from formerly state-controlled cooperatives whose political independence is doubtful (see Ponte 2004). FLO guidelines also require that producers follow some basic guidelines in terms of minimal use of agro-chemicals and environmental protection. So far, these guidelines have not been strictly enforced, although they are likely to become more prominent.[5]

Producer organizations are regularly assessed against a set of standards by FLO inspectors. One of the main criticisms that had been levelled against the fair trade system is that FLO was both the custodian and the certifier of the standard, while in other systems the two functions are kept separate. For a long time, FLO argued that this was necessary to keep certification and monitoring costs down. In the fair trade system, contrary to others, producer organizations did not pay for certification. FLO also argued that it attempted to address the power relations in trading, rather than putting the responsibility for matching a set of standards on the shoulders of producers, as often happens in other kinds of environmental and social certification. This situation may be changing somewhat with the establishment of a separate entity (FLO-Cert. Ltd) that will take care of certification on the basis of ISO standards for certification bodies (ISO 65). The new division of labour between FLO and FLO-Cert. is meant to provide more transparency in certification and auditing. National initiatives will continue part-funding certification with their contributions. However, FLO-Cert. will also have to finance its activities with registration fees paid by traders and producer organizations.

The main remaining difference between fair trade and other sustainable coffee certifications is that fair trade pays a minimum price to producers. The price paid by fair trade importers to farmer organizations is based on a social premium of at least US$0.05/lb of green coffee over the New York C and London LIFFE prices, plus or minus the relevant quality differential. Certified organic coffee bought from a registered farmer organization attracts an additional premium of US$0.15/lb. The overall fair trade minimum price varies according to the type and origin of the coffee (Table 5.7). As we can observe by comparing prices in Tables 5.7 and 5.8, at the time of writing fair trade importers paid a free-on-board (fob) price that was almost twice the price of conventional washed Arabica, and more than three times the price of conventional natural Robusta. As a result, the fair trade premium was extremely high: US$0.59/lb for washed (Mild) Arabica and US$0.75/lb for Robusta.

In 2000 a quantity of over 220,000 bags of coffee was sold as fair trade globally, for a retail value of US$393 million. The estimated production capacity of the over 300 cooperatives and farmer organizations in the coffee fair trade register is 1.2 million bags. This could be interpreted as a large oversupply. However, some observers argue that having many cooperatives from a number of origins is actually good for fair trade importers. In this way, they can choose among many different kinds of coffees and can be more demanding on quality. They argue that this is one of the reasons the overall quality of fair trade coffee has improved in recent years. On the other hand, the oversupply argument may be supported by the views of other actors in the movement who argue that there seems to be an unspoken

Table 5.7 Fair trade minimum prices (US$/lb, green coffee)

Type of coffee	Regular		Organic certified	
	Central America, Mexico, Africa, Asia	South America, Caribbean	Central America, Mexico Africa, Asia	South America, Caribbean
Washed Arabica	1.26	1.24	1.41	1.39
Unwashed Arabica	1.20	1.20	1.35	1.35
Washed Robusta	1.10	1.10	1.25	1.25
Unwashed Robusta	1.06	1.06	1.21	1.21

Source: FLO.

Table 5.8 International coffee market prices (September 2003 contracts; New York C for Arabica and LIFFE for Robusta) and fair trade premium level

	Market price (US$/lb, green)	Fair trade premium – Africa (US$/lb green)
Mild Arabica	0.67	0.59
Unwashed Robusta	0.31	0.75

Source: Market prices – CSCE and LIFFE databases; premium calculated as difference between minimum price (as in Table 5.7) and market prices.

moratorium on the entry of new coffee cooperatives into the FLO register.

The share of fair trade coffee in the global market is still small (0.8 per cent in 2000 by value, 0.2–0.3 per cent by volume). According to FLO, total imports of fair trade coffee in 2001 amounted to 278,000 bags – an increase of 19 per cent over the previous year. Forty-four per cent of these imports were fair trade and organic certified. In previous years, growth was as low as 6 per cent (2000) and as high as 24 per cent (1999). The US market is growing fast (45 per cent in 2001). Fair trade coffee represents a relatively high proportion of total coffee imports in the Netherlands (6.1 per cent), and Denmark (2.3 per cent). The largest markets by overall volume of fair trade imports are the Netherlands

(90,900 bags), Germany (53,500 bags), the US (50,700 bags), Denmark (25,000 bags) and the UK (24,000 bags). If we extrapolate the average rate of growth in fair trade coffee markets for the period 1999–2001 (16.5 per cent), fair trade coffee imports in 2003 should be in the region of 378,000 bags – 31,700 of which would be Robusta. This estimate, however, may be too optimistic. According to other analysts, fair trade purchase levels in most mature European markets are relatively stagnant (Potts 2003). Giovannucci and Koekoek (2003) estimate a global demand for fair trade coffee in 2003 at 298,000 bags (which is a more reasonable figure and has been entered in Table 5.4).

Shade-grown

Shade-grown is a relatively recent sustainable coffee certification initiative. Its main aim is to conserve forest cover through the production of coffee under the shade of forest canopy. Currently, the only labels offering independent verification are the Smithsonian Migratory Bird Center (SMBC) for 'bird-friendly' coffee (since 1997) and the Rainforest Alliance for 'Rainforest Alliance-certified' coffee (since 1996).[6]

In traditional farming systems, coffee is part of an integrated agroforestry system including indigenous tree species that provide shade and timber. It is also intercropped with other food crops such as maize and bananas. This system supports the long-term sustainability of coffee yields and conserves water, soil and biodiversity. Advocates of shade-grown coffee argue that the conversion from shade-grown to 'sun coffee' (also known as the 'technification' of coffee cultivation) that has taken place in Latin America in the last 20 years is threatening this ecological equilibrium. Of the permanent land planted in coffee, the amount of sun coffee systems ranges from 17 per cent in Mexico to 40 per cent in Costa Rica and 69 per cent in Colombia. Overall, an estimated 30–40 per cent of all Latin American coffee is technified – even excluding Brazil, where historically coffee has been almost all sun-grown. Sun coffee achieves higher yields in the short term due to higher coffee tree density and the application of external inputs. Concerns arise, however, about the long-term sustainability of these gains. Conversion from shade to sun coffee entails the cutting of forest trees. Clearing layers of vegetation impedes the replenishment of soil nutrients through natural mulching and decreases protection from soil erosion and water run-off, in addition to the increased run-off of agro-chemicals. A large plantation company investing in sun coffee in East Africa has reported a 'project cycle' of 5–7 years, after which it is more profitable to move to another piece of land rather than continuing with intensive cultivation.[7] The original tree-covered land, deforested and depleted of soil nutrients, would be abandoned at the end of this non-regenerative 'cycle'.

Coffee can be grown under a variety of types of shade – from a monoculture shade system (with only one type of shade tree) to a multi-layered system with a high diversity of species. The latter achieves a higher level of biodiversity than the former. This creates a problem when shade-grown coffee reaches the marketplace without third party certification, since the consumer does not know what level of shade is present on the farm. A consensus has now been reached among stakeholders (mainly those based in consumer countries) on a common set of Conservation Principles for Coffee Production, which provides a foundation for conservation-based certification programmes – including shade guidelines. The conservation principles have been published by the Consumer's Choice Council in collaboration with the Rainforest Alliance, the SMBC and Conservation International. Coffee operators can use them as a sourcing guideline or as a code of conduct. This is a step forward in terms of streamlining shade parameters. Companies can refer to these guidelines and publicize their content to consumers without necessarily using third party certification. In theory, the conservation principles outline conditions and practices that apply to farms and processing facilities in most coffee-growing regions of the world. However, this initiative, as well as the core of the market for shade-grown coffee, is centred on the US and its Central American and Andean suppliers. Furthermore, the costs and benefits of conservation principles have not been well worked through and presented to farmers – the initiative's proponents may be well-intentioned, but they are seen by some farmers as high-handed and idealistic.[8] Finally, African voices have been infrequently heard in this debate.

In North America, some shade-grown coffee is also known as 'bird-friendly'. This is because it provides an excellent ecosystem for migratory birds and other forest-dwelling wildlife. Studies have shown that the diversity of migratory birds plummets when coffee is converted from shade to sun: in Colombia and Mexico, 94–97 per cent fewer bird species were found in sun coffee than in shade coffee.[9] In

Mexico and the Caribbean Basin, shaded cocoa and coffee plantations are estimated to support the largest number of forest-dependent migratory birds of any agricultural habitat. On the basis of these observations, the SMBC has developed a certification system for the production, processing and marketing of shade-grown organic coffee that awards a bird-friendly label.

Farms that are already certified as organic (or that can simultaneously be certified as organic) are awarded the SMBC label on the basis of guidelines covering a number of criteria developed in relation to the optimal environment for birds migrating between North and Latin America. No such effort has yet been formalized in relation to birds that migrate between Europe and Africa, where criteria may differ.

The Sustainable Agriculture Network has also developed a sustainability certification for coffee. The secretariat for this network is the Rainforest Alliance, an environmental group based in the US. The Rainforest Alliance label combines environmental and social criteria. Coffee has to be grown under shade (although the shade criteria are less strict than in the Smithsonian certification). Use of agro-chemicals is kept to a minimum and strictly managed (therefore, the criteria are less strict than in organic certification). Fair treatment and good conditions for workers must be provided. However, no minimum price is guaranteed and large farms can be certified (contrary to existing fair trade criteria). Growers must not burn fuelwood and other waste wood from the pruning of coffee trees, and new farms cannot be established on cleared forest land. Finally, vegetation buffers must be used to mitigate the polluting effects of pulp run-off in rivers. Therefore, some landscape and biodiversity issues that are not covered in organic certification are addressed in Rainforest Alliance certification. In sum, the Rainforest Alliance tries to cover environmental, shade-specific and socio-economic issues, but its standards are less strict than in the organic, bird-friendly and fair trade certifications taken individually. In relation to shade, Rainforest Alliance standards only require that 'in those regions where coffee has traditionally been cultivated beneath shade trees, producers must maintain or establish a canopy cover of mixed native trees'. This requirement includes at least 12 species of native trees that are well distributed around the farm, a density of shade tree species of 70 trees per hectare, two shade strata, and a minimum proportion of evergreen species.

Shade-grown coffee was practically unknown in the market before 1997. In 2000/1, 50,000 bags of coffee were certified as shade-grown by the SMBC and Rainforest Alliance, but only about 9,100 bags were sold as such (with a retail value of US$16.2 million), almost all in North America (see Tables 5.1 and 5.2). A substantial amount of coffee (8,300 bags) was sold with reference to 'shade' although it was not certified. Many operators based in consuming countries use the concept of 'shade-grown verified' coffee. This coffee is not certified by a third party. The concept simply implies that the farm has been visited by someone to make sure that there is 'shade'. These verifiers are not independent and it is not clear what guidelines they use. Some coffee operators use the term shade-grown even where there are only a few trees on a farm, or only one species. This creates confusion, as consumers do not know which terms to trust, and provides opportunities for free-riding to less-committed operators.

In 2004, the SMBC coffee programme comprised 19 farms in seven Latin American countries (Brazil, Colombia, Costa Rica, Ecuador, Guatemala, Mexico and Peru), covering about 6,000 acres of shaded farmland. As of early 2004, Rainforest Alliance (which also certifies wood products and foliage, bananas, oranges, cocoa and cut flowers) had certified over 28,337 hectares of coffee land in nine Latin American countries (Brazil, Colombia, Costa Rica, El Salvador, Guatemala, Honduras, Mexico, Nicaragua and Panama). Only about 11 per cent of this area appeared to be cultivated by smallholders and their cooperatives and groups (a majority of which are found in Colombia and Honduras).

Future market growth assessments for shade-grown coffee are at 10–20 per cent per year. According to Rice and McLean (1999) several importers and roasters in the late 1990s reported that they saw limited market potential for non-organic shade-grown coffee, and had therefore decided to offer shade only in conjunction with organic coffees (SMBC certification and, more rarely, combined Rainforest Alliance and organic certification). This situation may be changing, however, as mainstream roasters (such as Kraft and Procter and Gamble) have committed to purchasing some Rainforest Alliance-certified coffee. In Europe, there has been a relative lack of interest in shade-grown coffee so far. As a result, Africa has not exported any certified shade-grown coffee.

According to one source, the average premium for shade-grown coffee at the import level is estimated at US$0.35/lb. The industry average is US$0.53/lb, with retailers pocketing an average of US$0.6/lb (see Table 5.3; Giovannucci 2001). Interestingly, these levels are slightly lower than those reported for organic coffee. The explanation for this is that half the market for shade-grown coffee is not certified, and, of the certified portion, only SMBC requires organic certification. Other sources estimate the premium at the retail level to be US$1–2/lb over coffees of comparable origin and grade. Yet there is no formal or standard price premium for shade coffee producers in the SMBC system. They usually receive the same price as for organic coffee. Although there are no added costs to farmers since certification is carried out jointly with organic, the lack of price premium gives no incentive to sun-grown coffee farmers to convert to shade. Rainforest Alliance has reported that sometimes farmers selling coffee under their label are able to charge a premium of US$0.1/lb. With a few exceptions, no premium is paid to producers of uncertified shade coffee (Rice and McLean 1999). Premiums reported by SMBC and Rainforest Alliance are said to range between 0.05 and 0.18 US$/lb.[10] Expenses to run these programmes are covered differently. SMBC charges US$0.25/lb for use of its label to roasters. Rainforest Alliance costs are covered by foundation grants. Direct costs of certification are in both cases paid by farmers.

According to a third source, farmers selling triple-certified organic, fair trade and Rainforest Alliance-certified coffee from El Triunfo (Chiapas, Mexico) earned a price of US$1.38/lb in 2001 (Damiani 2001). Considering that double-certified organic and fair trade coffee is bought at US$1.41/lb, there does not seem to be an extra premium for shade-grown coffee. This is confirmed by other shade-grown certified producers, who have reported that they do not necessarily end up earning an extra premium above organic certification (which is required by the Smithsonian standards). This means that instead of earning a premium, certification may just ensure that certified producers sell their coffee more easily (or earlier) than other producers. Yet this outcome could be conceived as an implicit premium. This happens if the price obtained as a 'first-in-line' supplier is higher than the price that would have been obtained by selling coffee later in the season. No estimations on this interpretation were available at the time of writing.

Utz Kapeh

Utz Kapeh (meaning 'a good cup of coffee' in one of the Mayan languages) is the name of a foundation based in Guatemala and the Netherlands. Originally set up with the support of the Dutch company Royal Ahold, one of the world's largest retail chains, it is now an independent initiative. It has developed a code of conduct for growing sustainable coffee on the basis of the 'Good Agricultural Practices' of the European Retailer Group (EUREP-GAP). EUREP-GAP started in 1997 as the initiative of a group of European large retailers, mostly British and North European. The main objective of EUREP-GAP is 'to develop widely accepted standards and procedures for global certification of Good Agricultural Practices'. EUREP-GAP was first dedicated to the elaboration of technical specifications for fruit and vegetables, but since its creation it has developed standards and procedures for an increasing number of products (sunflower, poultry, aquaculture), including coffee. On 1 October 2004, the Utz Kapeh code of conduct was officially recognized by EUREP-GAP.[11] In the words of the Utz Kapeh foundation, 'our programme is now EUREP-GAP plus. This means that our code meets the European retail standard for Good Agricultural Practices (EUREP-GAP) plus Utz Kapeh's additional social components, plus Utz Kapeh's unique traceability and sales system' (*Utz Kapeh Newsletter*, November 2004).

The Utz Kapeh code contains criteria on soil management, fertilizer use, integrated pest management, waste pollution management, worker health, safety and welfare, and other socio-economic and cultural aspects. Utz Kapeh's goals are to guarantee access to basic social services, guide producers to match standards for growing sustainable coffee, and provide assistance in implementing these standards. The foundation registers interested producers and provides the code of conduct. It establishes contact with an independent certification agency, which performs inspections and grants the certificate if standards are met. Roasters pay a US$0.02/lb fee to the foundation. Certifications were first achieved in 2002.[12] In addition to the original EUREP-GAP Protocol for Good Agricultural Practice, the code refers to standards of the ILO and to the Universal Declaration of Human Rights. At least on paper, the Utz Kapeh initiative aims at improving the living conditions of people who work in the coffee sector and at achieving environmental goals. It should be noted, however, that many of these entries in the coffee code are marked as 'should' and 'minor must'. This means that they have lower priority in the implementation protocol.

As of March 2004, Utz Kapeh had certified 42 farms and groups of cooperatives in twelve countries.[13] This amounted to a potential production of over 630,000 bags, of which 111,000 bags were Robusta (about 18 per cent of the total). In 2003 Utz Kapeh actually purchased 233,000 bags as certified coffee; in 2004, it purchased 355,000 bags (*Utz Kapeh Newsletter*, January 2005). One could interpret this demand–supply balance as oversupply; however, large roasters want a wide variety of origins to choose from. As a matter of fact, one of the reasons why the 'Big Four' roasters had not yet committed to buying large quantities of Utz Kapeh coffee until recently was that there was not enough certified coffee of various origins for their needs.[14]

Most of the demand for Utz Kapeh coffee until the early 2000s came from Ahold Coffee Company (a subsidiary of Royal Ahold), a roaster controlling about 12 per cent of the Dutch market and sourcing all its coffee as certified Utz Kapeh. As mentioned above, Sara Lee committed to buying 41,600 bags of Utz Kapeh coffee in 2004. Retailers such as Casino (France) and the former Safeway (UK) also began to buy Utz Kapeh coffee, together with another 40 roasters. It is clear that this certification scheme is growing fast and has reached a substantial size.

Originally, Utz Kapeh did not set fixed premiums for its certified coffee. The initiative was considered a 'preferred supplier program', in which roasters would buy directly from certified suppliers in producing countries that matched certain standards. In practice, it seems that producers ended up getting a premium of US$0.07–0.26/lb for Mild Arabica,[15] but it is not clear how much of this premium was linked to quality and how much to sustainability. When it was realized that certification costs in this system would have had to be borne by producers, the foundation started to consider a system of variable premiums specifically rewarding sustainability. This system was finally approved in May 2003.

Under this system, the total price of coffee bought with Utz Kapeh certification was supposed to be the sum of the reference price (New York C or London LIFFE) plus or minus the quality premium, plus a variable 'sustainability investment premium' that depended on the level of the international price. The lower-end price thresholds that triggered the sustainability premium were to be reviewed periodically by the Utz Kapeh board of directors. The review was initially scheduled to take place twice a year. This system (as originally designed) was not thought to be optional. Utz Kapeh stated that 'over time, buyers who consistently do not live up to the spirit of the Sustainability Differential will be de-listed from the Utz Kapeh programme'.[16] An analysis of Utz Kapeh coffee certification in Uganda carried out by one of the authors in 2003 suggested that neither farmers nor the exporter involved knew much (or at all) about the premium system (Ponte and Kawuma 2003). Interestingly, as large roasters became interested in Utz Kapeh, discussions of the premium system disappeared from Utz Kapeh's literature. It was not mentioned at all at the presentation given at the 2004 SCAA conference. One can only assume that the premium system has become strictly voluntary or that it has been abandoned altogether. The emphasis of this initiative seems to have shifted to ensuring full traceability and to providing producers with a 'ticket to entry' to an 'emerging market for mainstream certified responsible coffee'.[17] Utz Kapeh's current position on pricing is that 'a certified producer is "rewarded" in a market-oriented way and not in the form of a minimum price. . . . Therefore Utz Kapeh does not interfere in the price negotiations between roaster and farmer. We believe that the principle of supply and demand is the best way to provide a better price for a better product for the farmer.'[18]

Impact of certification systems on sustainability

The more direct measure of the impact of standards systems on the economic sustainability of coffee farmers is the level of premium offered. At September 2003 market prices, the highest premium by far was paid by fair trade importers. The fair trade premium for Mild Arabica coffee was almost four times what could be obtained for organic coffee and nine times larger than what would have been paid by Utz Kapeh had they applied their 2003 premium system. In the case of Robusta, the gap was even higher: the premium was seven times what was offered for organic coffee. The Utz Kapeh premium did not apply to Robusta (see Table 5.9).

The premium mechanism in the four certification options listed above works in different ways. As a result, changes in market prices affect them differently. Table 5.10 provides a sensitivity analysis in relation to changing market prices in three of the certifications where there is a premium (or there can be one in specific market circumstances). A 30 per cent *increase* in coffee market prices would eliminate the premium for Utz Kapeh Arabica (if the premium system was applied at all), would increase the level of the organic premium, and reduce the fair trade premium. In this scenario, the gap between fair trade and organic premiums would be still substantial but lower than in Table 5.9. A 30 per cent *decrease* in coffee market prices would trigger both Arabica and Robusta premiums for Utz Kapeh, decrease the premium for organic and increase the premium for fair trade.

Table 5.9 Premium levels for certified sustainability coffees (US$/lb, green coffee)

	Market price*	Utz Kapeh premium**	Organic premium	Fair trade premium	Shade premium
Mild Arabica	0.67	0.07	0.16	0.59	0.05–0.18
Natural Robusta	0.31	0.00	0.10	0.785	n.a.

Sources: Ponte and Kawuma (2003); Giovannucci and Ponte (2005).
* Prices refer to June 2003 (September 2003 New York C and LIFFE contracts).
** The payment of this premium is encouraged but not enforced.

The overall *income* impact of sustainability standards depends on the balance between the extra costs of matching these standards (including labour costs and the cost of certification where it is not covered by cooperatives and/or exporters) in comparison to the extra income earned from the premium plus/minus the impact of changing farming practices on yields and quality. In the case of organic coffee, yields and quality tend to increase in areas where agro-chemicals were not used previous to conversion. In other cases, quality is still likely to improve, but yields may suffer in the short term. The balance sheet for fair trade is usually positive, since until recently farmers' organizations did not have to pay for certification and inspection, the premium is high and the necessary changes in farming systems fairly limited. However, these impacts may be hard to maintain in the future in the fair trade system –

Table 5.10 Sensitivity analysis of premium levels for certified coffees in relation to changing coffee market prices (US$/lb, green coffee)

	Higher market price scenario				Lower market price scenario			
	Market price 30% higher	Utz Kapeh	Organic	Fair trade	Market price 30% lower	Utz Kapeh*	Organic	Fair trade
Mild Arabica	0.83	0.00	0.21	0.39	0.47	0.07	0.11	0.79
Natural Robusta	0.40	0.00	0.14	0.66	0.22	0.03	0.07	0.84

Source: Ponte and Kawuma (2003).

as oversupply continues and pressure for prices to descend increases. As for shade-grown certification, on the one hand, the impact on yields in the short term is negative and labour inputs increase; on the other hand, coffee quality often improves, weeding becomes cheaper, soil fertility improves, and coffee trees tend to live longer. No estimates are available for Utz Kapeh certification yet.

The process leading to some of the certifications examined in this chapter can stimulate farm incomes outside the coffee economy.

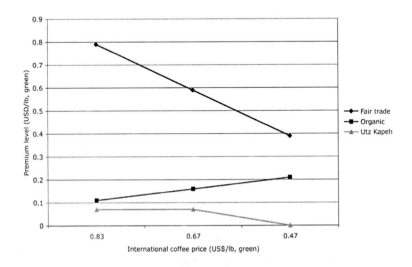

Figure 5.1 Premium variance in relation to coffee prices (Arabica)

Shade-grown certification stimulates reforestation; therefore, income from sale of forest by-products and fruit may increase. Organic and Rainforest Alliance certification relate to the farm rather than coffee alone; thus, markets can be sought for other farm products (a range of products in the case of organic, bananas in the case of Rainforest Alliance). However, these possibilities should not be overestimated: local markets for forest by-products vary, and some non-coffee organic products may suffer from the same demand problems as coffee does. Also, most organic projects focus on one or a small group of related crops for which the exporter has technical and market competence.

In relation to socio-economic and environmental impacts, in the case of organic and shade-grown certifications, spill-over effects have been observed on adjacent communities – in terms of improving both farming practices and coffee quality. In Uganda, for example, several observers mentioned that coffee quality and yields are improving even for non-participants who live in areas close to an organic coffee project. This is likely to be the result of 'copying' and their hopes of being incorporated in the project in the future. In fair trade, the main spill-over effect is achieved through community-level projects financed with part of the fair trade premium. In areas where fair trade and organic double certification has been achieved, the two sets of benefits have been cumulative (Ponte and Kawuma 2003).[19]

Other social benefits of sustainable certifications arise from the fact that marketing partners demand a certain degree of accountability and monitoring, usually through producer organizations. These organizations can help improve the bargaining position of farmers even for the part of the coffee harvest that is not sold through the sustainable channel. These organizations can also become an anchor for other rural development activities, such as micro-finance. However, sustainability certification is a costly and sometimes lengthy exercise. It requires setting rules and monitoring compliance. In the right circumstances and with the right dynamics, this can create a virtuous circle of empowerment and organizational strengthening. At the same time, farmer organizations may find it difficult to wade through rough times if the expected benefits do not materialize in the short term. The hidden costs of coordination (time spent in meetings, transport), uncertainty, and the limitations of collective action may dramatically decrease the overall net benefits of certification efforts.

A critical evaluation

In the previous sections, we have examined the sustainability certifications that are active in the coffee industry. Their main characteristics
are summarized in Table 5.11, and their impact on actual sustainability
(broadly defined) in Table 5.12.[20] A general problem in the realm of
certified coffees is that the quantity supplied is often above the market
demand. Therefore, producers may not be sure that investment in
certification and appropriate agro-ecological practices will be recouped.
For example, oversupply of organic coffee is a common problem in
some countries. In many agro-ecological and/or socio-economic
settings, coffee farmers perform agricultural practices that are close to
the organic model.[21] Yet organic agriculture is about more than not
using agro-chemicals. The conversion process can be elaborate and
expensive, may take years, and usually involves access to extension
services and technical assistance (although this is not the case if few
agro-chemicals were used before conversion). The costs of certification
for producers can be alleviated if NGOs or aid agencies are involved,
or if the certificate holders are export companies (in this case, however,
the exporter ends up controlling financial and information flows). The
premium received by farmers depends on the marketing system
(whether the certificate holder is a cooperative or an exporter), on the
number of farmers that are involved in the scheme, on what percentage
of total sales are certified organic (versus how much coffee has to be
sold as the conventional product), and on the costs of acquiring and
maintaining certification. The key to economic sustainability for organic
conversion is to find a reliable minimum market year after year.

Some of the same problems apply to shade-grown certification.
Certified producers have reported that they do not necessarily end up
earning an extra premium above organic certification (which is
required by the Smithsonian standards). In 2000/1, 50,000 bags of
coffee were certified as shade-grown, but only 9,000 bags were sold as
such (with a retail value of US$16.2 million), mostly in North America.

Fair trade certification is available only to small farmer groups,
organizations and cooperatives. The process usually takes six to twelve
months to be carried out – longer if organic certification is also sought.
Fair trade certification requires setting up formal organizational structures, auditing, and mechanisms of transparency and accountability.
Therefore, its cost depends on whether farmers in a certain area are

Table 5.11 Main features of certification systems for sustainable coffee

Name	Actors or organizations setting the standards	Characteristics	Geographic and farm-size coverage
Organic	International Federation of Organic Agriculture Movements (IFOAM) and affiliated associations	Accredited certification agencies monitor organic standards in production, processing and handling; formally, IFOAM basic standards make reference to issues of social justice, but do not set requirements	Global, but most organic coffee comes from Latin America, especially Mexico; all farms
Fair trade	Fair Trade Labelling Organizations International (FLO) and associated Fair Trade Guarantee Organizations	Minimum guaranteed price paid to registered small farmers' organizations that match standards on socio-economic development; non-profit organizations set/monitor standards and mediate between registered producers and fair trade importers	Global, but a sizeable amount of fair trade coffee is bought also in Africa; only smallholders
Bird-friendly coffee	Smithsonian Migratory Bird Center (SMBC)	Minimum standards on vegetation cover and species diversity (in addition to practices) needed to obtain use of label; also covers soil management	Standard applied only to Latin American coffees so far; mainly estates
Rainforest Alliance-certified	Rainforest Alliance	Certifies farms on the basis of sustainability standards; covers environmental protection, shade, basic labour and living conditions, and community relations	Latin American countries only; mostly estates but also some cooperatives
Utz Kapeh	Utz Kapeh Foundation	Code of conduct for growing sustainable coffee formulated on the basis of the 'good agricultural practices' of the European Retailer Group (EUREP); includes standards on environmental protection and management, and labour and living conditions	Mainly in Latin American countries, but growing also in Asia (India, Indonesia, and Vietnam) and in Africa (Uganda and Zambia); mostly estates, but also some cooperatives

Source: Adapted and updated from Ponte and Kawuma (2003).

already organized, and on what it takes for an organization to achieve 'fair trade status'. The rewards in terms of premium are known and substantial (as long as there is a fair trade market for the coffee supplied). They vary depending on whether the coffee sold is Robusta or Arabica, conventional or organic. Yet fairness issues in fair trade are not completely crystal clear. Better-off farmers are more likely to be involved in a farmer group or organization than more marginalized ones. In the same area, there may be a cooperative that is chosen as a fair trade partner and one that is not. Fair trade buyers may select a small cooperative that sells most of its product exclusively to the fair trade channel, making a few farmers relatively well off. Alternatively, they may buy from a large cooperative that sells a tiny percentage to

Table 5.12 Summary of impacts of selected coffee certification
systems on sustainability

	Utz Kapeh	Organic
Premium	A system paying a low premium only under certain market conditions was agreed in 2003 but subsequently abandoned	Premium paid (but overall levels of premium are decreasing in time)
Yields and quality	Possibly positive but limited	Short-term impact on yields may b negative; possibly positive impact on quality
Labour inputs	Moderately higher labour inputs	Higher labour inputs
Other income impacts	Not known	Possibility of selling other organic products from the farm; income diversification
Market access, networking	Number of buyers and markets are still limited, but increasing	Access to well-established and reliable market
Extension, credit	Potentially better extension services from supportive NGOs and some buyers, but limited support from public extension services	Possibly more effective extension from field staff supported by NGOs and some buyers, but limited support from public system
Organizational capacity; community impact	Strengthening organizational capabilities (if registration is done via farmer groups rather than individually)	Potential increase in mutual suppo among farmers to solve management problems in the farm
Environment	Limited environmental benefits	Potential adoption of new farming techniques to improve soil fertility as well as drought and erosion resilience
Risk, planning capabilities	Potential for some reduced pest management and social risks. Planning may improve	Risk reduction through reduced external inputs, no monocropping, improved soil resilience; planning may improve

Source: Adapted and updated from Ponte and Kawuma (2003). See also Giovannucci and Ponte (2005).

air trade	Shade-grown (SMBC and RA)
igh level of premium in current market; ome premium always assured	No assured premium (but may be paid in certain circumstances)
nly indirect (and possibly positive) impact on elds and quality (through higher income, us increased possibility of purchasing inputs nd hiring labour)	Negative yield impact; positive impact on quality
gher labour inputs linked to attending eetings, transport, coordination, etc.	Higher labour inputs
ossible indirect impact through establish- ent of new links with wider trade networks; ossibility of selling other fair trade products	Possibility of selling forest by-products and fruit
ccess to well-established and reliable arket; technical assistance from fair trade nporters; development of new networks of ontacts among participants	Buyers and markets are still limited, but likely to increase
ccess to trade financing and traditional credit ources due to the improved financial position f cooperatives	More effective agro-forestry extension from supportive NGOs but limited support from public system
ncreased organizational capacity of partici- ant farmers; access to training; strength- ned ability of organizations to serve their embers; community projects	Mutual support among farmers for forest management
ery limited or non-existent	Improved biodiversity and agro-ecological conditions; enhancement of soil fertility
etter planning for coffee production and ersonal and household needs; guaranteed rice reduces risk	Reduced pest management and social (Rainforest Alliance-certified only) risk; planning may improve

fair trade, which results in a small premium to a large number of farmers. The accountability and transparency record of some cooperatives, especially if formerly government-controlled, has also been questioned. Fair trade does not cover the conditions of workers in coffee estates. Finally, some countries offer much fair trade coffee, others do not.

When the fair trade market offers such a large premium over the mainstream market, these points of contention become even trickier to handle. FLO is considering a downward revision of the minimum price for unwashed Robusta, which would be a good idea if it made fair trade *espresso* blends cheaper at the retail level, and if this were to translate into a higher market share. Obviously, increasing the market share of fair trade coffee in general would have a positive impact on producers. For this reason, fair trade organizations, after targeting Starbucks, have started to mount campaigns against large mainstream roasters and roasters/retailers. This has led Procter and Gamble and Dunkin' Donuts to start offering fair trade coffee. However, at the same time, fair trade coffee faces strong challenges in making inroads into mainstream supply channels under the current pricing structure.

In relation to attempts at 'superlabelling', one of the problems so far has been the limited reach of such initiatives. Rainforest Alliance has granted certifications in the coffee sector mostly to estates, and all in Latin America. Utz Kapeh has certified large estates and some cooperatives, mostly in Latin America, but also (more recently) in Asia and Africa. In neither case are funds provided to producers for investments to comply with the standards and for certification (although both provide help in finding funds). Similarly, neither guarantees a living wage (only payments according to national laws). This has prompted criticism from advocates of traditional certifications, who fear that economic benefits to farmers are being watered down and that the multiplication of labels is confusing consumers.

The problem of equity in relation to sustainability revolves around the fact that raising standards (whether in terms of environmental protection or socio-economic conditions) heightens entry barriers. A first issue is whether higher standards are rewarded with higher prices to producers. This happens in fair trade and, at lower levels, in organic coffees. Utz Kapeh seems to have abandoned the idea of paying a (low) guaranteed premium in certain market conditions. Shade-grown coffee does not guarantee a premium. A second issue relates to the distribution of benefits to different coffee-growing regions under the various schemes. On this count, Latin America seems to be the clear winner over Asia and Africa, with the exception of fair trade. A third issue is whether one group of producers is disproportionately rewarded in comparison to another. On this count, smallholders emerge as winners only in fair trade and, to some extent, in organic certification. In the case of Utz Kapeh and shade-grown coffee, estates appear to have benefited more than smallholders and their organizations – although efforts are being made, it seems, to correct this imbalance.

Private and public/private initiatives on sustainability

General features
Coffee operators in consuming countries (international traders, roasters, retailers) are involved in sustainability issues in four ways: (1) they may buy and/or sell certified coffees, such as organic, fair trade, shade-grown and Utz Kapeh; (2) they may contribute to projects in favour of coffee-growing communities; (3) they may develop their own mission statements, codes of conduct and sourcing guidelines that include environmental and/or social parameters; and (4) they may adopt codes of conduct or sourcing guidelines that have been written by sectoral organizations, public/private initiatives and/or NGOs. In this section, we focus on private firms' adoption of codes of conduct and sourcing guidelines that are not verified by third parties (see also Ponte 2002c; Giovannucci and Ponte 2005).

An increasing number of companies are adopting the Conservation Principles for Coffee Production (see above, p. 178) to develop their own codes of conduct and sourcing guidelines. Among these, we find Green Mountain Coffee Roasters, Rapunzel Pure Organics and Starbucks. These companies (and others) have also been using their own guidelines. For example, since 1992, Green Mountain Coffee Roasters has been running a Stewardship Programme, which is geared to identifying those growers who have made measurable commitments in the areas of coffee quality, environmental protection and labour conditions.[22]

Thanksgiving Coffee Company has been running a rating system for buying coffee from growers based on social and environmental criteria since 1995. Thanksgiving Coffee also markets Song Bird coffee in a joint venture with the American Birding Association (ABA). This line of shade-grown coffees is 'verified' by the coffee company owner (therefore, it does not qualify as a certified coffee). The ABA endorses Song Bird coffee, while Thanksgiving markets the product. The company also returns 15 cents per package to the ABA. A similar process is taking place for the company's Bat Magic coffee. This is also a shade-grown coffee, and is marketed in relation to the preservation of bat habitat. A percentage of each sale of Bat Magic coffee supports Bat Conservation International and the Wildlife Trust, two non-profit environmental groups that are collaborating on grassroots bat conservation and public education projects around the world.[23]

Starbucks started a pilot programme in 2001 for the establishment of a preferred supplier program (PSP) of green coffee purchasing.[24] This is now known as the Coffee and Farmer Equity Practices Programme (CAFE). In February 2004, Starbucks announced that it intends to source more than 1.5 million bags of coffee through these guidelines within five years. If that happened, it would amount to almost twice the estimated 2003 size of all the sustainability certifications put together (see Table 5.4). This programme constitutes a set of standards and verification procedures for 'improvement in sustainable coffee production'. Starbucks defines sustainability as 'an economically viable model that addresses the social and environmental needs of all the participants in the coffee supply chain, from producer to consumer'.[25] This system is superimposed on the already-existing quality standards developed and applied by Starbucks to their suppliers.

The CAFE programme is a flexible points system that rewards performance in a number of categories of sustainability. A flexible point scale includes indicators grouped along three main headings and applies to farmers, processors, and vendors: social responsibility (maximum 40 points), coffee growing (maximum 45 points, mainly on environmental indicators), and coffee processing (maximum 20 points, mainly on water, waste and energy management). In this system, programme applicants who achieve 60 per cent of total performance rating and 60 per cent in each pertaining area are awarded 'preferred supplier status'. If they achieve a minimum of 80 per cent overall rating (and 60 per cent in each area), they qualify for 'strategic supplier status'. Preferred and strategic suppliers of individual origins and types are given purchase priority (starting from the highest score) over other offers received during a particular purchasing cycle. Strategic suppliers are awarded a one-year sustainability conversion premium of US$0.01/lb on all shipments that meet the CAFE programme guidelines, but only during the first crop year in which the score is achieved.[26] Continuous improvement is stimulated through a further premium of the same size awarded to suppliers improving by at least ten points above the 80 per cent score over the previous year. Starbucks has also outlined a system of independent verification to ensure credibility.

Mainstream roasters and international traders are also taking steps in the realm of sustainability. Nestlé has developed a procurement policy linked to the concept of sustainable agriculture in collaboration with the Sustainable Agriculture Initiative (SAI) Platform (which also sees the participation of other large international traders and roasters such as Ecom, Kraft, Neumann, Sara Lee, Tchibo and Volcafé). In a document entitled 'Action Plan for Sustainable Green Coffee Production', Nestlé lays out a points-based system (similar to the one developed by Starbucks) with which its suppliers will have to progressively comply. According to the Nestlé document, this system 'would enable the creation, for each origin, of a Sustainability ranking of suppliers. In future Nestlé will use this ranking in order to

> assure that our Green Coffee sourcing supports the long-term drive towards Sustainable Green Coffee Production. The Sustainable Green Coffee Production project will progressively establish full traceability of Nestlé Green Coffee supplies. (*Ibid.*)

In late 2004, Nestlé and Kraft were also thought to be about to launch their own 'ethically aware' brands in the hope of capturing some of the market share controlled by fair trade. In this context, Kraft proposed to pay farmers who adhere to its ethical criteria a 20 per cent premium on the price of green coffee beans on the open market.[27]

Another important initiative in the realm of sustainability in the mainstream coffee market is the public/private collaboration between the German Coffee Association and the German Ministry of Cooperation and Development. This initiative led to the writing of a code of conduct, the Common Code for the Coffee Community (or 4C) 'for growing, processing and marketing of mainstream coffee that is feasible for implementation and suitable for binding agreements'. According to its promoters, more than 70 representatives from coffee farmers, trade and industry, NGOs and trade unions were involved in the elaboration of the Code. The parties to the elaboration process included large roasters (Nestlé, Tchibo, Sara Lee and Kraft), international traders (Neumann and Volcafé), producing country representatives (from Brazil, Vietnam, Kenya, Colombia, Indonesia and several Central American countries), NGOs (Oxfam International and Greenpeace), and federations of trade unions (including representatives from coffee industry workers).

The Common Code 'is a market-based and open initiative to promote and encourage sustainability in the green coffee chain' (*Common Code for the Coffee Community*, 2004: 1). It is based on three dimensions:

- A *social* dimension, which calls for 'decent working and living conditions for farmers and their families as well as employees';
- An *environmental* dimension, aiming at protecting primary forests and conserving natural resources in production and post-harvest operations;
- An *economic viability* dimension, with 'reasonable earnings for all in the coffee chain, free access to markets and sustainable livelihoods' (*ibid.*).

The objective of the code is to 'foster sustainability in the "mainstream" green coffee chain and to increase the quantities of coffee meeting basic sustainability criteria within all three dimensions' (*ibid.*).[28] This initiative – in attempting to set a cross-sector standard developed with multi-stakeholder input – is a clear example of how the distinction between private and voluntary standards is becoming blurred. Furthermore, the Common Code basically embeds guidelines that seek to avoid the worst forms of labour exploitation and environmental destruction. These guidelines draw on existing UN conventions and other domestic regulations that are already in force in many producing countries. In this respect, the Common Code substitutes (failing) implementation of existing regulations by the state with voluntary compliance verified through auditing in the framework of tripartite agreements between governments, NGOs/unions, and the private sector. Finally, the Common Code is the broadest initiative seeking to mainstream sustainability.

Evaluation of private and public/private initiatives

The Starbucks CAFE initiative is a creative effort that can promote sustainable practices and provide economic stability to qualifying producers. However, a shortcoming of the programme is that it does not contemplate any permanent price differential to cover the extra costs embedded in meeting the 'sustainability criteria'. Suppliers have to improve performance and pay for independent verification. Yet, there is no long-term guarantee that they will receive higher prices than those already offered by Starbucks. Unless the system of points-based incentives is kept over the long term, instead of just one year, the CAFE programme runs the risk of merely raising barriers to entry for suppliers. This system is also much more sophisticated in relation to its environmental aspects than its social coverage, potentially rendering its impacts on the social and economic fronts less substantive. Finally, the Starbucks system is more easily applicable to estates than to cooperatives and farmer groups.[29]

The Nestlé and Common Code initiatives on sustainability are still in their infancy and thus difficult to assess. Nevertheless, until recently, there did not seem to be much scope for the designation of premiums or other direct economic benefits to producers from such systems, and so their long-term economic benefits for producers remained uncertain at best. This may be changing: we have seen that Kraft and Nestlé are about to launch their own 'ethically aware' brands. It is also encouraging that the Common Code initiative has made strides in involving producing-country actors in the setting of the basic standard. Yet, if one looks attentively at the content of the Code, producers do not come out as clear winners. The Code seeks to 're-arrange the transfer of added value toward the producers' (*Common Code for the Coffee Community* 2004: 1), but provides no indication of how this would take place. The main reference document states that '[t]he Common Code is not a solution to the current coffee crisis, but offers a long-term development perspective to suppliers and establishes a new basis for competition with regard to the quality of the product and the quality of sustainable production methods' (*ibid.*: 5). To the extent that it promotes a new concept of quality in mainstream coffee markets, the initiative is a step in the right direction. However, the Code does not address the way quality content is valued (that is, priced) along the chain, does not demand price premiums for new quality content (after all, it is a 'market-based initiative') and, unsurprisingly, does not question the structure of the coffee value chain *per se*. Thus, the likely outcome is that actors based in consumer countries will be able to sell a different 'quality content' of their coffee and at the same time expect actors based in producer countries to deliver this new content at the same price. In addition, the extra costs of auditing and management improvement will be transferred down to producers.

In sum, private initiatives are laudable in that they open up market channels for selling sustainable coffees. When points systems are used, they also provide opportunities for suppliers to follow a learning curve towards matching higher standards. The critical considerations raised in this chapter should be read in a comparative manner. To the extent that these initiatives enable the channelling of value-added to the producer (of any size), they still operate in a redistributive manner (between consuming and producing countries) and thus can play a role in correcting the trend towards increased transfer of wealth downstream in supply chains. However, so far they have had a patchy record in providing material incentives to producers (mainly, a premium). The proliferation of initiatives also means that inevitably there will be different definitions and procedural guidelines for sustainability, which is likely to add confusion in the marketplace. The Common Code initiative (and, to some extent, the Starbucks CAFE initiative) address some of these limitations. But even these initiatives do not address the power relations among actors in the coffee value chain, since they are often built upon them.

Conclusion

The global value chain for coffee has been one of the most important battlegrounds for the establishment of reference certifications and codes of conduct that address environmental and socio-economic preoccupations. As in other agro-food products, several groups and initiatives are trying to assert leadership. Coffee has been a leading product for fair trade organizations and environmentalists. Several labels have been created, including organics, fair trade and bird-friendly. Some recent initiatives, however, are attempting to mainstream sustainability and take the ground from the early labels: the Rainforest Alliance initiative, Utz Kapeh and the Common Code for the Coffee Community. The problem here is not just the fact that these firms adopt weaker substitutes to convey their sustainability efforts to their customers and shareholders. The greater danger lies in the possibility that their considerable marketing clout could generate consumer acceptance of modest or cosmetic standards, and subsequently erode more stringent (and internationally accepted) standards (Giovannucci and Ponte 2005).

The current process of elaboration of mainstream sustainability codes can be interpreted as the commoditization of sustainable coffee (or the commoditization of sustainability), a similar process to the standardization process that occurred at the end of the nineteenth century in the coffee trade in general. This is occurring alongside the commoditization of certification itself. For example, certifiers in the organic sector that originally formed as offshoots of the organic movement had a blurred role encompassing advice and inspection. These have evolved in the direction of a complete separation of advice, inspection and certification. They now get accredited to perform multiple certifications, and compete with each other around price and reputation.[30] Another possible way of looking at the impact of certification is that jobs in regulation, extension and research that were lost with market liberalization in producing countries are being replaced by private sector jobs in auditing and certification. This may lead to a not-so-appealing situation in which 'a whole army of people with clipboards will come to bother farmers'.[31]

The global value chain for coffee used to be regulated by domestic governments in producing countries and international commodity agreements at the level of international trade. It is not less regulated today, just regulated differently. Certifications such as organics and fair trade started this process in niche markets. Other initiatives are now taking 'new regulation' to mainstream markets. The outcomes of this process will indirectly determine the growth prospects of more radical initiatives such as fair trade. They will also directly determine whether farmers can get a better deal for their product and whether a fairer distribution of value along the chain can be obtained. Current indications suggest that this is unlikely to happen.

Is there still a clear role for regulation? While NGOs and other civil society organizations can at least partly represent the needs of growers in the South, their capacity to ensure a certain level of fairness is limited by their resources and the scope of their mandates. We can conceptualize standard-setting processes as new forms of social contract in which the state, rather than being directly involved between the parties, provides a form of basic guarantee while (more or less accountable) NGOs and firms are in charge of hammering out the bargains. Despite the increasing clout of multinational corporations (MNCs), regulation can help ensure that the voice of producers is heard. With balanced inputs from corporate, civil, and governmental sources, sustainability standards can play a key role in addressing inequalities (and indeed genuinely fomenting sustainability) in the coffee trade – and even more broadly in international trade (Giovannucci and Ponte 2005). Before laying out how this could be done, in the next chapter we examine a number of case studies on the distribution of value along coffee value chains in mainstream, specialty and sustainable sectors in selected countries. Then we lay out some key theoretical issues that will inform the practical policy suggestions and specific strategies for action presented in the last chapter of the book.

Notes

1   Note that the total volume of organic coffee in this table is almost certainly underestimated; it is unlikely that the organics market is smaller than fair trade, even considering the overlaps between the two. The estimate for organics given in Table 5.4 is likely to better reflect real levels.

2   This estimate takes into consideration that 44 per cent of fair trade coffee is also certified organic.

3   For various estimates of the organic coffee market, see Giovannucci (2001), Lewin, Giovannucci and Varangis (2004), Rice and McLean (1999), ITC (2002) and FIBL (2002). IFOAM, the Organic Coffee Association (OCA), the Organic Trade Association (OTA) and Naturland (Germany) were not able to provide statistics on the global organic coffee trade. The most reliable figures on organic coffee are the ones from the fair trade movement (see below). Fair trade and organic double-certified coffee, however, is only one segment of the organic trade.

4   No reliable data are available on the geographical sources of European and Japanese imports.

5   Fair trade requirements for producer organizations are divided in two sets: (1) minimum requirements, which all producer organizations must meet if they want to register (or that they have to meet within a specified period); and (2) process requirements, on which producer organizations

must show permanent improvement. Minimum standards are meant to ensure that fair trade benefits reach the small farmers and/or workers; that the farmer organization has potential for development; and that the fair trade instruments can take effect and lead to a development that cannot be achieved otherwise. The degree of progress which FLO requires from each producer organization depends on the level of economic benefits it receives from fair trade and on its specific context. Producer organizations are regularly inspected for compliance with these requirements. Fair trade importers have to match a set of FLO standards as well: (1) they must buy directly from the FLO-registered producer association on the basis of multi-annual contracts; (2) they must pay an FLO-determined minimum price and a social premium to the producer organization, plus an extra premium for organic coffee; (3) they must offer pre-financing for 60 per cent of the contract value upon request from the producer organization. In addition to these requirements, fair trade importers also provide technical support to producer organizations and play an advocacy role for producers in national and international fora. Farmer organizations use the fair trade premium for community projects, human resource development, environmental protection and business development. Part of the premium is also paid directly to farmers (FLO 2002).

6   Rainforest Alliance-certified coffee was formerly known as Eco-OK.

7   Own field interview, Moshi (Tanzania), December 2000.

8   Source: Peter Baker, personal communication, December 2004.

9   However, work at Cenicafé Colombia suggests that such dramatic declines may be exaggerated. Large declines may be the case for certain forest-loving species, but other species increase in sun-grown coffee (Peter Baker, personal communication, December 2004).

10 Reported to Daniele Giovanucci. See Giovannucci and Ponte (2005).

11 Source: http://www.eurep.org/about.html.

12 Utz Kapeh registers interested producers or cooperatives/farmer associations and provides the code of conduct. If desired by the producer, exchange of information starts between the Foundation and the producer to help comply with the code of conduct. When the producer is ready, Utz Kapeh establishes contact with an (Utz Kapeh-approved) independent certification body. The certification body performs inspections on the basis of the code of conduct and, when the producer complies, grants the certificate.

13 Utz Kapeh certifications as of March 2004 comprised: two cooperatives in Costa Rica, eight farms in Guatemala, one group of cooperatives in Honduras, eight farms in Brazil, one farm in Bolivia, one farm and one group of cooperatives in Colombia, six groups of cooperatives and farmer

groups in Peru, one group of farms in India, one group of farms in Indonesia, six farms in Vietnam, three farmer groups organized by an exporter in Uganda, and one farm in Zambia.

14 Source: sustainable coffee operator, personal communication 2 June 2003.

15 Source: Utz Kapeh presentation at the 2002 SCAA conference.

16 Source: Utz Kapeh, 'Guidelines on the pricing of Utz Kapeh Certified Responsible Coffee', document distributed at the 2002 SCAA conference, Anaheim, CA.

17 Source: http://www.utzkapeh.org/Utzkapeh/ukwebsite.nsf/portal? Openframeset.

18 Source: http://www.utzkapeh.org/Utzkapeh/ukwebsite.nsf/portal? Openframeset.

19 For more details on the impacts of organic, fair trade and shade certifications on socio-economic conditions of beneficiary communities and on the environment, see Ponte and Kawuma (2003).

20 For other assessments of fair trade coffee, see Mace (1998), Murray, Raynolds and Taylor (2003), Raynolds (2000; 2002), Raynolds, Murray and Taylor (2004), Renard (2003), Schmidt (2002), Tallontire (1999; 2000), Taylor (2005) and Waridel (2001). On sustainability in the coffee sector more generally, see also Vellema and Boselie (2003).

21 This is especially relevant after market liberalization in African countries producing Mild Arabica. Agro-chemicals have become much more expensive, especially if compared to coffee prices, and access to credit for smallholders has dried up (Ponte 2002a; 2002d). On the contrary, in areas producing Hard Arabica and Robusta coffee, farmers rarely used agro-chemicals, even before liberalization.

22 Interview, Anaheim, California, 5 May 2002. Green Mountain ranked 16th on the Forbes 200 Best Small Companies Ranking in 2001. Its coffee sales were valued at US$84 million in 2000 (see Luisa Kroll, 'Entrepreneur of the Year: Java Man', Forbes, 29 October 2001).

23 Amy Satkofsky, 'Sustainable Coffee Is for the Birds — and Everybody Else', Business Magazine, September/October 2001.

24 Source: http://www.scscertified.com/csrpurchasing/starbucks.html.

25 Sources: Starbucks, press release, 12 November 2001; 'Starbucks Green Coffee Purchasing Program. Pilot Program for Preferred Suppliers', mimeo; and interview, Anaheim, California, 3 May 2002.

26 It should be noted that in the original 2001 formulation of the pilot programme, the costs incurred by suppliers in switching to such a system were to be mitigated by an interim financial incentive programme. The PSP programme stipulated that Starbucks would pay a premium of up to US$0.1/lb above the contracted price, roughly one cent for each 10

points earned. The current incentive system, as we can see, is much less generous (*ibid.*).

27 Source: *Guardian*, 22 November 2004. At the time of writing, it was unclear how the payment of this supposed 20 per cent premium was to be operationalized. Kraft already purchases Rainforest Alliance-certified coffee for its Kenco Sustainable Development brand. However, Rainforest Alliance certification does not have a social premium provision embedded in it.

28 The code is completely voluntary. In theory, this is how it should work: actors wanting to get involved carry out a self-assessment procedure that provides basic information on their current practices. These actors, called Common Code Units, are any group or individual that can ensure traceability of an aggregated volume of coffee composing at least one container (approximately 18 tons or 300 bags of green coffee). These Units request an implementation audit and develop an improvement scheme (*ibid.*: 7). An independent third-party verifies the self-assessment against the requirements of the code, rates the current performance of the actor and refers the result to a National Common Code Body. On the basis of a successful verification, the Unit develops a management plan to remove all problematic areas within a maximum of two years. Reverification procedures check the level of compliance and monitor improvement. If verification fails, the Unit loses its licence to supply Common Code coffee until verification is made again.

29 The company has nevertheless demonstrated some concern for smallholders, as in the case of its collaborative project with the Ford Foundation, Oxfam America and Coordinadora Estatae de Productores de Café (CEPCO) (an association of smallholder coffee producers in Oaxaca, Mexico). This pilot project provides farmers with technical assistance (including the introduction or refinement of cupping skills for the farmer organization), market information and product quality feedback.

30 We owe this observation to Peter Gibbon.

31 Peter Baker, personal communication, December 2004.

6

Value chains or values changed?

Value distribution along coffee chains: empirical evidence

As illustrated in previous chapters, the coffee crisis has afflicted producing countries in the late 1990s and early 2000s, with farmers facing among the lowest prices in a century in real terms. This crisis has coexisted with a coffee revival in consuming countries, if not in terms of overall consumption *per capita*, at least in terms of increasing value of consumption of coffee-based products. This contradiction is at the core of what we call the 'coffee paradox'. Another aspect of this double process is that farmers are getting a decreasing share of the final price paid by consumers for coffee. This means that the value added (and rent extracted)[1] along the chain takes place increasingly in consuming countries. Consumers pay proportionally less for the material attributes of coffee quality, and more for their symbolic and in-person service attributes – including branding, packaging, consumption ambience, and sustainability content.

One way of documenting the process of restructuring in value distribution along the global value chain for coffee is to look at the distribution of total income in a historical perspective.[2] Talbot (1997a: 65–7) estimates that, in the 1970s, an average of 20 per cent of total income generated by roast and ground sales was retained by producers, while the average proportion retained in consuming countries was almost 53 per cent (see Figure 6.1).[3] According to his calculations, between 1980/1 and 1988/9, producers still controlled almost 20 per cent of total income; 55 per cent was retained in consuming countries. After the collapse of the ICA in 1989, the situation changed dramatically. Between 1989/90 and 1994/5, the proportion of total income gained by producers dropped to 13 per cent; the proportion retained in consuming countries surged to 78 per cent.[4] This represents a substantial

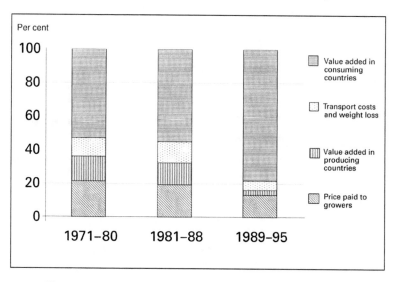

Figure 6.1 Distribution of coffee income along the coffee chain,
1971–80 to 1989–95 (%)

Note: Coffee income = weighted average of retail prices in ICO-member importing countries,
expressed in green bean equivalents. Monetary values of total coffee income for the periods
indicated in Figure 6.1: US$2.63/lb (1971–80); US$3.64/lb (1981–8); US$4.36/lb (1989–95)
(calculated from Talbot 1997a: 65–7).

transfer of resources from producing to consuming countries, irrespective of price levels. This kind of analysis was updated by Fitter and
Kaplinsky (2001) to cover the period up to 1999. Even given the international price peak of 1997, the average proportion of total income
accruing to farmers in the 1989/90–1998/9 period remained as low as
13.6 per cent. The share of income retained by producers in the early
2000s (the coffee crisis started in late 1999) is likely to have dropped
further owing to low prices for green coffee and the ability of roasters
and retailers to maintain consumer prices at relatively stable levels.

   Another way of assessing the distribution of value along the coffee
chain is through the use of proxies, such as the ratio between retail
prices for roasted coffee and international green coffee prices. While
green coffee prices almost halved between December 1999 and June
2003 (source: ICO database), average retail prices in the US between
December 1999 and December 2002 decreased by only 15 per cent
(*ibid.*). Figure 6.2 compares the evolution of green coffee import prices
in the US and the gross margin between retail and import prices.[5] It

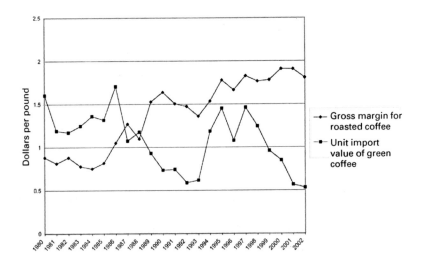

Figure 6.2 Unit import value for green coffee and gross margin for roasted coffee in the US, 1980–2002 (US$/lb)

Source: US Department of Labor (roasted coffee consumer prices, excluding sales tax) and FAO (green coffee unit import value).

shows a sharp decline in import prices occurring between the beginning of the 1980s and 2002. It also shows a marked increase in the gross margin, from a more or less stable level of US$0.8/lb at the beginning of the 1980s to US$1.8/lb at the beginning of the 2000s.

A broader perspective on changes in the value distribution is provided in Lewin, Giovannucci and Varangis (2004). What emerges from their analysis is that the ratio of import (cif) prices to retail prices in the five top importing markets decreased dramatically from 1995 (a period of high international prices) to 2001 (when the coffee crisis had already kicked in). The drop is most dramatic in the US (from around 38 per cent to around 19 per cent) and France (from 40 per cent to 25 per cent). Yet the ratio in the five countries in 2001 is fairly similar to the one in 1990 (another period of low prices) – with the exception of the US, where it fell from 25 per cent to about 19 per cent. The same authors also provide a breakdown of the coffee- and non-coffee-related costs that make up retail prices in the US. They argue that declining international coffee prices, as well as increasing non-coffee costs in the industry, are determining the declining proportion of the retail price of coffee that accrues to producers. We broadly agree with this perspective, but argue that a better way of looking at this phenomenon is not through the heading 'non-coffee costs', but rather through the creation of value that accrues to 'non-material' quality attributes of coffee at various points in the value chain. Furthermore, the ratio of farm-gate price to retail price (see our analysis below) is what most closely indicates the proportion of final price paid to producers, rather than import prices. Import prices also reflect the margins made by export companies in producing countries, many of which (especially in East Africa) are actually based in consumer countries.

An alternative approach to assessing the distribution of value is to analyse coffee value chains in specific cases rather than in the aggregate. Pelupessy (1999) applied this method to the Côte d'Ivoire–France and Costa Rica–Germany chains in the mid-1990s, with results that are fairly similar to Talbot's. In 1994, the grower's share of total retail price was 13.8 per cent in Côte d'Ivoire and 14.6 per cent in Costa Rica. Below, we carry out a similar exercise to provide more up-to-date results based on fieldwork by one of the authors in Uganda and Tanzania (as producing countries) and in the US and Italy (as the corresponding consuming countries). Our assessment provides only a snapshot picture of the distribution of value along specific chains in specific years. Yet it allows a comparison between different coffee blends (or single-origin products) of varying quality that are offered to consumers, between mainstream and specialty markets, and between roasted bean (or roast and ground) sales and sales of brewed coffee in bars and cafés. Table 6.1 and Figure 6.3 show the results for the value chain of Robusta coffee from Uganda to Italy in 2001/2. Ugandan Robusta is exported predominantly to Europe and used as a filler in mainstream blends in continental Europe and as a basic component of *espresso* blends of low to middle quality in Southern Europe (see Chapter 4). In Italy, Ugandan coffee is one of the top five origins by volume of Robusta imports and is usually blended with cheaper and harsher Robusta origins (from West Africa and/or Vietnam). The bottom end of the Italian market features 100 per cent Robusta blends, sold packaged in vacuum bricks in supermarkets for home consumption. This market channel is characterized by a branded offering, strong price competition and promotional sales. In term of product positioning, these vacuum bricks are the equivalent of branded coffee cans in the US mainstream market.

Table 6.1 Uganda–Italy value chain for Robusta (home consumption, sale at supermarkets, 100% Robusta blend), 2001/2

Value chain node	Details	US$/lb*	Proportion of retail price (%)
Farm gate	Selling price to local trader	0.14	6.6
Export	FOT (free on truck) ex-Kampala	0.21	10.3
Export harbour	FOB (free on board) ex-Mombasa	0.26	12.4
Import harbour	CIF (cost, insurance & freight) ex-EU Import harbour	0.30	14.3
Roaster	Selling price to supermarket chain	1.81	86.5
Retail	Consumer price at supermarket**	2.09	100.0

Note: * Roasted coffee equivalent weight (conversion factors: hulled/unhulled = 0.55; green ready for export/hulled = 0.95 due to drying and sorting losses in export preparation in Uganda; roasted/green = 0.80).
Average exchange rate: US$1 = ITL1,743 (average October 2001–September 2002; source: www.oanda.com).
** VAT excluded.
Sources: Own fieldwork data.

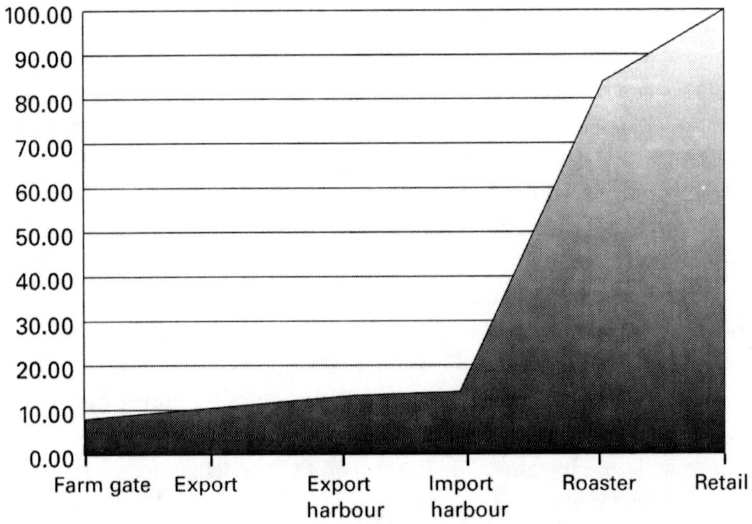

Figure 6.3 Proportion of retail price at various nodes (%): Uganda–Italy value chain for Robusta (home consumption, supermarket channel, 100% Robusta blend), 2001/2
Source: Table 6.1.

Given the lack of comparative value chain data from other Robusta origins, in our analysis of a 100 per cent Robusta blend sold at a supermarket chain in Italy, we have assumed that only Ugandan Robusta is used. This yields an estimate of the proportion of the retail price that accrues to the farmer that is probably higher than in reality, since Ugandan Robusta commands a premium over many other Robusta origins.[6] In our approach, rather than presenting weight loss (due to hulling, drying, export preparation, and roasting) as a proportion of the final price (as in Talbot 1997a and Fitter and Kaplinsky 2001), we calculated the prices paid at various nodes in the value chain in terms of the equivalent weight of roasted coffee. This means that the price indicated at the farm level is not the actual price received by the farmer for dry cherry coffee, but the equivalent price once all the weight losses are accumulated.

Table 6.1 and Figure 6.3 suggest that the process of squeezing the farmer (in terms of proportion of the final price paid at the farm gate) that started in the 1990s has progressed further in the early 2000s. Farm-gate prices in this particular value chain represent less than 7 per cent of the retail price. Even at the import (cif price) level, the proportion is lower than 15 per cent (a value in line with the one calculated by Lewin, Giovannucci and Varangis 2004 for the Italian market). What is presented here is a simplified picture of a complex series of transformations and passages. Between the farm gate and the export point, Robusta coffee in Uganda goes through the hands of various layers of traders, processors and an exporter. It gets hulled, transported, dried, sorted and prepared for export. Information on the net margins that various actors make along the chain is hard to come by, even through extensive fieldwork. However, what can be safely argued in relation to the Ugandan domestic market is that there is extreme competition at all levels of the value chain, and that net margins are slim. This shows in the relatively small difference between farm-level and export prices. The gap is smaller than the difference between import (cif) and export (free-on-truck Kampala) prices, owing to expensive transport between Kampala and Mombasa and clearing, forwarding, insurance and shipping charges. At the import point, even if coffee goes through intermediaries (such as international traders, or local importers/agents), their margins are also small (3–5 per cent). In other words, it is not the local traders, exporters and international traders/importers handling the material

Table 6.2 Tanzania–Italy value chain (home consumption, sale at supermarkets, weighted prices depending on blend composition), 1999/2000

Value chain node	Details	Low-end blend (100% Robusta)		Mid-range blend (50% Robusta, 30% Hard Arabica, 20% Mild Arabica)		High-end blend 100% Arabica, of which 60% Hard Arabica, 40% Mild Arabica)	
		US$/lb*	Proportion of retail price (%)	US$/lb*	Proportion of retail price (%)	US$/lb*	Proportion of retail price (%)
Farm gate	Selling price to local trader	0.20	8.7	0.25	4.7	0.31	3.9
Auction	Ex-Moshi for Mild Arabica; ex-Kemondo Bay for Hard Arabica and Robusta	0.47	20.7	0.57	10.4	0.66	8.2
Export harbour	FOB (free on board): ex-Tanga for Mild Arabica; ex-Dar es Salaam for Hard Arabica and Robusta	0.53	23.3	0.63	11.5	0.72	8.9
Import harbour	CIF (cost, insurance and freight) ex-EU import harbour	0.56	25.0	0.66	12.2	0.76	9.4
Roaster	Selling price to the super-market chain	1.99	88.0	4.61	85.0	6.51	80.0
Retail	Consumer price at super-market**	2.26	100.0	5.43	100.0	8.14	100.0

Note: * Roasted coffee equivalent weight (conversion factors for Mild Arabica:
green/parchment = 0.80; roasted/green = 0.80; conversion factors for Robusta and Hard
Arabica are the same as in Table 6.1). Average exchange rate US$1 = ITL2,010 (October 1999
–September 2000; source: www.oanda.com).
** VAT excluded.
Source: Own fieldwork data.

content of the 'generic' coffee product who are making a killing in the value chain. It is branded roasters and, to a lesser extent, retailers.

Given that retail margins vary between 12 and 20 per cent depending on the quality of the roasted blend (see Chapter 4), it is clear that most of the value added is generated by roasters. As argued earlier in the book, roasting, blending, grinding and vacuum packing are relatively low-tech operations. Thus most value is generated in symbolic production. At the low end of the market, symbolic production is mostly generated through branding and associated promotional and advertising costs.

The next issue to be unpacked is whether these results apply only to low-end coffees blends in Italy. Are higher-quality coffees distributed in supermarket chains better in terms of distribution of value along the chain? What about consumption in the bar segment? In order to answer these questions, we use another East African origin, Tanzania. Tanzania is helpful in this respect because it exports all three kinds of coffee that can be used in middle-range and high-end *espresso* blends in Italy: Hard Arabica, Robusta and Mild Arabica. The results of this analysis (see Table 6.2) refer to hypothetical blends of different kinds of coffees, all coming from Tanzania. This is not a real-life situation, as blends are usually composed of various origins. However, it can offer a reasonable approximation.

If one held the view that higher-quality coffees offer a better deal to farmers, the results of Table 6.2 would come as a surprise. Although the equivalent aggregate farm-gate prices are higher in absolute terms for better blends (owing to higher proportions of more expensive coffees such as Mild Arabica), farmers get a higher proportion of the retail price of coffee for lower-quality blends. The proportion accruing to farmers in Tanzania for a 100 per cent Robusta blend in 1999/2000 (8.7 per cent) is fairly similar to the one exhibited in the Uganda case in 2001/2 (6.6 per cent).[7]

As we move up one step in the quality ladder, to mid-range blends, the proportion of the final price paid to the farmer drops to less than 5 per cent. For high-end blends, it is even lower, less than 4 per cent. This suggests that differentiation at the retail level pays off disproportionately for roasters and retailers. Their mark-ups for what is sold as better quality (or simply higher price) are proportionately higher than the increased cost they incur to procure the raw material.[8] For example,

Table 6.3 Tanzania–Italy value chain for *espresso* blends (bar consumption, weighted prices depending on blend composition), 1999/2000

Value chain node	Details	Mid-range blend (50% Robusta, 30% Hard Arabica, 20% Mild Arabica)		High-end blend (100% Arabica: 60% Hard Arabica, 40% Mild Arabica)	
		US$/lb*	Proportion of retail price (%)	US$/lb*	Proportion of retail price (%)
Farm gate	Selling price to local trader	0.26	1.2	0.31	1.4
Auction	Ex-Moshi for Mild Arabica; ex-Kemondo Bay for Hard Arabica and Robusta	0.59	2.7	0.72	3.3
Export harbour	FOB (free on board): Ex-Tanga for Mild Arabica; ex-Dar for Hard Arabica and Robusta	0.65	3.0	0.78	3.6
Import harbour	CIF (cost, insurance, freight) ex-EU import harbour	0.69	3.2	0.82	3.8
Roaster	Selling price to bar owner	7.24	33.3	8.14	37.5
Retail	Consumer price at the bar**	21.71	100.0	21.71	100.0

Notes:
* Roasted coffee equivalent weight (see conversion factors in previous tables).
** Based on a bar price of ITL 1,200 minus VAT and an exchange rate of US$1 = ITL2,010 (average for 1999/2000) and a dosage of 10g of coffee for each *espresso*.
Source: Own fieldwork data.

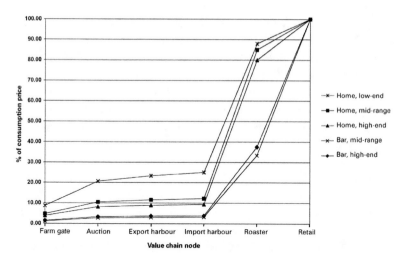

Figure 6.4 Tanzania–Italy value chain (supermarket and bar channels, weighted prices depending on blend composition), 1999/2000

Source: Previous tables.

the ratio of the cost of the raw material at the import level between a high- and a low-end blend is only 1.35. Yet, the ratio at the retail level is 3.6. This phenomenon is particularly odd in the Italian context because home consumption coffee is not marketed through explicit references to quality. The same brand will offer different blends at different price segments. Brand recognition, rather than material quality, is the main message conveyed to consumers. Because of the limited quality consciousness of consumers, branded roasters can sell a differentiated blend at a higher price without a proportional improvement in the material quality of the blend. In sum, in the home consumption segment of the Italian coffee market, value is added mostly through branding. The higher the price segment of the blend is, the higher the returns for roasters (and, marginally, for supermarket chains).

In the bar consumption segment of the market, farmers fare even worse. As shown in Table 6.3, farmers receive 1.2–1.4 per cent of the retail price of a coffee brewed as straight *espresso* at one of the thousands of bars in Italy (for milk-based *espresso* drinks, the proportion is even lower). In this segment, most of the value is added at the bar through brewing and the offering of in-person services. Brand recognition, as mentioned in Chapter 4, is not a major factor in this case. The market is extremely fragmented. Thus, oligopoly-inspired explanations of the distribution of value along the chain do not apply. Roasters still make healthy margins, but these are based mainly on service offerings to bar owners (financing, provision of cups, brewing and grinding machinery on loan, technical assistance, weekly supplies) rather than on branding as in the retail segment. The incentives for offering better blends (for both roasters and bar owners) are limited by the fact that consumers expect more or less the same price in all bars, not only across one particular area, but country-wide as well. At the same time, because margins are so high, it does not pay to offer a very poor blend, such as a high-proportion Robusta. While preparation with a stove-top coffee maker at home transfers only some of the qualities of the coffee into the cup, an *espresso* preparation with a professional machine transfers much more – taints as well as good qualities. Yet because 100 per cent Arabica blends are harder to handle properly at the brewing stage, most bars will offer a mid-range blend.

Figure 6.4 consolidates the analysis so far by combining quality segments and sales channels. In terms of their share of the final price for coffee, farmers fare best in the supermarket channel at the low end of the quality range and worst in both quality profiles in the bar channel. Roasters fare best in the supermarket channel in high-end blends (if success is measured by the difference between the proportion of final price at the roaster and import levels). Supermarket chains fare better with higher-end blends. Bar owners, proportionally, fare best of all actors. Up to the roaster level, coffee is sold mainly in relation to its material quality attributes. Roasters, retailers and bars sell the symbolic attributes and in-person services connected to coffee. Most of the value added is created here.

Is this picture peculiar to the Italian market? Is the US specialty market any better in terms of distribution of value along the coffee chain? The results summarized in Table 6.4 indicate a broader application of the argument beyond mainstream markets and beyond Italy. This table shows the distribution of value along the Tanzania–US chain for a specific kind of Tanzanian coffee that is appreciated almost exclusively in the US specialty market: single-origin Kilimanjaro peaberry. Peaberry is a whole coffee bean that has not split in two halves. It is sought for its odd shape and because it is believed (at least in the US) to provide a better taste profile in the cup than a regular half bean. The

Table 6.4 Tanzania–US value chain for single-origin Kilimanjaro peaberry coffee in specialty markets (roasted beans and brewed), 1999/2000

Value chain node	Details	Roasted bean sale (specialty outlet)		Brewed sale at a café chain	
		US$/lb*	Proportion of retail price (%)	US$/lb*	Proportion of retail price (%)
Farm gate	Selling price to local trader	0.49	4.1	0.49	1.0
Auction	Ex-Moshi for Mild Arabica; ex-Kemondo Bay for Hard Arabica and Robusta	0.91	7.6	0.91	1.8
Export harbour	FOB (free on board): ex-Tanga for Mild Arabica; ex-Dar es Salaam for Hard Arabica and Robusta	0.97	8.1	0.97	1.9
Import harbour	CIF (cost, insurance and freight) ex-US import harbour	1.03	8.6	1.03	2.1
Roaster	Selling price to specialty outlets or café chains	9.60	80.0	9.60	19.2
Retail	Consumer price at specialty outlet or café**	12.00	100.0	50.00	100.0

* Conversion factors: see previous tables.
** Sales price at specialty outlet based on average price of US$12/lb – sales tax excluded (1999/2000). Sales price at café based on Starbucks average price for 1999/2000 (US$1.10, sales tax excluded) for a cup (six fluid ounces or 180 millilitres) prepared with two tablespoons of ground coffee (10 g).
Source:
http://www.starbucks.com/ourcoffees/coffee_edu9.asp?category%5Fname=The+Four+Fundamentals

coffee price paid at the farm level is the same as for other coffee. The separation of peaberries from regular beans occurs at the curing and grading stages before export. Therefore, some value is created by those who carry out this operation before selling the coffee at the auction. Peaberry is sold as a specific grade at the Moshi auction in discrete lots. Therefore, precise price information is available at all levels of the coffee chain in Tanzania. On the US side, we have split the analysis in two: (1) sales in specialty outlets as whole roasted beans; and (2) sales of brewed coffee at a café chain (at Starbucks-level prices). The latter calculation is somewhat arbitrary, since peaberry is usually sold in roasted bean form. However, the comparison helps us to understand the level of value addition that takes place in café chains in the US.

The picture emerging from the Tanzania–US chain is one that, at the farm level, does not differ much from the Tanzania–Italy chain. In the bean sale segment, farmers get about 4 per cent of the final price (similar to the proportion they get in the mid-range blend in the supermarket channel in Italy). In the café segment, farmers get about 1 per cent, almost the same as in the bar segment in Italy. The proportion of the final price at the import level for bean sales in the US specialty market is similar to the high-end blends offered in Italy through supermarket chains (8.6 per cent and 9.3 per cent respectively). For brewed coffee sales, the US proportion at the import level is similar to the one in the bar segment in Italy (about 2–3 per cent). What this suggests it that, in terms of distribution of value along the chain, the US specialty coffee is similar to the Italian mainstream market, both in relation to sales of beans/blends and in relation to sales of brewed coffee at US cafés and Italian bars. The second part of this statement comes as no surprise, in the sense that in both places value is created mainly through symbolic and in-person service attributes other than branding. In US cafés, selling ambience and a certain lifestyle is more important than in-person service *per se*. In Italian bars, it is mostly in-person services that are sold with the coffee; not much emphasis is placed on material quality, nor is information provided on the origin of the coffees in the blend.

The equivalence between the Italian mainstream value chain and US sales of specialty coffee beans is more intriguing. The two establishments could not be more different. Specialty retailers in the US offer single-origin coffees and quality blends; they provide plenty of information on the origin of the coffee and its material attributes; in small roaster–retailer establishments, relationships with consumers are often personalized, so that in-person services are also offered; average consumers are more quality-conscious than in mainstream markets. The Italian mainstream market (as well as the US one), still offers mainly symbolic attributes, but almost exclusively related to branded offerings of mediocre to poor quality with no effort to communicate quality information to the consumer and no in-person service. Quality is embedded in the brand and the price category. Roasters' focus is on offering a constant quality profile in time and space. It is a mass market of anonymous consumers. Whether or not consumers participate in the creation of symbolic and in-person service attributes, the value added in this process is captured by café chains, bars, supermarket chains and roasters in consuming countries.

In Chapter 5, we examined the role and limitations of sustainable coffees in improving the livelihoods of coffee farmers in developing countries. In that context, we focused our discussion especially on the level of prices (and premiums) offered to farmers for sustainable coffees. Here, we apply a further test to sustainable coffees in terms of the distribution of value that they exhibit along their chains – both in their own terms and in comparison to other mainstream and specialty coffees. We do this via the analysis of the ratio of producer price to retail price in the Tanzania–Italy and Tanzania–US coffee chains for sustainable coffees of similar quality to the mainstream and specialty coffees presented above. Table 6.5 summarizes the results of this analysis for two kinds of sustainable coffees (fair trade and organic) and two quality/price range profiles (mid-range blends sold in supermarket chains in Italy in roast and ground form, and single-origin peaberry Kilimanjaro Mild Arabica sold in roasted bean form in US specialty outlets).[9]

Table 6.5 shows that, for organic coffees, the proportion of the final coffee price paid to the farmer (adjusted for processing and roasting weight losses) in both Italy- and US-bound value chains is similar to their non-organic value chain equivalents (around 4–5 per cent). Although organics provide higher prices at the farm level, they do not provide a higher proportion of the retail price to farmers. In terms of fairness, they are equivalent to mainstream coffees. With regard to fair trade coffee, one major caveat should be presented at the outset. The fair trade prices included in Table 6.5 are prices paid to the cooperative society, not farm-gate prices. Therefore, the comparison with other

Table 6.5 Value distribution in fair trade and organic coffee chains
(Tanzania–Italy and Tanzania–US)

Value chain	Type of sustainable coffee	Node	Price (US$/lb)*	% of retail price
Italy	Fair trade (mid-range blend)	Ex-coop price	1.31	21.0
		Retail	6.24	
	Organic (mid-range blend)	Farm-gate price	0.32	4.4
		Retail	7.33	
US	Fair trade (single-origin Kilimanjaro peaberry)	Ex-coop price	1.45	11.5
		Retail	12.65	
	Organic (single-origin Kilimanjaro peaberry)	Farm-gate price	0.62	4.9
		Retail	12.64	

* Roasted coffee price equivalent, 1999/2000; ex-coop price is different from the minimum prices for fair trade coffee in Table 5.7 owing to three factors: (1) it is an aggregate price for the three kinds of coffee used in the blend; (2) it is a roasted coffee price equivalent; and (3) fair trade minimum prices are fob prices, from which levies, transport and handling costs need to be deducted to arrive at the net ex-coop price. Retail prices exclude VAT/sales tax.
Sources: Fieldwork data.

value chains should be made with caution. The price that farmers actually receive will depend on the size of the cooperative, the proportion of coffee that the cooperative sells through the fair trade channel over the total amount of coffee sold, and the amount of the premium that is used for community projects or other business projects by the cooperative (see Chapter 5).

With these caveats in mind, fair trade coffee (and by implication double-certified fair trade/organic coffees) fares much better. In the Tanzania–US chain, the proportion of the consumer price paid to the cooperative is about 12 per cent. This is much higher than for organics, but markedly lower than in the Tanzania–Italy chain. This is because Italian *espresso* blends contain a high proportion of Hard Arabica and Robusta coffees. Since the late 1990s, these fair trade coffees have attracted higher premiums over conventional coffees than Mild Arabicas (see Chapter 5). Again, lower-quality species and/or processing seem to offer better deals for farmers at least in terms of proportional distribution of value along the chain.

In Italy, fair trade coffee distributed in supermarkets is sold at only modest premiums over conventional coffees of similar quality. However, the price paid to the cooperatives for this coffee is markedly higher than for conventional coffee. Therefore, the percentage of the price paid to the cooperative over the retail price is a whopping 21 per cent. This proportion is similar to the one shown by Talbot (1997a) for all coffees in the 1970s and 1980s under the ICA system.[10] In a sense, we can argue that fair trade has substituted the quota system as the guarantor of a fair distribution of value along the coffee chain. The notable difference is that fair trade represents less than 1 per cent of the market, while the ICA covered a major proportion of the coffee trade.

In conclusion, fair trade seems to be the only coffee value chain where the proportion of the consumer price paid to farmers/cooperatives reaches levels that are similar to those for mainstream coffees under the ICA regime. All other chains, including specialty and organics, have seen a dramatic fall in the proportion of the final price that accrues to the farmer. This does not mean that paying a higher price for quality (of whatever nature) at the farm level is useless: quite the contrary. What it means is that a qualitative jump towards a more equal distribution of value along coffee chains (and markedly higher farm-gate prices) can only occur when producing countries are able to generate symbolic quality attributes for which they get paid directly (in-person service provision is trickier, given the distance between production and consumption). If these attributes are added further downstream in the value chain, little ends up in farmers' hands. These conclusions and the evidence accumulated throughout this book so far bring us back to the issue of 'solving the commodity problem' that was posited at the beginning. In the next section, we unpack this problem from a theoretical point of view. In Chapter 7, we provide some policy suggestions and specific strategies for action.

Solving the commodity problem: theoretical approaches

In the previous section, we have argued that higher prices and a fairer distribution of value in coffee chains is unlikely to occur unless producers embed symbolic content in the material things they sell, secure property rights on this symbolic content, and obtain higher prices in doing so. These observations provide the framework for theoretical and practical approaches in solving the commodity problem (and the coffee paradox). In this section, we highlight three theoretical dimensions linked to the solution: (1) changing quality conventions; (2) promoting transparency and consumer–producer connectivity; (3) territoriality as a vehicle for embedding value at the production level; and (4) consumers (and other actors along the chain) as agents of change.

Changing quality conventions

Part of the solution to the commodity problem entails embedding symbolic quality attributes into commodity production in developing countries. Coffee, like other agro-food products, is prone to quality variance due to the vagaries of the weather. Although there are some minimal regulatory requirements for coffee to be 'fit for trade', the focus of economic agents is on a number of different quality attributes, depending on where along the chain the transaction is taking place (see Chapter 4). As explained earlier, in the mainstream coffee market, roasters have maintained a dominant position through – among other things – effective management of the asymmetry of information on quality. Essentially, roasters buy coffee with complete material quality information from international traders. Once coffee is blended and roasted, it is sold to consumers under a brand name with essentially no further information on its material quality. That means that roasters use brand reputation as a proxy for variance in material quality. This does not mean that a higher price necessarily buys a better coffee. Packaging, shelf placing and advertisement also play a large role in establishing consumers' ideas of quality. The important point here is that roasters have complete information on material quality when they buy coffee, and they release next to no information on material quality to their clients.

The major threat to mainstream roasters' dominance of the global value chain for coffee comes from changing quality conventions that are emerging in the specialty and sustainable coffee industries. At least in parts of these industries, not only do consumers require more information on (and higher levels of) material coffee quality, they also include environmental and socio-economic aspects in their consideration of quality (symbolic content). Roasters operating in this segment are under pressure to provide a means of measuring complex quality content. As certification and auditing systems are developed, however, mainstream roasters can also enter this market. At the same time, more successful specialty operators are streamlining their operations and adopting strategies that resemble the ones carried out in the mainstream coffee market. In a sense, the distinction between the specialty and mainstream coffee markets becomes more blurred.

As noted in our brief discussion of convention theory in Chapter 1, Thévenot (1995; but also Raynolds 2002; 2004) suggest that, against the background of a return to the dominance of a market convention, domestic and civic conventions can still be observed in certain sectors. Some agro-food analysts (Murdoch, Marsden and Banks 2000; Murdoch and Miele 1999) actually argue that domestic and civic conventions are becoming more important. However, the case study of coffee (and of other commodities, see Gibbon and Ponte 2005) suggests that purely market-related quality conventions are actually far from dominant and that industrial norms are being applied to the management of quality control. Furthermore, the purported resilience of domestic conventions is problematic in at least two respects: (1) domestic conventions, with their reference both to localistic and brand-based justifications, include remarkably different mechanisms of quality negotiation and arbitration; and (2) the nature of these mechanisms has shifted over time, limiting the category's explanatory power.

The case of specialty coffee suggests that shifts within 'domestic' forms may be as important as between these and other forms. Information on quality in the mainstream coffee market at the retail level is normally embedded in brands. In the specialty coffee sector, much more information on quality is passed on to the consumer, but largely in relation to coffee origin – thus on the basis of narratives of place (domestic trust). At the same time, there is a specific attempt to encode information about ambience of consumption in the language of quality (quality of consumption environments and/or experiences, and of individual consumers). In some cases, these narratives tend to be replicated in a standardized manner for mass consumption (Starbucks) – thus recalling industrial quality conventions. Origin-based 'trust' narratives also tend to be replaced by certified quality systems (the coffee standards on material quality being developed by the SCAA, for example) that partially de-link quality from place. In any event, strictly domestic conventions are under threat in relation to the protection of indications of geographical origin (IGOs). The preservation of unique IGOs has been

222 · The coffee paradox

part of high-level struggles at the WTO level, with traditional producers of wine and spirits (chiefly, France and Italy) pitched against 'new world' producers (Australia, Chile, US, Argentina and South Africa). The latter argue that some geographical denominations, including those for some cheeses and meat preparations, have lost their relation with locality and have become simply generalized ways of producing a specific food or beverage (more on this topic below).

Overlaps between conventions also arise along value chains. For example, in mainstream coffee value chains, relational contracting between roasters and importers, and between importers and exporters, usually takes place in an environment of fairly accurate information on material coffee quality (industrial convention). In producing countries, on the contrary, most transactions take place with only limited information on quality communicated. When differences in quality are not so important (Robusta coffee), a market convention dominates in the exchange between local producers, traders and exporters. When quality differences are more important (Mild Arabica coffee), lack of certainty on quality is resolved through repeated personal interactions (domestic convention).

The literature also argues that 'civic content' is becoming more important in the negotiation of quality content (as is argued by Thévenot 1995, among others). In practice though, this trend is often counteracted by others. Raynolds (2002) and Renard (2003), for example, explain how fair trade coffee embodies not only civic norms (paying a fair price, helping small farmers' organizations), but also a more direct, but still virtual, contact between consumers and producers (invoking a domestic convention). At the same time, labelling and certification are organized in terms of an industrial convention, and relationships with some mainstream marketers who carry fair trade coffee are based on a market convention.

The setting of strict and 'objective' quality standards in many initiatives that promise sustainability can also be interpreted as an attempted incorporation of industrial conventions, which in the process subordinate engagement with domestic and civic norms to other ends. In other words, mainstream roasters may attempt to fold the threats to leadership arising from the increasing importance of civic conventions into the operational environment of the market-industrial convention (codifying such parameters into broader standards, certification and labelling).

If a broad historical interpretation can be attempted at all using convention theory categories – considering the overlaps and complexity of quality conventions within and between value chains – we would argue that industrial conventions are increasingly embedding traits that according to convention theory are domestic (branding), but that could be better distinguished on the basis that they are owned by powerful actors. At the same time, civic conventions tend to shorten the distance between geographically separated actors, allowing virtual repeated interactions, the building of trust, and the generation of new configurations of proximity. Thus, there is a blurring of the boundaries between domestic and civic conventions.

We would also argue that, as knowledge of quality becomes embedded in technical instruments such as standards, modules and codes of conduct, there is less need for repeated interactions and the building of the personalized relationships that are the third leg of domestic conventions (the other two being branding and geographical origin); in a sense, we can say that trust becomes institutionalized in the label or code of conduct, rather than by reference to a specific firm. At the same time, the reputation of the certifier can be an important issue for the credibility of the label. We would then argue that, as brands, standardization and certifications become globally known and/or accepted, the boundaries between market and industrial conventions become increasingly blurred, while different forms of domestic conventions arise (linked to the reputation of the certifier rather than the actor/firm handling the coffee).

In sum, what is taking place in coffee value chains is a reconsolidation of the compromise between industrial and market quality conventions – rather than an outright dominance of market conventions, as argued by Thévenot. This becomes clearer when one considers the underlying bifurcation of quality experiences in the coffee value chains. On the one hand, increasingly complex quality content is codified in equally complex standards. On the other hand, in some branches of the coffee sector, quality content is vulgarized, or becoming so. This is happening against a weakening and/or restructuring of domestic conventions based on trust and repeated social interactions. Domestic conventions based on geography of origin, and civic conventions that cater to specialty and sustainability markets, could be considered forms of resistance against this trend. In a sense, there may be more continuity in the market–industrial compromise than previously thought – as some features of domestic and civic conventions are absorbed into industrial conventions, and as the differences between industrial and market conventions may be decreasing with improved prospects for standardization within a large number of differentiated product lines.

Policy and strategic approaches attempting to improve the situation of coffee farmers should be built on these reflections. This means acknowledging that mainstreaming approaches to sustainability, based on generic and voluntary codes of conduct or standards that are designed by Northern actors on behalf of supposed Southern beneficiaries, are likely to muffle the voice of farmers. Only acceptance (by consumers and other actors along the value chain) of truly domestic and civic conventions can deliver a more transparent system for farmers. This process can be built on promoting intimate consumer knowledge of the commodity *and* the places of production (rather than brand recognition by itself), and on taking responsibility for environmental and socio-economic impacts of production and trade not only in general, but also in relation to specific places. In the next two sections, we examine how this can take place through transparency and the use of locality to embed symbolic (and sometimes in-person service) quality attributes. In the final section, we examine the role of retailers and consumers in promoting change of this kind.

Transparency and producer–consumer connectivity

The second dimension of solving the commodity problem is to promote transparency and consumer–producer connectivity. This entails finding ways of improving information flows in value chains so that prices, the content of quality, and the identity of actors involved in production, processing and exchange situations are known to other actors along the chain. The key issue here is that if producers embed symbolic content in a commodity, consumers need to know what this content is, value it, and pay for it – rather than expecting it as an integral part of a redefined but standardized offering (based on a market–industrial quality convention).

Increasing connectivity also entails two-way transparency in trade networks – not a 'looking-glass', one-way gaze that provides consumers with more information about producers, but does not tell producers who the consumers are, or what they want. In theoretical terms, we draw critically on the 'material culture' approach (Appadurai 1986), particularly on the role of disjuncted knowledge as a source of continuing marginalization of commodity producers, and on the production of commodity mythologies. We link this approach to other insights emerging in agro-food studies dealing with commodity fetishism – that is, 'the necessary masking of social relations under which commodities are produced from which capitalist commodity production gains much of its legitimacy' (Guthman 2002: 296 – drawing on Marx). This is done to understand what is hidden and what is communicated in value chains that are supposed to be more transparent (such as sustainable coffees). From this perspective, enhancing transparency and connectivity between producers and consumers could be a (more or less effective) process of unveiling commodity fetishism. We discuss the extent to which various sustainability initiatives in the coffee sector effect this unveiling, and to what extent their codification and embedding in standard codes and certifications leads instead to a double fetishism – the masking of social relations of production combined with the commoditization of the knowledge about the commodity itself (Freidberg 2003c).

The material culture approach is based on the argument that commodity status is given by the situation of exchange, not by the intrinsic properties of objects. According to Appadurai (1986), objects can move in and out of 'commodity status' – that is, they have social lives (see also Kopytoff 1986). Drawing on Simmel (1976), Appadurai sees commodities as objects of economic value, where value is a judgement made by subjects on objects, rather than an inherent property of objects (*ibid.*: 3). He highlights that it is the 'standards and criteria (symbolic, classificatory, and moral) that define the exchange-ability of things in any particular social and historical moment' (*ibid.*: 14). In other words, this approach helps us focus on how a thing can be exchanged under a specific name and origin, with particular attributes at a specific time in a particular place, and how the value of this thing reflects one or more situationally and historically dominant classificatory regimes (or conventions). This does not imply that there are always *shared* understandings of exchange situations among the actors involved. In some cases, the standards and criteria governing exchange are widely understood and accepted; in others, all that is agreed upon is a 'minimum set of conventions regarding the transaction itself' (*ibid.*).

Appadurai (1986) explores the role of knowledge in ways that directly speak to our discussion of transparency and connectivity between producers and consumers. He argues that commodities represent complex social forms and distributions of knowledge at the levels of production, exchange and consumption. Technical knowledge at the sites of production, applied within cosmological, social and ritual boundaries, is mediated by degrees of knowledge of markets, consumers and destinations of things. In this process, '[l]arge gaps in knowledge of the ultimate market by the producer . . . [may lead] to high profits in trade and to the relative deprivation of the producing country or class in relation to the consumer and the trader' (Appadurai 1986: 43; see also Spooner 1986). As we have argued elsewhere in this book, quality information is used by mainstream roasters to maintain a dominant position in the mainstream coffee market. We have also seen that sustainability certifications and direct contacts between specialty roasters and producer cooperatives do not necessarily provide transparency of the kind and at the level that facilitate a process of producer empowerment.

Appadurai argues that 'when the spatial, cognitive, and institutional distances between production, distribution and consumption are great' (Appadurai 1986: 48), specialized mythologies about commodity and commodity flows are generated. 'Mythological understandings of the circulation of commodities are generated because of the detachment, indifference, or ignorance of participants as regards all but a single aspect of the economic trajectory of the commodity' (Appadurai 1986: 54). He argues that one such mythology (the mythology of circulation) is generated in relation to commodity futures market, where the trade is about contracts (paper trade) and the physical commodity is rarely exchanged. This could be seen as an instance of 'meta-fetishization, where not only does the commodity become a substitute for the social relations that lie behind it, but the movement of *prices* becomes an autonomous substitute for the flow of commodities themselves' (Appadurai 1986: 50; original emphasis).

Other scholars have argued that commodity fetishism does not refer simply to the masking of social relations but also to the masking of society–nature relations that are concealed in commodity production (Allen and Kovach 2000; Guthman 2002; Hartwick 1998). In this respect, consumer (or NGO) demands for transparency in agro-food production and trade could be seen as 'lift[ing] one corner of com-modity fetishism' (Goodman 2004: 5) because they provide information on ecological and production relations that would otherwise be con-cealed from distant consumers. Some of these scholars also draw on Durkheim's idea of the totem as a symbol representing rather than hiding social relationships. According to Goodman and DuPuis, 'a "totemic" perspective infuses studies of food as symbols of cultural identity and solidarity' (2002: 11). Similarly, Guthman sees the political meaning of ethical foods as deriving from the visibility of material claims (no child labour, environmentally sound practices), rather than concealment (com-modity fetishism) (2002: 306–7). In this reading, sustainability initiatives are imbued with symbolic values meant to show solidarity, responsi-bility, and care for environmental and socio-economic concerns.

Recent work on struggles around organic standards and the 'indus-trialization' of organic practices (Raynolds 2004; Guthman 2002; 2003) suggests that some of these transparency demands themselves may conceal as much as they reveal in terms of socio-economic relations of production and trade. On these lines, Freidberg (2003a; 2003b; 2003c; 2004) sees the emergence of concerns with socio-economic conditions, environmental protection and locality as an instance of 'double commodity fetishism'. In her case study of the marketing of tropical fruit and ethnic cuisine, she argues that marketing strategies 'embellish consumers' relatively superficial geographical knowledge and curiosity about the faraway, the exotic and ethnic . . . [and obscure] the social relations and exploitative practices of production' (Freidberg 2003c: 29; drawing also on Cook 1994; and Cook and Crang 1996). She also argues that current supermarket practices embedded in codes of conducts actually contribute to the process of fetishization. In addition to this, the costs of compliance are moved down to producers, and thus a clean conscience comes cheap. Freidberg suggests that supermarket chains have moved from a 'don't ask, don't tell' approach to obliging suppliers to tell everything about the production process. In turn, super-markets are eager to tell consumers that food has been produced following the highest environmental and social standards. 'The appear-ance of transparency ... has become the new *packaging* model' (Freidberg 2003c: 29; original emphasis; see also Freidberg 2004) in the same way that traceability has become a standard part of supply chain risk management.

> The conventions providing information about the production process ...
> serve to facilitate marketing because, like the transparent plastic box, they
> assure buyers ... that all is clean, nothing hidden. But they are only effective
> if buyers value those conventions and, indeed, accept them at face value
> ...[T]he conventions themselves have become fetishized commodities.
> Like the plastic box and other forms of packaging, labels and codes of
> conduct are produced for exchange ... and invested with meanings.
> (Freidberg 2003c: 29)

While the notion of commodity fetishism provides helpful analytical
insights in understanding issues of transparency, we do not subscribe to
an orthodox Marxist interpretation of it. An orthodox interpretation
would be linked to a notion of value as an inherent property of commodities – fixed by the labour power invested in them. If this were the
case, by definition all conventions would be fetishistic, since they
would mediate the act of exchange.[11] In this sense, Appadurai's take on
the relational aspects of commodity, and convention theory's claim that
there are no essential referents lying behind the languages and norms of
quality evaluation, are more nuanced points of departure. Our aim here
is: (1) to use instances of mythologies of exchange and commodity
fetishism to examine transparency in coffee value chains; and (2) to
understand how asymmetry of information confers power on actors
based in consumer countries *vis-à-vis* coffee producers.

Our study suggests at least three mythologies that obscure true transparency in coffee value chains. First, in relation to simple fetishism, the
mythology of 'Italian' coffee promotes the complete disappearance of
social relations of production (and producers themselves). This mythology is in fact double: (1) the 'Italian' identity is based on a specific
method of brewing combined with the use of particular blends; this
obfuscates the fact that the coffee itself comes from the tropics; and (2)
espresso preparation (and/or branding) is also portrayed as incorporating
the material qualities of coffee, making it 'good' whatever the quality of
the raw material. As a direct result, in *espresso* markets, image is brand
(or venue of consumption), and very little emphasis is given to the
origins of coffee. The best one generally gets is the not-so-useful information that a blend is '100 per cent Arabica'.

Second, coffee mythologies are also generated in sustainable coffee
initiatives, where harmonious relations between nature, place and
community are portrayed. They are transmitted through consumer

information placed on the final coffee pack, related leaflets, websites and/or other marketing and promotional materials. Yet, the 'distance' between consumer and producer is shortened only on the side of consumers – producers do not acquire additional knowledge about consumers, and often they do not get higher prices for the coffee sold in this value chain, either. Furthermore, the social relations behind the production and exchange of coffee are still to a large extent veiled, especially with regard to 'environmental' coffees (see Chapter 5). If this information is summarized and guaranteed in labels and certification, double fetishism takes place.

Finally, mythologies are generated in fair trade coffee as well, where the consumer supports ideas of cooperation, minimum prices and support for smallholder farming. While this happens in some cooperatives in some countries, other experiences tell a different story. For example, the fair trade premium paid to a large cooperative that sells only a small proportion of its coffee through fair trade channels will be divided among many farmers. The result is that the cooperative's financial survival is enhanced, but individual farmers will not feel the impact directly in their livelihoods. In fieldwork conducted in East Africa, one of the authors also observed that very few farmers in these large cooperative unions know about fair trade, let alone what it means.[12]

In sum, transparency in a value chain suffers when there are discontinuities in the distribution of knowledge and/or myth creation. However, and to some extent counter-intuitively, transparency may also suffer when information on commodity production and circulation is embedded in standardized and externally verified labels and certifications. The label then becomes a cheap substitute for intimate knowledge of the commodity and of producers. Certifications and auditing procedures can actually facilitate a blinding of producers in relation to the specific requirements that consumers want. This happens when producers' enhanced knowledge is limited to the requirements set in standards. Matching these requirements does not mean knowing markets and consumers any better. Can intimate knowledge of producers and commodities be generated in shorter value chains? Can 'local' be sold as a mark of quality in ways that generate higher returns for producers? How can producers in distant lands sell territoriality to consumers as a symbolic content of quality? These are some of the questions that are addressed in the next section.

Territoriality

The third dimension of solving the commodity problem relates to *territoriality* as a vehicle for embedding value at the production level. Here, we examine how rewarding it is for producers to embed symbolic quality attributes that are tied to a particular location. Three ways of offering territoriality (or *terroir*, 'locality') are analysed: (1) as a generic offering signalled in labels of origin that are not guaranteed by regulation and thus are prone to imitation and extra-local competitive offering; (2) as an offering devised by producer associations, guaranteed by regulation and administered by independent institutions – as in the appellation systems for wine in France and Italy; and (3) as an offering that embeds elements of certification and codification for socio-economic and environmental preoccupations into specific places, thus placing responsibility for a specific location on the shoulders of both producers and consumers (in the first two ways, quality is guaranteed by place but there is no necessary provision for specific environmental and socio-economic clauses).

For these discussions, we draw from some of the agro-food literature in economic geography and rural sociology to understand the complex relations between: local producers and distant/spread-out consumers; *terroir* and quality; and regulation and producer empowerment. But before turning to territoriality issues of direct relevance to tropical commodity producers, we first examine the record of developed country farmers in selling locality to consumers.

According to the alternative agro-food networks (AAFNs) and the 'quality turn' literatures (Murdoch and Miele 1999; Murdoch, Marsden and Banks 2000; Ploeg *et al.* 2000; Ploeg and Renting 2000), consumers in developed countries have moved away from consuming industrial agro-food products and towards consuming niche and specialty products. AAFNs, however, remain a small segment of the agro-food industry. What is sold to consumers as high quality in AAFNs includes products characterized by organic or low external inputs practices, specific locations or regions, or supplied through farmers' markets, short/local food supply chains, agro-tourism and other kinds of multi-functional agricultural enterprises. The 'quality turn' is explained in part by the heightened reflexivity of consumers (in relation to both product quality and production/process methods) and in part by reactions to repeated food scares in the 1990s (BSE, e-coli, salmonella).

In particular, labels of origin and growing consumer demand for products that carry them have been taken as an indication of the emergence of a new rural development paradigm (Marsden, Banks and Bristow 2000; Murdoch, Marsden and Banks 2000; Ploeg and Renting 2000). In marked contrast to the literature on commodity fetishism, these authors argue that there has been an improvement in true transparency in agro-food networks. Murdoch, Marsden and Banks (2000), for example, argue that quality is coming to be seen as inherent in more local and natural foods, thus that 'quality food production systems are being reembedded in local ecologies' (2000: 103), and that the quality turn is leading to the reassertion of nature over capital.

We, along with others, question how beneficial AAFNs and short networks/value chains are for producers and for social justice, even within developed countries (Goodman 2003: 3; and other contributions in the same issue). Allen et al. (2003) argue that reference to locality does not necessarily entail environmental and/or social objectives, nor the germination of oppositional challenges. They assert that silence about social relations in alternative food initiatives in California (and elsewhere) indicates that rural communities and family farmers do no necessarily embody social justice (Allen et al. 2003: 74). Goodman suggests that the AAFN literature neglects 'social processes and relations of power that produce, reproduce and restructure the scale of the local ... [L]ocal embeddedness of economic forms [does not preclude] exploitation' (Goodman 2004: 5). He also highlights that it is important to assess the durability and magnitude of income flows deriving from AAFNs (2004: 8) and the location of the actors who capture them (see Chapter 5).

The threats to locality (as a way to improve returns to producers) come from at least two sources. First, the growth of products claiming territorial identity (without regulatory protection as in the AOC system, see below) has triggered corporate responses, such as requirements of traceability, Hazard Analysis and Critical Control Point (HACCP), other quality assurance protocols, sourcing and labelling of local foods, and own-label territorial identity foods. These put pressure on margins downwards, and tend to shift economic rents away from the farm (Goodman 2004: 9). Second, the sourcing strategies of AAFNs that have expanded beyond locality tend to resemble the ones adopted by large corporate actors (like Starbucks) – partly because of scale-related standardization of operations, and partly as a result of downward pressures on margins by industrial imitators (see the example of Parmigiano Reggiano in Roest and Menghi 2000). As supply chains are extended, the relational connections that are typical of short chains are more difficult to reproduce.

In short, 'strategic imitation and convergence on the modalities used to represent territorial identities raise the very real prospect that quality differentiation by AAFNs will be trivialized and economic rents redistributed from the farm level and other local actors' (Goodman 2004: 9–10; see also Neilson 2004). We argue that these challenges are even more pronounced in naturally long value chains such as coffee, and (below) that territoriality/*terroir* as a symbolic quality attribute is profitable to the producer only when a regulatory framework sustains it. We draw from the organization of the wine industry in Europe (specifically in France and Italy) to understand the advantages and limitations of exporting this model to commodity production in developing countries.

Barham argues that increasing demand for *terroir*-related products in Europe comes from a rediscovery of the sense of history and authenticity (a contested terrain) as part of an 'ongoing construction of a collective representation of the past through food that is perhaps largely unconscious for consumers' (Barham 2003: 132). However, at the same time, she questions the general applicability of labels of origin as an engine of rural development by underlining that different ways of technically organizing these labels have different outcomes, especially in relation to whether the state is the protector, monitor and administrator of the system (as in the AOC system in France and the Denominazione di Origine Controllata (DOC) system in Italy). Barham (*ibid.*) claims that, ultimately, geographical appellations (labels of origin that enjoy state protection) challenge conventional agricultural practice with their reference to place or *terroir*. They also provide the means for rural development that empowers producers and more marginalized areas. Barham's approach, although providing a more realistic path towards solving the commodity problem than the one outlined in the more populist literature on locality, still obscures several problems.

First, the AOC system in France is being challenged by the labelling strategies (based on brand names and grape varieties) of New World wine producers. Second, the French AOC system is dependent on a specific institutional tradition that includes producers, producer associations, processers, traders, regional state administrations, national government and the EU itself. These may be important limiting factors for the possible success of this system elsewhere. Third, AOC labels, and IGOs more generally, as symbolic mediators of quality, attempt to conserve the histories of people and place, but in extending material and symbolic exchanges between worldwide consumers and situated *terroir,* they incur a loss of direct presence through processes of abstraction (Goodman 2004: 10). This could lead to 'label fatigue' and a process of 'competitive territoriality'. Fourth, AOC systems can be subjected to internal fraud (for example, wine produced outside an appellation area may be imported and mixed/relabelled). Finally, some observers argue that the AOC system itself privileges prestigious producers and areas over others. For Moran (1993), the AOC system is a form of territorialization that favours Burgundy, Bordeaux and Champagne producers over the 'industrial' producers of the Midi. It also places restrictions on the use of grape varieties and on cultural practices that tend to crystallize a certain structural distribution of benefits. In other words, powerful actors can appropriate quality through geographical association in ways that marginalize smaller, traditional producers (Ilbery and Kneafsey 1999). Because actors in networks of producers, consumers and institutions engage in processes of representation of quality, '[t]he outcome of the process of [contested] representation will be the empowerment of some networks and the disempowerment of others' (*ibid.* 2218).

With specific reference to coffee value chains, trademarks and IGOs compete in influencing the opinion of consumers. Both can be used to qualify the final product: roast and ground coffee. Unlike wine production, coffee value chains are characterized by the geographical disintegration of the transformation process. Mainstream roasters do not have any link to a specific coffee *terroir* – quite the contrary. To be able to produce a distinctive and stable taste, roasters must be able to blend coffees coming from different origins. The acknowledgment and valorization of any IGO by the consumer adds a constraint, unless this origin offers a sufficient diversity of taste profiles, which is by definition contrary to the IGO project.

Despite these cautionary notes, we argue that IGO systems could be helpful in solving the commodity problem as posited in this book. IGO systems can be designed to: (1) facilitate the enforcement of intellectual property rights in relation to geographical indications of origin and truth in labelling; (2) promote regional or country-specific recognition; (3) build consumer trust and loyalty; and (4) improve and maintain quality.

In terms of the possibility of exporting the AOC system to other products and institutional situations, a study conducted by Barjolle and Sylvander (2000; 2002) sheds some light on requirements for the development of IGOs in finding that:

- The nature of the product is not particularly important in determining the success of an IGO (2002: 16).
- 'The country of origin is of some (but not overwhelming) importance' (ibid.: 16). An IGO can be promoted in countries without a tradition for such initiatives.
- A high number of firms in the supply chain is not a constraint on coordination efforts;
- Product specificity and market relevance are important for success, but an even more influential factor is coordination betweens firms.[13] Coordination is facilitated where 'channel captains' exist (a single or few processors dominating the supply chain, for example).
- Success depends on the capacity of firms to collectively set objectives in relation to territorial and sectoral governance on the basis of their individual competences (technology, know-how, strategic management, innovation). It also depends on the capacity to ensure compliance with the basic rules of the system, coupled with the capacity to maintain some flexibility so that 'each operator can be involved in the project while developing its own strategy' (ibid.: 17).

Contrary to generic certifications and labels applied to environmental protection and social conditions of production (which signal how a commodity has been produced), IGOs (and related labels) can also link responsible practices to specific places – although not necessarily so. In the coffee industry, the process of IGO development is at its early stage. In general, IGO areas have been defined by pre-existing boundaries, such as a town or district, or have been created specifically for a new IGO. Coffee IGOs have been developed for 'Jamaica Blue Mountain' and '100 per cent Colombian Coffee', and are under formulation in Kona (Hawaii), Antigua (Guatemala), Veracruz (Mexico),

Peru and Uganda. There are two basic ways of developing an IGO system. A more exclusive one (AOC in wine, Jamaica Blue Mountain in coffee) is to require a set of minimum standards for inclusion. This means that even though a farm is physically located within the IGO boundaries, it may qualify for an IGO only if it matches a certain plant variety, a certain processing method, or a minimum quality standard. A second, and more inclusive, system is one that simply defines and legally recognizes areas (the South African Wine of Origin and American Viticulture Area systems in wine, 100% Colombia in coffee). However, hybrid situations could also be developed, where stricter sub-IGOs are developed within a generic IGO (such as Napa Valley in California).[14] The general rule of thumb is the greater the detail, the more interesting the story, the higher the entry barrier.

The process of IGO development (especially the promotion and registration of marks in consuming countries) is expensive, and requires technical assistance and/or financial aid at various points. However, the gains for producers can be substantial. Specialty buyers are likely to pay higher prices in exchange for the warranty that a particular coffee comes from a specific geographical origin. When IGO systems are run by producer organizations, they make for good stories of cooperation. These stories, and the exotic aspects that are embedded in them, help the roaster/retailer to add value to the coffee. The guarantee of intellectual property rights helps channelling parts of this value back to the producer.

IGO systems can also be engineered to cater to the needs of smallholders, especially in the more inclusive versions.[15] Boundaries can be set to cover mainly smallholder-based producing areas. An additional step that could be taken is one of adding social and environmental concerns to IGO systems, so that civic concerns are tied to specific places. Finally, state support and enforcement of IGOs can avert private appropriation of geographical origin (as in the case of the exclusive use of the coffee label 'Toraja' granted to a Japanese firm – see Neilson 2004). Regulation is also needed to avoid misuse of the system by unscrupulous actors.[16]

In short, social and environmental concerns should be blended with IGO systems supported (or approved/monitored) by the state. With this combination, locality can be held responsible for possible exploitative practices, while at the same time generic socio-economic and environmental responsibility practices can be attached to a place. In other words, both producer and consumers can be held accountable for their actions in relation to a particular place (see also Barham 2003). In order for this to work, regulation needs to be used to transform local knowledge into property.[17]

IGO protection requires first of all the existence of a national regulatory framework. According to the Trade-Related Intellectual Property Rights (TRIPS) agreement (Article 24.9), 'There shall be no obligation under this Agreement to protect geographical indications which are not or cease to be protected in their country of origin, or which have fallen into disuse in that country.' Currently more than 60 countries have elaborated such regulatory frameworks but many coffee-producing countries have not.

The protection offered by TRIPs for all products (see Chapter 1) allows the use of an IGO if some other indication informs the consumer of the real origin of the product. For example, Antigua coffee produced in São Paulo could be sold by adding 'made in Brazil' to the label. Moreover, when producer organizations want to defend an IGO, they must prove that the consumer has been misled by the enterprise (not located in the region covered by the IGO) that has used the geographical indication.

An important issue for coffee IGOs is the possibility of extending the TRIPs agreement that provides additional protection for wines and spirits (Article 23) (Addor and Grazioli 2002). For these products, IGOs are protected whatever the risk of misleading the consumer. It means that the use of expressions such as 'kind', 'type', 'style', and 'imitation' on the label is prohibited, even when the true origin is indicated. Article 23 also prohibits the use of trademarks which contain or consist of an IGO identifying wines and spirits for those not produced in the indicated origin. With such an extension of Article 23, a designation like 'Antigua-style coffee, produced in Brazil' would be prohibited. The use of Antigua as a trademark would also be prohibited.

As part of current WTO negotiations, the EU has proposed such an extension of Article 23 to other products. The EU proposal also includes the elaboration of a register listing IGOs protected across international bodies. Several countries have opposed this proposal, mostly countries with a history of European immigration (such as Argentina, New Zealand, Australia or the United States) where local agricultural products have been named after European IGOs. In October 2003, the Dispute Settlement Body of the WTO agreed to study the EU rules on IGOs at the request of Australia and the US. But even in the US some are now arguing in favour of a reinforced international regulatory framework (Babcock and Clemens 2004). Actually, IGOs are viewed as a solution in many countries where agricultural policy reform is eliminating historical protection and financial support to farmers. This could be deftly turned around to benefit developing countries as well (see Chapter 7).

Agents of change? The politics of consumption and the role of retailers

The fourth dimension of solving the commodity problem is one of agency. More specifically: (1) How can civil society actors, intermediaries (traders, agents), service providers (logistics, finance providers), the agro-food industry, retailers, mediators of taste (like celebrity cooks or lifestyle consultants), consumer associations and individual consumers promote the processes of changing quality conventions, enhancing producer–consumer connectivity and developing IGO systems? (2) How could these processes be made to work for the benefit of commodity producers – that is, how can additional symbolic (and in-person service where applicable) quality attributes generate better returns to small farmers/producers in developing countries? (3) Can this be achieved with progressive change within mainstream channels, or does it necessitate a radical break with established power dynamics in global value chains?

Overall, these questions beg reflection upon market structures, business strategies of major corporations, and regulation. They also require a return to convention theory's preoccupation with how certain justificatory regimes of action come into place, how they are tested and legitimized, and how they succumb to – or absorb challenges from – other ways of doing things that are linked to different value frames.

The material presented in this book shows that, in the current situation, coffee farmers are being paid low prices for the coffee they produce – as a result of oversupply, production innovations in Brazil and Vietnam, oligopolistic markets at the roasting level, and the appropriation of symbolic and in-person service quality attributes in consuming countries. The mainstream retail market is characterized by low-quality blends offered under brand names. Higher-quality coffee supplied through the specialty markets does not necessarily translate into higher farm-gate prices, unless it is bought directly from the farm (or, more likely, the large estate). Geographical origin coffees are still a very small niche market. Sustainable coffees, with some exceptions, do not provide substantial extra income to farmers. In most coffee value chains, farmers are getting smaller proportions of the final consumption price. In the last section, we have sketched an approach to addressing this situation that combines regulation on geographical origins, intellectual property rights, and environmental and socio-economic concerns. This approach should also assure premiums at the farm level.

This is all fine on paper. However, no change can be imposed from the production side alone. Other actors have to be involved in promoting changes in practices and related quality conventions. In this section, we explore the complex web of representations of consumer interests to explore the role of consumers vis-à-vis (or in addition to) political action stimulated by NGOs. We also examine the possibility of cooperation and/or resistance by mainstream retailers and roasters. We start from the point of view that consumption is not a mechanical response to social manipulation, nor is it the result of a universal desire for whatever objects happen to be available (Appadurai 1986; Douglas and Isherwood 1981). Because quality is constantly renegotiated, powerful actors (including roasters and retailers) can appropriate the term to their own advantage. '[S]upermarkets . . . [are not just] places where people buy and attach meanings to food but also firms that profit … from their role as protectors of "consuming interests"' (Freidberg 2003a: 5).

The 1990s witnessed a surging interest in how retailers govern agro-food networks and in how they influence consumption patterns. Wrigley and Marsden (1996) argue that retailers have achieved not only economic, but also political power in the UK – as the state has delegated responsibilities over managing and policing the food provisioning system to them. Retailers have also delivered new 'rights to consume' to newly empowered consumer groups, and have defined consumption interests around their own notions (Marsden and Arce 1995). Once such rights (for example, the right to new exotic food products) are released to a widening group of consumers, they can rarely be retracted afterwards (ibid.).

Arce and Marsden (1993) suggest that speaking for consumers is one of the ways in which retailers attempt to portray demand in a way that benefits their interest in competition with other actors. Yet they alone cannot succeed in changing consumption patterns. Consumer associations demand safer and better quality produce. New socio-cultural perceptions of nature arise. These are linked to the rise of the environmental agenda, the importance of diet and health (partly as a result of food scares), new ways of consuming nature and place (tourism, exotic places), and representations of lifestyle.

Similarly, the literature on the geographies of consumption (Jackson and Thrift 1995; Wrigley and Lowe 1996) emphasizes that consumers are not passive targets of advertising. They are 'knowing agents actively constructing consumption, as well as being constructed by it' (Hartwick 1998: 424). Hughes (2000), in her work on the cut flower trade from Kenya to the UK, argues that retailers use 'knowledges' circulating at different points in the network to reshape the relationships between these points to their advantage (Hughes 2000: 183). At one level, one may think that knowledge of consumers is constructed through market research and translated into representations that are used to manipulate the flower production process. Yet, there are more agents that construct these representations in the network than just retailers. Innovations in bouquet design are often generated through dialogue with top-level designers and florists; they are spread through lifestyle magazines and programmes, and negotiated with consumers via consumer surveys and focus groups. This makes it difficult to discern who spearheads innovation, although it seems to be clear that retailers can manipulate these knowledges to their advantage. On this last point, Lockie (2002) argues that the consumer is made governable and knowable through the application of technologies of knowledge – such as market research, survey data and point-of-sale record keeping. He shows, for example, that the people most likely to be stereotyped as 'organic consumers' by retailers are those best placed to consume the products that give retailers the highest margins.

According to Callon, Méadel and Rabehariosa (2002), one of the main concerns of retailers is to prompt consumers to question their preferences and, indirectly, their identities. Thus, they try to steer spontaneous and gradual processes of qualification and requalification of products to their advantage. They do so, *inter alia*, by setting up forms of organization promoting collaboration between suppliers and consumers in the qualification of products. In this way, competition can be thought of as turning on 'the attachment of consumers to products whose qualities have progressively been defined with their active participation' (*ibid.*: 212). In other words, consumption is influenced through the 'formatting of socio-technical devices [such as advertising, shelf positioning, presentation of products, focus groups, evaluation forms, point-of-sale data] which, distributing and redistributing the material bases of cognition, format the bases of calculation and preferences' (*ibid.*: 213). These processes of explicit and implicit collaboration between economic agents are said to apply to material products and service provision alike, but to be functioning more strongly in the services sector, where the mechanisms of 'singularization' and (re)qualification can be operated on a more continuous basis.

For the purposes of this book, the arguments summarized so far suggest that consumers are active agents, along with others, in formulating how the qualification of products should occur – and therefore in the governance of global value chains. At the same time, it is suggested that consumer preferences can be manipulated by other agents to the advantage of the latter. Wilkinson (2002: 340), for example, shows how 'functional foods' have been developed 'in a climate of constant opposition from consumer associations, [which means that] leading agrofood players are committed to imposing strategies that fly in the face of a "demand-oriented food system"'. The apparent paradox is the development and marketing of products that are unwanted by consumers but are nevertheless based on marketing strategies depending on consumer dialogue.

One interpretation of these complexities is that consumers can be enrolled in processes of social change, but that mainstream retailers (and roasters in the case of coffee) will not be the initiators of these processes. This is clearly the case in the mainstream coffee industry, which has embraced different quality conventions only when it perceived a serious threat from alternative conventions (in relation to the growth of specialty markets, for example). The opening up to different conventions, however, seems to be coming full circle in the process of mainstreaming, both in the specialty and sustainable coffees industries. Similarly, Guthman's work on organic agriculture in California (2002; 2003) attests to this in a developed country context. She documents a growing 'disjuncture between representations of organic agriculture and the political economy of organic food provision' (2002: 295), in particular how the market growth of organic produce has transformed the meaning of organic, the structure of the value chain and the distribution of value along it. She argues that, rather than representing a paradigmatic shift in food consumption, contemporary organic agriculture suffers from some of the very problems implicated in industrial agricultural methods and related exploitative labour relations (Guthman 2003).

So, if consumers alone will not bring social change, if retailers will try to mainstream efforts to initiate it, and if alternative agro-food networks do not necessarily work in that respect, what else is left? Hartwick suggests that a 'politics of reconnection' may facilitate the use of information about the sites of production and exchange to make consumers agents of social transformation (1998: 433). She sees this new politics of consumption as a complex undertaking involving a variety of actors: consumers, consumer associations, cultural critics, media activists, unions, women's groups, NGOs, churches and civil rights organizations (Hartwick 1998: 423). Citing Kaplan's (1995) work on the Body Shop, she underlines that 'an entrepreneurial consumption politics of "profit with principles" enables endless diversion and self-glorification' (ibid.). Drawing from work on consumption campaigns against fur, she stresses how 'self-righteous organizations assert the right to speak for silent others' (Hartwick 1998: 433). Yet her own work on gold and jewellery suggests that consumers seem to be the most silent actors, while other groups are far from silent. She concludes that the 'problem is more one of connecting and joining ongoing struggles, rather than a politics of speaking for others' (ibid.). She advocates a politics of consumption that is not media-driven and diversionary or fragmentary, but one that joins actors involved in consumption, representation, distribution, production and reproduction in political networks and alliances (Hartwick 1998: 434).

What can be gathered from Hartwick's approach (but also in Crewe 2000; and Freidberg 2003c) is that retailers and brand owners are susceptible to NGO pressure, bad press, and consumer action backlash, and that alliances with other groups can empower consumer politics and resistance. Thus action is possible, but it is complex. It has to be taken in a variety of fora and through a variety of actors. It involves the transformation of quality conventions and reference frameworks. It is 'voting with your dollar' but also media campaigns and boycotts. It entails material and mental change. It involves producer associations. It acts through different mechanisms, from lifestyle messages to good old regulation. We explore these possibilities in the next chapter.

Notes

1 We mention both 'value addition' and 'rent extraction' here to underline that value added by branding or selling other symbolic quality attributes (and in-person services) may also generate rents, especially in oligopolistic situations. This implies that the value added itself may not explain the entirety of the net profits that value chain actors in consuming countries obtain. However, this does not mean that rent extraction and value creation are two distinct components of consumer prices. In this book, we argue that final prices and value are determined by the consumer's evaluation of the quality attributes of a good. This evaluation is socially constructed (there are no exogenous preferences), but also depends on the competences and capabilities of consumers (in particular, the ability of measuring some material attributes and appreciating/interpreting symbols and their meanings). Thus creation of value can support the extraction of rent, but consumer price is not the sum of value added plus rent. For the sake of brevity, in the rest of our discussion we use exclusively the terminology 'value addition' or 'value creation'.

2 Talbot (1997a: 63) defines the total income generated along the coffee chain as 'equal to the total amount of money spent by consumers to purchase coffee products for final consumption'.

3 The remaining shares of total coffee income are: (1) transport costs and weight losses; and (2) value added in producing countries.

4 Talbot's (1997a) calculations are based on weighted average prices for all ICO member countries at various nodes of the chain.

5 Green coffee import prices were calculated using FAO data and by dividing the value of green coffee imports by the volume of imports. The gross margin is the difference between the average consumer price for roasted coffee, provided by the US Department of Labor, and the import price – taking into account the transformation ratio of 0.8 between green and roasted coffee (one pound of green coffee will yield, after roasting, 0.8 pounds of roasted coffee). The gross margin does not measure the profit generated by coffee for roasters and retailers, but evaluates the value created in the part of the coffee value chain located in the US.

6   The estimate of the proportion of the final price paid to the farmer based on a 100 per cent Robusta blend coming from Uganda and a cheaper origin (Vietnam, for example) would be lower because the final price would be the same, but the cost of the raw material would be lower.

7   It is a bit higher in Tanzania in 1999/2000 than in Uganda in 2001/2002, probably because international prices were higher at that time, while retail prices did not change substantially. There may also be an exchange rate factor involved. Tanzanian and Ugandan Robusta are very similar in quality. As a matter of fact, international traders often treat the two origins as one.

8   Fitter and Kaplinsky (2001) argue that coffee product and price differentiation at the retail level in UK supermarkets does not trickle down to farmers. As a matter of fact, they show that the spread of coffee prices, which has increased at the retail level, has actually fallen in international trade. What this means is that roasters are buying a more homogeneous product (at least in the mainstream market) and differentiate their offering through product proliferation.

9   As explained above, these are blends and single origins that may not represent real retail offerings, but are examined as approximations.

10 However, caution should be exercised in directly comparing the two figures, owing to differences in method. Talbot (1997a) groups weight losses in a separate category (together with transport costs). We provide unit prices for roasted equivalent weight at all levels, thus evening out the weight losses along the chain.

11 We owe these insights to Peter Gibbon.

12 For more details, see Ponte (2004). On the mythology of the smallholder see also Freidberg's (2003c; 2004) discussion of out-grower schemes in Zambian horticulture, where the members of the schemes are part of the Zambian professional and bureaucratic elite, and rely on hired labour.

13 In a separate study, Réviron, Chappuis and Barjolle (2003) also emphasize the importance of coordination and the 'vertical alliances' involved in PDO/PGI value chains. These vertical alliances put together operators acting at several levels of the supply chain. The Gruyère value chain is a good example of such a vertical alliance. A general assembly and a committee gathering representatives of milk producers, cheese makers and cheese ripeners direct the Interprofession du Gruyère. The Interprofession du Gruyère assumes a large number of functions: 'quality control of the product with respect to its code of practice, information and advice to the enterprises, collective promotion of the designation "Gruyère", research and development, development of a standard contract between cheese makers and ripeners, arbitration between members of the *interprofession,*

management of volumes and fixing of internal indicatory prices within the supply chain' (*ibid*: 3).

14 Mike Ferguson, 'Uncharted Territory: Exploring the Possibility of Specialty Coffee Appellations', www.scaa.org/stories.cfm?st2=stories/ 110501.cfm

15 If minimum quality requirements are set in IGO systems, relatively well-connected farmers and those who have access to technical assistance or extension may benefit more than more marginalized farmers – even within the same smallholder category.

16 Efforts in developing appellation programmes, together with certification and trademark registration in consuming countries, gained momentum in the coffee industry following the so-called 'Kona scandal'. In 2000, Michael L. Norton of Berkeley (California) was indicted by a US federal grand jury on account of fraud. He sold coffee as '100 per cent pure Kona' (from Hawaii), while about 87 per cent was found to be much cheaper coffee from Central America (see Stuart Adelson, 'Justice for Java: An Update on the Kona Coffee Fraud', http://www.scaa.org/stories.cfm? st2=stories/ 032001.cfm).

17 Techniques that are being developed to implant a genetic marking in agro-food products could facilitate this process through assuring the traceability of a product not exclusively for the sake of food safety risk minimization, but also (and mainly) for guaranteeing geographical intellectual property rights to producers.

7
A way forward

Governance and the coffee paradox

The global value chain for coffee is characterized by a paradox: a coffee crisis in producing countries, with international prices at the lowest levels in decades, and a coffee renaissance (also known as the *latte* revolution) in consuming countries, with the growth of specialty and sustainable coffee consumption and the fast expansion of coffee bar chains. This paradox exists because farmers and other producing country operators sell coffee in its material quality attributes. Consuming country operators create and appropriate value by selling the symbolic and in-person service quality attributes of coffee. Under the international regulation system managed by the International Coffee Organization (ICO) up to the late 1980s, selling material quality attributes was enough to guarantee to producing countries a fair share of the value of the coffee sold to the consumers. This is no longer the case.

The present crisis faced by coffee farmers and producing countries is not simply one of overproduction, but one relating to changes in the governance structure of the global value chain for coffee, including the ownership of stocks (see Chapter 3). Previous to the end of the International Coffee Agreement (ICA) regime in 1989, producing countries had some influence in the governance of the global value chain for coffee. Entry barriers in farming and in domestic trade were often mediated by governments and producer organizations. Governments also managed quality control systems and set quality standards to apply at the export level. In the consuming country segment of the value chain, roasters were increasing their leading role through branding, advertising and consolidation. Yet their control of the global value chain was limited by the quota system and government control of exports and stocks in producing countries.

In contrast, the post-ICA regime exhibits many of the characteristics of an explicitly buyer-driven chain – a roaster-driven one, to be more precise. The bargaining power of operators based in consuming countries now allows them to dominate actors in producing countries, especially farmers and their governments. Strategic choices made by roasters in the last decade or so have shaped the terms of participation in the value chain not only in the roaster segment, but also in other segments upstream (closer to the producer). Their outsourcing of supply management to international traders means that stocks are more readily available, leading to a previously unknown situation of low levels of stocks and low international prices. Meanwhile, a substantial proportion of total income generated in the coffee chain has been transferred from farmers to consuming-country operators.

The institutional framework of the global value chain for coffee has moved away from a public-controlled system where producers had a substantial say towards one that is more private and buyer-dominated. Fewer players control the bulk of the international trade and roasting segments of the chain, although some market segmentation has taken place, especially in the US with the emergence of the specialty coffee industry. Consolidation of the industry has taken place at the roasting and international trade levels. In producing countries, coffee state agencies have been reformed or suppressed and local actors have either allied themselves with international traders or disappeared. In most cases, they are losing control of processing, domestic trade and export functions. Further consolidation seems inevitable throughout the industry. Smallholder farmers, however, do not have easy consoli-dation options. Their cooperatives find it difficult to compete with local subsidiaries of international trading firms. As governments retreated from the regulation of domestic coffee markets, farmer organizations lost a political forum of negotiation. Under these con-ditions, even a supply shortage is unlikely to lead to price increases of the magnitude experienced in the past. In the coffee paradox, producers end up on the losing side of things.

These observations should not be interpreted in ways that place the blame exclusively on the shoulders of large roasting companies. In a way, these roasters have been playing according to the current rules of the game and the conventions that underpin them. And for those companies that are quoted on stock markets, this means above all maximizing shareholder value (see Gibbon and Ponte 2005). These rules of the game (and the governance structure that ensues from them) crystallized with the advent of a broad neoliberal project starting in the 1980s. International institutions, such as the World Bank and the IMF, spent that decade and a large part of the 1990s advising governments in the South to extricate themselves from their economies and permit market liberalization in their agricultural sectors (Ponte 2002d). As a result, governments in the South to a large extent were forced to step out of input, credit and service provision to farmers and from stock management. Indeed, some of the pre-liberalization marketing systems were marred by corruption and incompetence. Many state-controlled cooperatives operated on the basis of political patronage rather than in the interests of their members. The liberalizers had no shortage of ready-to-hand examples to justify their claims. Some producing countries under the ICA system adopted beggar-thy-neighbour strategies − and even during the current coffee crisis the blame game among ICO members (particularly against Vietnam) has been more evident than efforts of cooperation that could result in feasible supply management solutions. Meanwhile, governments in the North abandoned the idea of supply management in the tropical commodities sector, while subsidizing and tightly regulating agricultural markets at home. Evidently, we cannot blame roasters alone for the plight of coffee farmers.

There are indications that the rules of the game may be changing. WTO negotiations have been the focus of calls to end protectionism in the North. While these calls are ironically based on some of the tenets of neoliberalism, they do differentiate between instruments that should be used in the North and those that are appropriate in the South, and seek to justify protectionism and subsidization in the latter on the basis of the principle of 'special and differentiated treatment'. In the coffee industry, civil society groups have been mounting campaigns against large roasters to sway consumers and public opinion against them. Because brands are vulnerable to image damage through these actions, these companies had to take corrective measures, even if only cosmetically. The emergence of specialty and sustainable coffees and their subsequent mainstreaming may also be undermining the current governance system and the conventions that sustain it. These initiatives have facilitated a change in ideas of what content should be valued in coffee among an increasing number of consumers. They appear to support more direct relationships between producers and consumers, a better flow of information on markets and prices, and increasing customer demand for 'sustainability' and/or 'territoriality'. When sustainability and other premiums are paid, they improve the distribution of value in coffee chains to the advantage of producers, at least in comparison to mainstream coffees. Including producers in the standard-setting process provides a more equitable forum for governing relations and activities along the value chain.

Yet the best initiative currently available (fair trade) manages to return between 12 and 21 per cent of the final coffee price to producer cooperatives, depending on the specific value chain analysed. In the first place, this level is broadly similar to the one achieved by farmers in the mainstream market before the coffee crisis. In the second place, it is similar to what farmers achieved in the mainstream market under the ICA system in the 1970s and 1980s. Obviously, the development impact of these initiatives (real and potential) derives not only from higher prices for coffee, but also from the possibility of strengthening producer organizations and related outputs – service provision, forging of new trading contacts, creation of economies of scale, and so on. But only the older sustainability initiatives (fair trade and organics in particular) have proved relatively successful in these terms. Thus copycat strategies developed by mainstream industry actors, who are trying to achieve recognition while minimizing costs, endanger the potentially positive outcomes of sustainability initiatives – not only in terms of payment of premiums to farmers and the opportunity to get better prices at the consumer level, but also in terms of development prospects more broadly. In a sense, mainstream roasters want to be seen to be playing by what could become the new rules of the game, while subverting their intended objectives.

The end of regulation as we know it

Can regulation as we know it help to re-establish a fairer coffee regime to the advantage of farmers and their organizations? Can it solve the commodity problem more generally? In the last few years, there has been renewed interest in promoting supply management in tropical commodity markets (see, among others, Robbins 2003). Although we are broadly sympathetic towards this project, we also realize that the record of attempted supply management through regulation in the coffee market in the post-ICA era is not encouraging. Since the end of the ICA regime in 1989, the ICO has kept a relatively low regulatory profile. While this may have been justified in the mid-1990s in view of the high international coffee prices of 1994/5 and 1997, the advent of the so-called coffee crisis since 1999 has reinvigorated the debate on the role of regulation in international coffee markets. At the same time, coffee-producing countries are slowly realizing that a revival of the ICA system with quotas and price bands does not seem to be possible in the short term. There is no public or political support for quotas in consuming countries nor – with the end of the Cold War – is there a foreign policy reason for it. Although in February 2005 the US rejoined the ICO, this does not entail support for the re-establishment of a quota system.

Retention schemes through producer cartels, such as the efforts organized by the now-defunct Association of Coffee Producing Countries (ACPC), have not been able to influence markets in the presence of an excess of supply, the absence of state agencies able to control exports and organize storage, and high levels of market concentration at the level of international trade and roasting. Another example of failure to revamp international commodity agreements more generally is the Common Fund for Commodities (CFC), which was negotiated within UNCTAD from 1976 to 1980 and became effective in 1989. CFC's original mandate was mainly to facilitate the conclusion and functioning of commodity agreements of particular interest to developing countries, to finance international buffer stocks, and to coordinate national stocks internationally. This never took place. The CFC's current mandate is instead 'to enhance the socio-economic development of commodity producers and contribute to the development of society as a whole. In line with its market-oriented approach, the Fund concentrates on commodity development projects' (http://www.common-fund.org).

A regulatory option that has been proposed in the coffee sector is the establishment of quotas on production. In theory, this could be an easier solution than the re-establishment of ICAs, but it is the opposite of what governments have been promoting in the past in their own countries – that is, higher rather than lower production. This option also fails to take into account the current ability of governments or industry associations in producing countries to monitor and control coffee cultivation at the field level effectively following market liberalization. In most academic and policy circles, even more critical ones, it is increasingly accepted that a return to the domestic regulatory systems based on marketing boards and stabilization funds would be extremely difficult to achieve – given the systematic and donor-enforced retreat of state action in these realms and the related weakening of producer organizations.

The closest the ICO has come to reasserting its regulatory power has been through the Coffee Quality Improvement Programme (CQP). In September 2001, the ICO established a Quality Committee with a mandate to recommend standards and procedures for the withdrawal from the market of low-quality coffee. This committee, comprising twelve experts from exporting and importing members, together with private sector representatives, formulated recommendations that were adopted by the ICO in February 2002 under Resolution 407. Resolution 407 established the CQP and spelled out the minimum standards for exportable coffee based on defect count and maximum moisture content. A higher defect count was allowed for Robusta than for Arabica. The wording of the resolution implied binding standards that were to be followed by ICO exporting members and monitored by importing members. The original formulation implied that exporting members were expected to develop and implement national measures ensuring compliance with these standards. This would have been a particularly important change in those countries that do not have mandatory quality control procedures for coffee exports. Finally, the resolution mandated that coffee that was not exportable would have to be used for non-human consumption purposes.

The short-term goal of the programme was to reduce the supply of exportable coffee, thereby increasing prices. In the longer term, the programme aimed at raising the overall quality of coffee exports. However, it was never clear what mechanisms would be used to compensate countries and farmers likely to be affected by the programme. The programme found support from some consuming-country governments and private sector operators, but the ICO encountered problems in ensuring compliance by producing countries. It did not take into account that public management of quality control had disappeared in many countries after liberalization. The programme also faced strong reluctance from the US, which was negotiating re-entry to the ICO after having left the organization in 1989. Reflecting these difficulties, and following a review of the impact of the first phase of the project, in May 2004 the ICO passed a new resolution (Resolution 420) that makes the CQP voluntary rather than mandatory. This means that all coffee passing the minimum quality test is labelled distinctively, but all coffees are exportable. In a sense, the CQP has lost its regulatory bite, and with it any chance to make a difference. This *realpolitik* outcome is the latest sign of the weakness of international regulation (outside the WTO), which may explain why, in February 2005, the US returned to the ICO.

Another way of addressing the plight of coffee farmers through old-style regulation is compensation for the macroeconomic impacts of price and terms of trade shocks. In the 1960s the IMF established the Compensatory Finance Facility and the Buffer Stock Financing Facility, which were both used extensively prior to the mid-1980s, especially by middle-income countries. Through STABEX (Stabilization of Export Earnings), the EU supported ACP countries with balance of payments problems resulting from commodity prices. Falling commodity prices in the early 1990s and the end of commodity agreements led to major resource disbursements and increased eligibility for assistance. The IMF facilities have hardly been used in the 1990s. STABEX ran into serious problems and in 1990–1 was able to pay out only 42 per cent of eligible claims. Repayment rates also collapsed. In 2000, with the signing of the Cotonou Agreement, the EU replaced STABEX with FLEX (the Flexibility Instrument), based on much more stringent criteria for eligibility and lower levels of compensation. After sharp criticism from ACP countries, rules were relaxed in 2004. Yet, even under the new rules compensatory levels are unlikely to reach the ones achieved under STABEX (DFID and ODI 2004; Gibbon 2004).

At the same time as old forms of regulation seem to offer only few and limited avenues of solution to the coffee crisis, and the commodity problem more broadly, new forms of international regulation are being vented in unorthodox policy and academic circles. Two of these relate to negotiations and debates taking place within the WTO calling for: (1) the elimination of producer subsidies in the North; and (2) global regulation against oligopolistic behaviour. The first point features prominently in the Doha Round trade negotiations and has found strong political support among civil society groups, many governments in the South, and some governments in the North as well (Oxfam 2004). Its implementation, however, will benefit mainly farmers in more advanced developing countries. Least-developed countries (LDCs) are starting to recognize that the benefits for them are limited, and that they can even incur losses (banana producers in the Caribbean and LDC sugar producers, for example, who in the past have benefited from preferential treatment by the EU) unless more advanced developing countries eliminate their subsidies as well. In relation to coffee, the subsidy issue is not relevant. Tariff escalation is more of an issue for producing countries, but mainly in relation to exports of instant coffee (chiefly, for Brazil). Exports of roasted coffee, given the shorter shelf life of this product and the general preference for blending various origins, are unlikely to increase dramatically, anyway.

Global regulation of oligopolistic behaviour (through competition or anti-trust regulation at the WTO level) has also been raised as a possible way of addressing unequal trade relations. As highlighted by Gibbon (2004), so far this approach has focused on a discussion of what changes would be necessary within the WTO to advance an international anti-trust agenda, rather than on identifying economic criteria that would measure the exercise of monopoly or monopsony power, or on exploring the legal basis for possible action. Gibbon argues that the little evidence available is based on the study of the relation of final prices to marginal costs, the magnitude of price transmission, and (as in this book) on the distribution of gross margins along value chains. However, national anti-trust laws are 'based mainly on observed evidence about (a limited range of) types of actions by individual firms and collusive behaviours, rather than on the structural characteristics of given markets' (*ibid.*: 22). Finally, even if anti-trust behaviour could be legally proved, there is still the problem of what kind of remedies would benefit developing country producers.

The most usual of these are fines collected by national authorities from companies found to have acted abusively. In the case of proposed mergers that can lead to a dominant market position, the most usual remedy is prohibition of the merger or (more frequently) actions ordered to dilute its effects. While there are possibilities to make orders for restitution/

compensation in relation to collusion between firms and abuse of dominant market position, these have been employed only rarely. (*Ibid.*)

Gibbon then argues that a better way of tackling oligopolistic behaviour may be to 'regulate opportunism' through transparency. We broadly agree with this perspective. However, we also think that deterrence and public relations damage to leading brands created by losing cases against an international anti-trust law could be effective in taming some of the abuse of oligopolistic positions.

In sum, regulation *per se* can still be an effective tool for twisting power relations in favour of farmers and their organizations. Some old-style regulatory tools could be readopted and adapted, such as partial re-regulation of marketing systems in producing countries on a case-by-case basis. Undoing 20 years of structural adjustment and market liberalization will not be an easy task. But even the World Bank, these days, advocates a stronger role for the state (see next section). Public forms of coordination (or the facilitation of private forms) could be re-established – especially in relation to quality control and quality-related pricing, provision of inputs and credit, and delivery of extension and research services.

But an exclusive focus on old-style regulation is out of place in the current historical context and the new governance structures in value chains for tropical commodities. Efforts should be directed towards developing new regulatory tools. Rules on transparency in product information and labelling (in the case of coffee, blend composition, proportions of Arabica and Robusta employed, countries of origin of coffee used in blends, and perhaps the proportion of final price paid to producers) and international anti-trust law are two promising avenues. Regulation would also be central in supporting the establishment of IGO systems in producing countries, and in defending these systems internationally through a legally binding WTO register of geographic indications that goes beyond wine and spirits.

Business and donors to the rescue?

Solutions to the commodity problem and the coffee crisis have been proposed on the basis of standpoints very different to regulation. At the other end of the spectrum, segments of the business world and more orthodox academics, policy makers and think tanks argue that the solution is embedded in the problem: oversupply causes low prices, uncompetitive farmers move out of the cultivation of a specific crop, supply decreases, and prices rise again. Less orthodox, but still market-based solutions have also been presented. In specific relation to coffee, according to TechnoServe (2003), the best three 'business solutions' for solving the coffee crisis are: (1) promoting consumption in producing countries and in emerging markets; (2) diversifying production; and (3) promoting specialty coffee.

The problem with promoting consumption in producing countries is that growth of consumption in Brazil in the last few decades is used as a successful example; yet, only Brazil and Ethiopia have a truly domestic coffee culture to build upon. Most other producing countries do not, nor do they have the resources that Brazil can muster. Emerging markets, with the exception of Eastern Europe and Russia, are traditionally tea-drinking. Also, it is not clear who would pay for generic promotion in these countries. Coffee producer organizations and industry associations are cash-strapped. Large roasters are the only ones with enough capital to invest in (brand-specific) promotion in these locations.

Diversification out of coffee cultivation is extremely difficult in some locations. Alternative crops may not be any more attractive in terms of price and returns to labour; they may not be agro-ecologically compatible (or may have serious environmental implications, especially in mountain areas); market structures and traders handling these crops may not be present. Also, cultural attachments to coffee cultivation are strong in many locations (Scholer 2004). Finally, diversification is hard to engineer: if alternative crops (or economic activities) were present, feasible, and culturally acceptable, producers would already have adopted them (and, to some extent, they have – coca leaf cultivation in Colombia, *khat* in Ethiopia, vanilla in Uganda).

The third TechnoServe solution, supporting specialty coffee, is broadly reasonable – given the changes in consumption patterns that have taken place in the last decade or so. The main cautionary note here is that, as we have shown in this book, specialty coffee (intended as high-quality) does not necessarily entail higher prices for better quality coffee at the farm gate (especially among smallholders), nor does it lead to the strengthening of producer organizations in the absence of other favourable factors.

In another evaluation of coffee markets, the World Bank came up with a series of policy suggestions that could be characterized as 'donor-oriented' (Lewin, Giovannucci and Varangis 2004). Refreshingly, the World Bank report recognizes the structural changes that have taken place in the coffee market in the last two decades, and the limitations of exclusively business-oriented solutions. Not surprisingly though, it steers away from regulatory solutions. In substance, the report provides a mild endorsement of 'differentiated coffee markets' (specialty and sustainable) with emphasis on market access rather than on premiums. It takes market liberalization as a given in producer countries and recommends that governments create the 'appropriate business environment'. Finally, it advocates that governments (through externally supported programmes) help producer organizations so that they can link up with buyers in the North and supply farmers with the services once provided by the state (research, extension, risk management, and marketing). This set of recommendations does not differ substantially from those presented in another major policy study carried out by Rabobank for the Dutch Ministry of Foreign Affairs (RIAS 2002), which additionally supported the ICO Coffee Quality Programme and the establishment of public–private partnerships.

Among the tools highlighted here, the World Bank has been particularly active in promoting price risk management in the last decade. This involves the use of a combination of 'put options', price insurance transactions and warehouse receipt-based finance. In this system, producers can buy price risk management instruments as part of wider arrangements with international traders and local credit institutions involving the sale of a crop and possibly the provision of inputs. Yet the International Task Force created by the World Bank in 1999 for this purpose has so far set up only two pilot schemes of this kind – covering a few thousand coffee producers in Uganda and Tanzania. As Gibbon (2004) argues, price risk management instruments may not be so popular among producers and their organizations for a variety of reasons: they cover for price and not volume risk; they cover a time period of only two years in theory, and often shorter than that in practice; they do not hedge commodity price premiums; their cost is high; and they require a high level of liquidity. For these reasons, it is

> only likely to be very large-scale, volume-secure, credit-worthy and globally oriented producers who will be able to make much use of such

markets, in the absence of subsidies, technical assistance, donor-brokered financial intermediation or all three.... As for the behaviour of 'real' commodity markets themselves, these instruments are broadly neutral. Their role is to reduce the effects of price volatility for individual actors, rather than to reduce volatility in aggregate. (*Ibid.*: 16)

The fundamental problem with the approaches summarized in this section is that they are, to a large extent, based on ignoring the role of power in determining the functioning of value chains. Prices at different nodes of a value chain are not exclusively determined by the volumes of demand and supply. They are also determined by oligopolistic behaviour, the ownership of stocks, and the actions of investment funds in futures markets. Furthermore, price discovery at various points of a value chain is based on what quality attributes can be discovered and assessed and by whom. The kind of measurement devices and the metrics used depend on the quality convention employed at that point, location and time. Conventions refer to different fundamental values (and related implicit and explicit rules of the game), utilize different measurement and testing devices, and are justified in different ways. Value chains are driven by powerful actors who, among other things, are actively involved in shaping these conventions. Without due consideration of these elements, the menu of solutions to the coffee crisis, or the commodity problem more broadly, will remain the same – old-style regulation, market-based solutions, and narrow donor projects.

What role for transparency?

In critical thinking on commodity trade, much faith has been placed upon the role of certifications and labels in providing more information to consumers and improved market access possibilities for producers. This approach is based on the premise that, provided with enough information, consumers would vote with their dollars and thus promote change in the way commodity trade is carried out. Yet, certifications and labels do not necessarily promote trading relations that are significantly different from those in mainstream trade. Transparency in certified coffees often operates only in one direction, providing more information to consumers. Farmers are unlikely to know any more about consumers' demands and preferences in these schemes. Also, certification and auditing can provide the means for mainstream and larger specialty roasters and retailers to outsource troubleshooting. These processes can provide low-cost conscience cleansing while not necessarily leading to better conditions for farmers. In the extreme case, certifications promote the creation of mythologies and double fetishism, where social relations behind commodity production are apparently unveiled, but in reality such relations are concealed through the commoditization of information about them.

Through certifications and auditing, powerful actors can hide their influence on trading networks. They also operate a subtle transfer of responsibility and surveillance activities – away from them and towards multi-stakeholder fora, auditors, certifiers, and accreditation agencies. In turn, the latter are not directly responsible for corporate behaviour; their job is to ensure that actual practices match the benchmarks defined in standards, protocols and codes of conduct. When producers are made participant (if not in practice, at least on paper) in the writing of codes and standards, they are enrolled in the formation of justificatory regimes that underpin quality conventions. Producer participation in the Common Code for the Coffee Community, for example, justifies the existence of the mainstream coffee market against the criticism levied against it from a socio-economic and environmental standpoint. Justificatory regimes are then validated through self-monitoring (from producer to retailer) and external verification.

In short, producers are made part of a process of qualification of a product that is supposed to be for their benefit, but rarely is. The process of participation is then part of an enrolment effort that allows powerful actors (international traders, roasters and retailers) to claim that they are speaking in the name of producers. These same actors also enrol consumers and civil society – through representation in multi-stakeholder fora and the use of consumer surveys and focus groups of dubious design. Finally, consumers are enrolled in 'self-governance' via decision making about buying the 'right' product – a process aided by labels and other product-sourcing information.

Our contention is that for consumer–producer connectivity to mean anything for smallholder farmers and farm workers in developing countries it has to be based on two-way transparency. Producers need to know what kind of symbolic attributes are to be embedded in 'quality', and how – whether through ideas, design, craft or culture;

and whether by invoking tradition, *terroir*, exotic places, agro-tourism, gastronomy, nature, or simple living. Systems of dual connectivity have to reward higher quality content with attractive remuneration or a premium for producers. This can be done by making sure that environmental, social, economic or hedonistic content is paid with minimum premiums at the farm level over products of similar material quality that do not embed this content. Producer organizations and supportive exporters can play a key role in transmitting this knowledge and in organizing transactions on this basis. Thus, these systems may also facilitate collective action and help farmers reap the benefits of aggregation in producer organizations. The most effective way to make this happen is to combine new content with 'place' through IGO systems guaranteed by regulation in producing countries and at the global level. This is one of the areas where regulation still has a substantial role to play.

This approach involves radical change in the functioning of trade networks, in consumption patterns and in the valuation of quality content. It requires a proactive change in quality conventions and in the related processes of justification and legitimization of action. In the rest of this chapter, we provide a series of ideas on policies and strategies that have either not been seriously considered in policy circles, or have received lower priority. These are built upon our focus on the coffee paradox rather than on the coffee crisis, and thus reflect the analytical and theoretical discussions carried on throughout this book. This also means that policies and strategies have to shift from an exclusive focus on the material attributes of coffee and towards coffee farmers' production of (and remuneration from) symbolic attributes and (where possible) in-person services.

Our agenda is also built upon the recognition that the separation between mainstream and specialty or niche solutions is misleading. First, sustainability initiatives are becoming mainstream. Second, the boundaries between mainstream and specialty are increasingly blurred. Third, condemning some solutions as good only for niche markets reflects lack of imagination: mainstream in two decades could well resemble niche today; but the fundamental decisions about how incentives work, what is fair and what is not, and how standards are designed are being taken now. In twenty years, it will be too late to undo the damage of decisions that affect farmers negatively, in the same way that it is too late now to undo much of the damage caused by market liberalization in agricultural sectors in the South. So, the reader should interpret the next section as a strategy that is not only about niche markets, but also about how mainstream markets could be working in the long term.

Policies and strategies: an alternative agenda

Improving sustainability certifications

Despite the criticism we have levelled at certifications and other initiatives on sustainable coffee, there are ways of making these initiatives appeal to consumers while simultaneously leading to substantive improvements in farmers' livelihoods and their participation in the setting of standards. In particular, we highlight the role that could be played by a Sustainable Coffee Cooperation Forum (SCCF).[1] This forum could be used for:

- promoting the discussion of sustainability standards in terms of their content and of their possible coordination, harmonization and/or equivalency;
- ensuring that the voices of producers (especially smallholders) are heard in relation to the appropriateness and the costs/benefits arising from such standards;
- coordinating efforts to raise funds for technical assistance;
- making sure that the extra efforts that are entailed in matching sustainability standards yield extra incomes to producers, rather than being an extra demand to be matched at the same price; a focus on market access rather than premiums delegitimizes calls for improved prices at the farm level;
- promoting mechanisms of cost minimization in certification, through multiple certifications, group auditing, accreditation of local certification agencies, and the development of internal control systems that are easy to administer;
- evaluating the best way of approaching public agencies in the process of development and enforcement of standards.

Furthermore, there are various ways of promoting cooperation among individual certification initiatives with the goal of increasing the coverage of sustainability in the coffee sector. We will present them in order of increasing difficulty. The order of presentation can also be read as a step-by-step programme for SCCF activities.

The most immediate form of cooperation, and one that is already happening anyway, is the process of facilitating *multiple certifications*. These are more likely to take place among the stricter certification options (fair trade, organic, bird-friendly) than with options that are perceived as attempts to combine economic, social and environmental criteria at a lower threshold (Utz Kapeh, Rainforest Alliance, Common Code for the Coffee Community). In this sense, it will be difficult to involve all the certification initiatives in such an effort. Yet, multiple certifications (in whatever form) achieve economies of scale and save on costs of certification. Furthermore, the SCCF could be a vehicle for a possible discussion of 'low bar' versus 'high bar' sustainability thresholds in view of a future development of a sustainability 'umbrella seal' based on points rather than absolute standards (see below). In this realm, a 'low bar' version could be based on the Common Code, the Rainforest Alliance standard and/or Utz Kapeh, while the 'high bar' could be triple certification: fair trade + organic + bird-friendly.

A second step in the process of expanding the sustainability coverage is to further *develop economic, social and environmental standards within individual initiatives*. This is also something that is happening already (fair trade is considering stricter environmental standards; the organic movement is considering the inclusion of shade parameters). These processes are made possible through exchange of information among various initiatives. At the institutional level, collaboration among different certification initiatives has taken place within the International Social and Environmental Accreditation and Labelling (ISEAL) initiative, which facilitates communication between various certification bodies and runs joint field certification experiments in the field (Wunderlich 2002: 23). The SCCF could create a spin-off (or linked) initiative with specific reference to coffee. Again, stricter standards would have to be rewarded by higher premiums, otherwise they would represent just higher entry barriers.

A third step would be the creation of a sustainability umbrella label. This could be developed on the basis of the principle of equivalence. Different certification agencies would use their own criteria but agree on a set of common principles that should be respected within each individual certification (TerraChoice 2000: 41). This option would allow for more flexibility in matching different social and environmental conditions, and at the same time would provide a common framework of reference. Yet different certifications adopt standards that focus on one area more than another, and it may be difficult to find common ground in terms of accepting what a minimum requirement of sustainability means. If this were possible at all, it would probably happen in terms of developing a label in addition to the ones already known to the consumers (an umbrella label) rather than a superlabel that would replace them. Such an umbrella label could be developed as an absolute set of standards or on the basis of a 'points' system of sustainability (depending on how many aspects are covered by the different combination of certifications) (see also Rice and McLean 1999: 105–6). We understand that individual labels are the *raison d'être* of many sustainability certifications. However, inaction is likely to entail leaving the ground open for mainstream sustainability initiatives. This may result in the some of the old certifications being pushed out of the market.

The most far-fetched process in the development of sustainability standards in the coffee sector is *harmonization*. Harmonization is based on the idea that one set of criteria is used for the definition of all sustainable coffee: given the plurality of initiatives and the complexity of the content of sustainability, this is unlikely to happen. Even within well-established subcategories of the sustainability family, such as organics, it has been extremely difficult and laborious to come up with universally accepted standards. Also, it may not be possible to come up with standards that are applicable to all agro-ecological conditions.

Nevertheless, there is no point in setting sustainability standards without the participation of their intended beneficiaries. Standards as a general rule raise entry barriers, which are likely to be more pronounced for smallholders than for estates (with the exception of fair trade). Technical assistance is one of the ways of ensuring compliance with new standards. Yet, the coverage of technical assistance is spotty, sometimes politically motivated, and tends to concentrate in areas that are less disadvantaged and more likely to show 'success'. Technical assistance also tends to be reactive (filling the gaps after they arise), while the coffee industry needs to be proactive. Therefore, the SCCF could be involved in fund raising and coordination for activities that promote broader development objectives:

- farmer credit (for improvements related to matching sustainability standards);
- training and organizational assistance for cooperatives and other kinds of producer associations;
- facilitating direct marketing between these organizations and buyers in consuming countries;
- lobbying for the re-establishment of coordination mechanisms in producing countries, especially in relation to quality control and quality incentives;
- simplifying smallholder compliance with standards (in organics, for example, auditing of a sample of farmers in a catchment area is sufficient; the alternative, auditing all farmers, would make certification much more expensive);
- facilitating the creation of IGO systems (see below);
- promoting processes and institutions that facilitate the creation of symbolic and in-person service quality attributes by producers and their associations;
- facilitating producer participation in the setting of standards for an umbrella seal, and in revisions of individual certification requirements.

Coffee operators should also accept the idea that matching sustainability standards is expensive for producers. Thus, any initiative demanding improvements in the sustainability content of coffee should include provisions for offering mandatory premiums based on actual costs of production. Indications of the levels of these premiums and/or the proportion of the final price that goes to the farmer should be put on the label. As mentioned earlier, regulation in consuming countries could be devised to make it mandatory to provide this kind of information for all coffees, (currently) mainstream coffee included. Additional required information could be the proportion of Mild Arabica, Hard Arabica and Robusta contained in a blend. Pressure for the establishment of these rules is unlikely to come from the mainstream coffee industry — as is obvious from reading the content of mainstream sustainability codes of conduct.

Levels and types of premiums could be discussed by industry actors, public agencies and NGOs within the SCCF, rather than being left to market forces. This approach draws on a quality convention that offers 'something for something', rather than improved quality content at the same price. Its legitimating narrative is based on the fact that prices are not determined solely by demand and supply equilibrium, but by the valuation of different quality attributes in the various stages of production, exchange and consumption. Thus, if the consumer wants (or is led to want) a minimum proportion of the retail price to be paid to the producer, this is 'what the market wants'. Some actors in the industry argue that consumers will not pay higher prices for sustainable coffees. However, if anything, the experience of the specialty coffee industry actually suggests that consumers are willing to pay higher prices for the symbolic attributes of the coffee they drink and the in-person services attached to it. The problem is not how to get consumers to pay, but how to transfer a bigger proportion of the final price down to producers.

Most sustainability initiatives have developed within the realm of voluntary and/or private standard setting. It is unlikely that governmental intervention will be needed in the process of coordinating/combining sustainable standards and certifications. However, public regulation may play an important role in achieving recognition of the content of certification and ensuring the validity of claims made under it. As explained above, regulation could also play a role in forcing the provision of more information on premiums and rough blend composition through stricter labelling requirements for both specialty/sustainable and mainstream coffee. Finally, the experience of organic certification suggests that there is a role for public regulation in facilitating harmonization – as long as rules are flexible enough to accommodate variation. The SCCF could be the catalyst to bring together private sector actors, NGOs, and public regulators to discuss these issues.

Finally, the SCCF could provide an institutional framework for designing industry-wide strategies on sustainable coffee. So far, sustainability issues have been addressed mainly in niche markets. The 'long haul' strategy of some of the 'high-mark' certification initiatives (such as fair trade and organic) has been to grow at the expense of commercial coffees and/or through attempts to get commercial roasters to certify coffee – without compromising sustainability standards and by paying a premium. However, some of the sustainability initiatives tailored for the mainstream market (such as Utz Kapeh and the Common Code for the Coffee Community) pose serious challenges for the high-mark initiatives because they provide an aura of sustainability to consumers at no extra cost, and offer no premium and limited direct benefits to farmers. Success under such an approach could conceivably drive out other approaches to sustainability through a 'watering down' process.

This analysis suggests that win-win strategies are possible but that such outcomes will crucially depend upon considerable dialogue, trust-building and cooperation, hence the need for something akin to the SCCF. In short, the sustainable coffee industry should seriously consider ways of expanding the market for its coffee in ways that:

- do not substantively water down the content of sustainability;
- provide for extra resources to farmers to comply with standards;
- involve the supposed beneficiaries at all steps of formulation;
- are practical and flexible enough to allow for widespread adoption.

Material and symbolic quality: the role of IGO systems and intellectual property rights

Even in their best configurations, and with the participation of producers in standard setting and monitoring, generic certifications do not provide an immediate link between consumer and producer. Often, information flows from South to North, but not vice versa. Certifications can also be used to externalize troubleshooting and diffuse responsibility. However, there is nothing in principle against linking certifications guaranteeing socio-economic and environmental quality content with specific places. In this section, we argue that IGO systems are imperfect but promising institutional set-ups to facilitate improvement in quality attributes (material and symbolic) and to ensure that these improvements benefit producers.

In addition to improving sustainability initiatives and broadening their market coverage, solving the coffee paradox requires improving coffee quality, raising the reputation of individual origins, and refining marketing skills in producing countries. The key for would-be producers of high-quality coffees is to know how to sell the right coffee to the right people at the right prices by emphasizing the right quality attributes. They need to know which quality characteristics are appreciated where, what kind of premiums will be paid, and what motivations are needed for consumers to take a product seriously.

Coffee is labour-intensive, and material quality improvement does not necessarily require large capital outlays. Groups of smallholder farmers in Tanzania, with the help of NGOs, have been able to produce high-quality coffee that is sold directly at the export auction. The higher prices they fetched generated positive returns to the extra efforts required. This shows that smallholder (and often poor) farmers can produce and handle high-quality coffee, get higher prices and improve their livelihoods – if they receive institutional support and are exposed to quality-related market incentives. Unfortunately, the tendency for traders in many producing countries after liberalization has been to buy all coffee at one price. No price differentials are offered to smallholders for good-quality coffee, which reduces their incentive to improve quality. Exporters who cater to specialty markets rely increasingly upon estates through vertical integration or long-term contracts. Small farmers are being marginalized.

Producing countries need to support small farmers in achieving – and reaping the benefits of – improvements in material coffee quality. They can do so by: (re-)establishing forms of coordination (public or private) that restore quality-related payments for coffee; tackling market failures in input and credit markets; and facilitating the establishment of farmer groups and producer associations. Consumer countries can pass stricter labelling requirements so that consumers know how much of the price they pay goes down to the farmer, or how much Robusta there is in a purported high-quality blend.

Yet improving the material quality attributes of coffee and getting paid for it remains a necessary, but not sufficient strategy for producers. The value-added that can be captured at the farm gate in improving material quality is limited. Producers need to sell the symbolic quality attributes of coffee as well – territory, a story, ideas, and the exotic. They need consumer information so that they can provide individualized material and/or symbolic offerings. Albeit more limited, some in-person service provision is also possible through agro-tourist networks, safari-and-coffee farm tours, and the establishment of café chains controlled by producer organizations (Fedecafé of Colombia opened the first two Juan Valdez cafés in Washington, DC and New York in 2004).

This strategy entails the valorization of resources that have geographical identity, and thus a quality convention based on place. In practical terms, this is done by marketing the territory itself, or by encapsulating territory/culture within specific products (see also Ray 1998). In order for this process to be producer-led and -controlled, the construction of territorial identities should be done through IGO systems (based on uniqueness and geographical determinism) and related producer associations. IGOs should be recognized and defended in national and international regulation via a justificatory regime based on the defence of intellectual property rights. The logic of intellectual property rights, so far used mainly in relation to defending innovation in developed countries, should be turned on its head and used to defend producers in developing countries against expropriation of the geographical indications of places where they live. A similar process is taking place in defence of biodiversity and against biopiracy in the South, and some of the same instruments could be used. At the WTO level, discussions related to the establishment of a register of indications for wine and spirits should be broadened to include products that are of interest to the South (see Chapter 6 for details).

This overall process should aim at: (1) transforming geography and local knowledge into property; (2) making sure that product identity feeds back into territorial identity, becoming intellectual capital that is available to other (non-coffee) producers in the area (through the promotion of other products by association, for example); and (3) strengthening of producer associations, which could support members in other ways (such as the provision of credit or the defence of contractual rights). The establishment of an IGO strengthens producer organizations because it provides them with a focus and a clear business plan – instead of a more generic push 'to get themselves together'. Thus, local producers could not only benefit from higher prices for their products, but also from wider developmental impacts.

IGO-related organizations could spearhead broader territorial strategies (constructed around tourism, crafts, other agro-food products, music, gastronomy, etcetera), drafted in collaboration with regional governments, commercial associations, donor agencies/NGOs, Northern marketers or local producer groups. With this approach, it would not only be locations producing high-quality coffees that would qualify and/or benefit from an IGO-led initiative, but also locations where the material attributes of coffee may not be so attractive, but other material and symbolic offerings and in-person services may be.

Making hedonism work for the South

Any long-term solution to the historic slide of coffee prices needs to target what is now considered the mainstream market. Most mainstream consumers will continue to buy branded coffee in the foreseeable future. These consumers rely on brands for a consistent consumption experience in time and in space. Branded coffee roasters, however, are more concerned with homogeneity in the short term than in maintaining a high quality profile in the long term. This objective will not change, even with the adoption of the mainstream Common Code for the Coffee Community.

It is widely known in the coffee industry that material quality in the mainstream market deteriorated dramatically in the US in the last 30 years. Coffee roasters in Germany were using strictly Arabica coffee in their blends as recently as a decade ago. Now Germany imports a sizeable proportion of Robusta. The proportion of Robusta employed in *espresso* blends in Italy has increased as well. These are indicators that brands are not necessarily an insurance against deteriorating quality in time, although they tend to ensure a relatively homogeneous consumption experience in space.

Much branded coffee consists of a blend of various coffee types and origins. Some branded coffee also specifies whether it consists of 100 per cent Arabica or not. When consisting of a single-origin coffee, branded coffee is sometimes sold with the identification of the producing country. However, in the mainstream market, there is little information available to consumers about the coffee they drink. Branded roasters never specify the composition of a blend in terms of origin and coffee type. Perhaps, the most problematic aspect is that consumers do not know how to assess coffee quality. They simply do not have the language and the knowledge to discern the many characteristics of coffee.

This relative ignorance mirrors to some extent where the wine industry was 20–30 years ago. Most mainstream consumers did not know much about wine or how to assess its quality. Nowadays, most of these consumers have at least a rudimentary knowledge of different types and origins, their taste characteristics, and how to match food with a particular wine. It has become fashionable – not only among the wealthy – to be a wine expert, tasting courses have become popular, and most restaurants offer a wide selection of wines. On the contrary, most coffee consumers are left in the dark. They may know of Ethiopian coffee, for example, but little on why it is special. Few know that particular coffees go better with milk than other coffees, or that you could match a dessert type with a specific kind of coffee. Even fancy restaurants that offer an impressive selection of food and wines often serve unspecified coffee.

One of the main differences between the wine and coffee industries is that the wine industry was able to undergo a radical transformation in the absence of a strong branded environment (although this has changed). In the coffee industry, branded roasters have no interest in providing information that waters down brand identification and attachment. Also, wine is offered to the consumer as an end product, often served straight from the bottle, while coffee can be spoiled in many ways on its way from producer to consumer, not least at the brewing stage. Yet consumers who have already learnt how to appreciate good wine are also likely to be interested in educating their nose and tastebuds in relation to coffee. The fact that the vocabulary used in professional coffee tasting borrows heavily from wine tasting helps. Is it too far out to think of coffee tastings being organized at Starbucks outlets? Why not let consumers compare different kinds of mainstream coffees on the supermarket isle?

A consumer who knows how to discern the material qualities of coffee will look for particular kinds of coffee and be willing to pay more for its specificity. If the added value of informed consumption is then transferred up the value chain (through IGO systems, for example), it can have a positive impact on producers. More informed consumers are also a market-based guarantee of higher demand for better-quality coffee. Finally, they can address power imbalances in the global coffee chain by facilitating market fragmentation in consuming countries.

The ICO, international NGOs, aid agencies and producing country governments should build alliances and promote initiatives aimed at cultivating consumers rather than more coffee. At a general level, these initiatives should include the organization of tasting sessions in coffee bars or institutional environments, where consumers could receive basic information on types and origins of coffee, and acquire the basic language and techniques of tasting. This should be coupled with a wide-ranging information campaign in the media and in coffee retail outlets (coffee bar chains, specialty coffee retailers, and selected supermarket chains). These activities should include the promotion of IGO coffees, which by design are more likely to pass on symbolic value to producers.

Strategically, these initiatives should not be marketed under a developmental agenda. They should be directed to mainstream consumers for the sake of increasing their perception of sophistication. A hedonistic approach to commodity trade that works for the South is based on extracting value for producers from the symbolic content of quality demanded by consumers. This entails a quality convention based on connoisseurship. The strategy is based on promoting the consumer's sense of self through enhanced aesthetic cognition, identity choice/making/remaking, 'travelling through taste', and an intimate relation to *terroir* (or symbolic ownership of a place). The key issue here is to channel the hedonistic value to the producer level in the South through IGO systems controlled by local institutions. This strategy is based on a broad alliance between 'makers and mediators of taste' (celebrity cooks, lifestyle consultants, designers), consumer associations and producer-controlled, IGO-based organizations.

Coffee, commodity trade and development

The commodity problem has been at the centre of many debates in development circles in the last half-century. At various times, the elusiveness of the promise of development has been attributed to different factors. From the 1950s to the 1970s, it was blamed on historically declining terms of trade for commodities due to differences between agriculture and manufacturing, and the fallacy of composition. It was tackled through international commodity agreements. Starting in the 1980s, a case was built against public intervention in commodity production and trade at both the domestic and international levels. As a result, liberalization and deregulation policies ensued (at least in the South).

More recently, unfair rules of trade and abuse of market power have been highlighted, accompanied by calls for agricultural sector liberalization in developed countries, more transparency in trade rules, and political pressure against large multinational corporations.

Box 7.1 Summary of proposals for an alternative agenda

Regulatory approaches
- International anti-trust regulation;
- Regulation forcing the disclosure of more information on the label of coffee sold at the retail level (proportion of various kinds of coffee used, origin, etcetera);
- Rules requiring public verification of claims made under sustainability certifications (by national standards bureaux, for example);
- Extension of the protection offered by the TRIPS agreement for wine and spirits to other agricultural products; establishment of a WTO-level binding register of IGOs that covers more than just wine and spirits and that is favourable to developing countries;
- Domestic regulation in producing countries, giving legal backing to IGO systems;
- Partial reregulation in producing countries – especially in relation to the enforcement of coffee quality assessment rules and the payment of price incentives on quality.

Hybrid approaches
- Creating a Sustainable Coffee Cooperation Fund (SCCF) that:
  - provides a cooperation forum to various sustainability initiatives;
  - promotes the payment of premiums for coffee that matches sustainability standards;
  - avoids the watering down of sustainability standards at the same time as simplifying compliance by smallholders;
  - provides training and organizational assistance to producer associations;
  - helps farmers participate in standard setting and monitoring;
- Establishing IGO systems and broader IGO-based territorial strategies in producing countries;
- Providing quality improvement infrastructure;
- Strengthening producer organizations (better if related to IGO systems, which provide a more focused business plan);
- Promoting private and/or public–private forms of coordination for the provision of inputs, credit and services to farmers.

Commercial approaches
- Promoting IGO coffees in consuming countries;
- Consumer education on quality – information campaign, organization of coffee tastings in venues of consumption, involvement of coffee experts, restaurateurs and celebrity chefs;
- Promoting agro-tourism; coffee, lodge and safari tours; opening of producer-controlled cafés in consuming countries.

For a large part of the twentieth century, producing countries in the coffee sector were quite successful in their attempts to control exports and limit the effect of overproduction on prices. This happened first thanks to a Brazilian near-monopoly of production and later to the ability of producing countries to act collectively (with the cooperation of consuming countries). With the end of international regulation and the retreat of the state from domestic market regulation and the management of stocks, producing countries have lost much of their leverage in the global value chain for coffee. Solutions to this situation that focus solely on the material content of coffee, however, are bound to be ineffective.

In this book, we have argued that a more nuanced analysis of the commodity problem and its impact on development has to be based on a different approach to what we mean by a commodity and how we evaluate quality attributes in goods. First, we have argued that coffee, like other agricultural products that are internationally traded, is a commodity not because of a curse of nature, but because peculiar institutions made it such. Specific standards, grades and futures markets have been organizing its interchangeability across time and space for more than a century. Second, we have observed that many developing countries are stuck in producing and exporting goods that are valued only in their *material* quality attributes. *Symbolic* and *in-person service* quality attributes are generated and controlled elsewhere. Thus market power is not only a question of market share (and abuse of it), but also of capturing the most valuable attributes while undermining the value of the attributes that need to be purchased.

In the last twenty years, several solutions have been proposed with a view to decommoditizing agricultural products, mostly based on the idea of supplying different product forms. Creating new material attributes is one of these solutions. But the agro-food processors and retailers that buy these agricultural products do not necessarily demand differentiated material offerings. Their own differentiation strategy is based on the ability of creating differences from the same raw material and above all on adding symbolic quality attributes to the products they sell.

Adding new symbolic attributes is another solution, one that is at the core of specialty markets and various sustainability initiatives. However, agro-food processors and retailers have also entered the fray of new symbolic offering and are proposing their own concepts of specialty and sustainable products. In this process of mainstreaming, producers have been cut off from many standard-setting processes. They do not seem to gain much from some of the initiatives that are marketed in the name of their own benefit, either. As the standards that producers have to match proliferate and become more complex and stringent, doubts have also emerged on the long-term feasibility of small-scale production in the South more generally. We may be witnessing the re-emergence, in a different guise, of the plantation model that characterized commodity production and trade between the fifteenth century and the second part of the nineteenth. Given that many agro-food commodities are produced overwhelmingly by small-holders, the potential impact of such an evolution should not be taken lightly.

Who will decide the content of new agro-food standards that are being set on quality and sustainability? Who will own the intellectual property rights of related labels? What kinds of benefits can small producers in the South expect from matching these standards? Who will benefit from selling symbolic attributes and in-person services? Could IGO systems provide a viable framework for collective action and for increasing farmers' control of symbolic production in the South? The answer to these questions will determine the future relationship between commodity trade and development.

Note

1 This does not entail the creation of yet another initiative on sustainable coffee. The SCCF (or any other appropriate form and name) could be developed, for example, as a loose alliance of 'old certification' initiatives – possibly linked to the existing Sustainable Coffee Initiative (SCI) that was set up by the International Institute for Sustainable Development (IISD) and UNCTAD.

References

Addor, F. and A. Grazioli (2002) 'Geographical Indications beyond Wines and Spirits: A Roadmap for a Better Protection for Geographical Indications in the WTO TRIPS Agreement', *The Journal of World Intellectual Property* 5(6): 865–97.

Akiyama, T. (2001) 'Coffee Market Liberalization since 1990', in T. Akiyama, J. Baffes, D. F. Larson and P. Varangis (eds.), *Commodity Market Reforms: Lessons of Two Decades*. Washington, DC: World Bank.

Akiyama, T. and P. Varangis (1990) 'The Impact of the International Coffee Agreement on Producing Countries', *World Bank Economic Review* 4(2): 157–73.

Allaire, G. and R. Boyer (1995) 'Régulation et conventions dans l'agriculture et les ISS', in G. Allaire and R. Boyer (eds.), *La grande transformation de l'agriculture: Lectures conventionnalistes et regulationnistes*. Paris: INRA–Economica.

Allen, P. and M. Kovach (2000) 'The Capitalist Composition of Organic: The Potential of Markets in Fulfilling the Promise of Organic Agriculture', *Agriculture and Human Values* 17: 221–32.

Allen, P., M. FitzSimmons, M. Goodman and K. Warner (2003) 'Shifting Plates in the Agrifood Landscape: The Tectonics of Alternative Agrifood Initiatives in California', *Journal of Rural Studies* 19: 61–75.

Appadurai, A. (1986) 'Introduction: Commodities and the Politics of Value', in A. Appadurai (ed.) *The Social Life of Things: Commodities in Cultural Perspective*. Cambridge: Cambridge University Press.

Arce, A. and T. Marsden (1993) 'The Social Construction of International Food: A New Research Agenda', *Economic Geography* 69(3): 291–311.

Babcock, B. and R. Clemens (2004) *Geographical Indications and Property Rights: Protecting Value-Added Agriculture Products*. MATRIC Briefing Paper. Armes, Iowa.

Baffes, J. (2005) 'Tanzania's Coffee Sector: Constraints and Challenges', *Journal of International Development* 17: 21–43.

Barham, E. (2003) 'Translating *Terroir*: The Global Challenge of French AOC Labeling', *Journal of Rural Studies* 19(1): 127–38.

Barjolle, D. and B. Sylvander (2000) *PDO and PGI Products: Market, Supply Chains and Institutions*. Bruxelles, European Commission: FAIR 1 – CT 95 – 0306.

—— (2002) 'Some Factors of Success for Origin Labelled Products in Agri-Food Supply Chains in Europe: Market, Internal Resources and Institutions', *Economies et Sociétés* 25(9–10): 1441–61.

Bates, R. H. (1981) *Markets and States in Tropical Africa: The Political Basis of Agricultural Policies*. Berkeley: University of California Press.

—— (1997) *Open-Economy Politics: The Political Economy of the World Coffee Trade*. Princeton: Princeton University Press.

Bernstein, E. M. (1960) 'International Effects of US Economic Policy', in Joint Economic Committee (ed.), *Study of Employment, Growth and Price Levels*. Washington: Joint Economic Committee.

Bettendorf, L. and F. Verboven (2000) 'Incomplete Transmission of Coffee Bean Prices: Evidence from the Netherlands', *European Review of Agricultural Economics*, 27(1): 1–16.

Bhuyan, S. and R. Lopez (1997) 'Oligopoly Power in the Food and Tobacco Industries', *American Journal of Agricultural Economics* 79: 1035–43.

Binswanger, H. and M. Rosenweig (1986) 'Behavioural and Material Determinants of Production Relations in Agriculture', *Journal of Development Studies* 22(3): 503–39.

Bleaney, M. and D. Greenaway (1993) 'Long-run Trends in the Relative Price of Primary Commodities and in the Terms of Trade of Developing Countries', *Oxford Economic Papers* 45(3): 349–63.

Boltanski, O. and L. Thévenot (1991) *De la justification. Les économies de la grandeur*. Paris: Gallimard.

Borrus, M. and J. Zysman (1997) 'Wintelism and the Changing Term of Global Competition: Prototype of the Future', *BRIE Working paper*. Berkeley: University of California.

Bourdieu, P. (1979) *De la distinction: Critique sociale du jugement*. Paris: Les editions de minuit.

Boy, L. (2001) 'Propriété intellectuelle: l'agriculture en première ligne avec l'accord ADPIC', in *DEMETER 2002: Nouveux enjeux pour l'agriculture*. DEMETER. Paris: Armand Colin.

Brown, J. G. (1991) 'Agro-Industry Profiles: Coffee', *EDI Working Papers*. Washington, DC: World Bank.

Busch, L. and K. Tanaka (1996) 'Rites of Passage: Constructing Quality in a Commodity Subsector', *Science, Technology and Human Values* 21(1): 3–27.

Callon, M., C. Méadel and V. Rabeharisoa (2002) 'The Economy of Qualities', *Economy and Society* 31(2): 194–217.

Cardoso, F. H. and E. Faletto (1979) *Dependency and Development in Latin America*. Berkeley: University of California Press.

Chamberlin, E. (1933) *The Theory of Monopolistic Competition*. Cambridge: Harvard University Press.

Chandler, A. D. (1977) *The Visible Hand: The Managerial Revolution in American Business*. Cambridge, MA: Belknap Press.

Christensen, M. F. (2005) 'The Postmodern Coffee Consumer: A Consumer-driven Global Value Chain Analysis of the Coffee Market'. MA thesis, Copenhagen: Copenhagen Business School.

Claessens, S. and R. C. Duncan (eds.) (1993) *Managing Commodity Price Risk in Developing Countries Using Financial Instruments: Case Studies*. Baltimore and London, published for the World Bank by the Johns Hopkins University Press.

Clarence-Smith, W.G. (1994) 'The Impact of Forced Coffee Cultivation on Java, 1805–1917', *Indonesia Circle* 64: 241–64.

—— (2000) *Cocoa and Chocolate, 1765–1914*. London and New York: Routledge.

Common Code for the Coffee Community (2004), available at www.sustainable-coffee.net/code_of_conduct/index.html

Common Fund for Commodities (CFC) (2000) *Study of Marketing and Trading Policies and Systems in Selected Coffee Producing Countries*. Amsterdam: Common Fund for Commodities.

Cook, I. (1994) 'New Fruits and Vanity: Symbolic Production in the Global Food Economy', in A. Bonanno, L. Busch, W. Friedland, L. Gouveia and E. Mingione (eds.), *From Columbus to ConAgra: The Globalization of Agriculture and Food*. Lawrence: University of Kansas Press.

Cook, I. and P. Crang (1996) 'The World on a Plate: Culinary Culture, Displacement, and Geographical Knowledges', *Journal of Material Culture* 1: 131–53.

Crewe, L. (2000) 'Geographies of Retailing and Consumption', *Progress in Human Geography* 24(2): 275–90.

Cronon, W. (1991) *Nature's Metropolis: Chicago and the Great West*. New York: W. W. Norton.

Crowe, T. (1997) 'Coffee Futures Price Behavior and Fund Investment', *ICO Coffee Newsletter* (4). London: ICO.

Curtin, P. D. (1990) *The Rise and Fall of the Plantation Complex: Essays in Atlantic History*. Cambridge and New York: Cambridge University Press.

Damiani, O. (2001) 'Organic Agriculture in Mexico: Case Studies of Small Farmer Associations in Chiapas and the Yucatan peninsula'. Rome: Office of Evaluations and

Studies, International Fund for Agricultural Development (IFAD).

—— (2002) 'Organic Agriculture in Guatemala: A Study of Producer Organizations in the Cuchumatanes Highlands'. Rome: Office of Evaluations and Studies, IFAD.

Darby, M. R. and E. Karni (1973) 'Free Competition and the Optimal Amount of Fraud', *Journal of Law and Economics* 16: 67–88.

Davatz, T. (1980) *Memorias de um colono no Brazil (1850)*. São Paulo: Ed. da Universidade de São Paulo.

Daviron, B. (1993) *Conflict et cooperation sur le marché international du café: une analyse de longue periode*. Thèse de Doctorat. Montpellier: Ecole Nationale Supérieure Agronomique de Montpellier.

—— (1994) 'La crisis del mercado cafetalero internacional en una perspectiva de largo plazo', in M. Samper (ed.), *Crisis y perspectivas del café latinoamericano*. San José, Costa Rica: ICAFE–UNA.

—— (1996) 'The Rise and Fall of Governmental Power on the International Coffee Market', in M. Griffon and P. Guillaumont (eds.), *Economics of Agricultural Policies in Developing Countries*. Paris: Editions de la Revue Française d'Economie.

—— (2002) 'Small Farm Production and the Standardization of Tropical Products', *Journal of Agrarian Change* 2(2): 162–84.

Daviron, B. and T. Voituriez (2003) 'Les paradoxes de la longévité du projet de stabilisation des marchés agricoles au XXe siècle: quelques enseignements de la pensée anglo-saxonne', *Economies et Sociétés* 37(9): 1579–1609.

Dean, W. (1976) *Rio Claro: A Brazilian Plantation System, 1820–1920*. Stanford, CA: Stanford University Press.

Deininger, K. and J. Okidi (2003) 'Growth and Poverty Reduction in Uganda 1992–2000: Panel Data Evidence', *Development Policy Review* 21(4): 481–510.

Delaporte, G. (1976) 'Le café : prix imposés ou prix négociés', *Revue Tiers-Monde* XVII(66): 433–47.

Desai, M. (2002) *Marx's Revenge: The Resurgence of Capitalism and the Death of Statist Socialism*. London: Verso.

DFID and ODI (2004) 'Rethinking Tropical Agricultural Commodities'. London: Department for International Development.

Dialosavvas, D. and P. L. Scandizzo (1991) 'Trends in the Terms of Trade of Primary Commodities, 1900–1982: The Controversy and its Origins', *Economic Development and Cultural Change* 39(2): 231–64.

Dicum, G. and N. Luttinger (1999) *The Coffee Book: Anatomy of an Industry from the Crop to the Last Drop*. New York: The New Press.

DiFulvio (1947) *Le café dans le monde*. Rome: Institut Internationale d'Agriculture.

Dijk, J. B. van, D. H. M. van Doesburg, A. M. A. Heijbroek, M. R. I. A. Wazir and G. S. M. de Wolff (1998) *The World Coffee Market*. Utrecht: Rabobank International.

Dorn, J. A., S. H. Hanke, and A. A. Walters (eds.) (1998) *The Revolution in Development Economics*. Washington, DC and Lanham, MD: Cato Institute.

Douglas, M. and B. Isherwood (1981) *The World of Goods*. New York: Basic Books.

Duque, O. and P. S. Baker (2003) *Devouring Profit: The Socio-Economics of Coffee Berry Borer IPM*. Chinchiná: The Commodities Press–CABI–CENICAFÉ.

Durevall, D. (2003) 'Competition and Pricing: An Analysis of the Market for Roasted Coffee', in Swedish Competition Authority (ed), *High Prices in Sweden – A Result of Poor Competition?* Stockholm: Swedish Competition Authority.

Emmanuel, A. (1972) *Unequal Exchange: A Study of the Imperialism of Trade*. New York: Monthly Review Press.

Eymard-Duvernay, F. (1989) 'Conventions de qualité et formes de coordination', *Revue Economique* 40(2): 329–59.

Fairtrade Foundation (2002) *Spilling the Beans on the Coffee Trade*. London: Fairtrade Foundation.

FAO (1962) *L'économie mondiale du café*. Rome: Food and Agriculture Organization (FAO).

—— (2001) *The Role of Agriculture in the Development of LDCs and Their Integration into the World Economy*. Rome: FAO.

—— (2004) FAOSTAT database.

Feenstra, R. C. (1998) 'Integration of Trade and Disintegration of Production in the Global Economy', *Journal of Economic Perspectives* 12(4): 31–50.

Fernando, M. R. (2003) 'Coffee Cultivation in Java, 1830–1917', in W. G. Clarence-Smith and S. Topik (eds.), *The Global Coffee Economy in Africa, Asia and Latin-America, 1500–1989*. Cambridge and New York: Cambridge University Press.

Feuerstein, S. (2002) 'Do Coffee Roasters Benefit from High Prices of Green Coffee Beans?' *International Journal of Industrial Organisation* 20: 89–118.

FIBL (2002) 'Organic Coffee, Cocoa and Tea'. Frick (Switzerland): Research Institute of Organic Agriculture (FIBL).

Fine, B. (2002) *The World of Consumption: The Material and Cultural Revisited* (second edition). London and New York: Routledge.

Finnemore, M. (1996) *National Interests in International Society*. Ithaca, NY: Cornell University Press.

Fitter, R. and R. Kaplinsky (2001) 'Can an Agricultural "Commodity" Be Decommodified, and If So, Who Is to Gain?' *IDS Working Paper* No. 37. Brighton: Institute for Development Studies.

FLO (2002) 'Fairtrade Standards for Coffee', Bonn: Fairtrade Labelling Organizations International, 25 April.

Fogel, R. W. (1989) *Without Consent or Contract: The Rise and Fall of American Slavery*. New York: Norton,

Font, M. A. (1990) *Coffee, Contention, and Change in the Making of Modern Brazil*. Cambridge, MA and Oxford: Blackwell.

Fortunel, F. (2000) *Le café au Viêt Nam: de la colonisation à l'essor d'un grand producteur mondial*. Paris: L'Harmattan.

Freidberg (2003a) 'Not All Sweetness and Light: New Cultural Geographies of Food,' *Social and Cultural Geography* 4(1): 3–6.

—— (2003b) 'Culture, Conventions and Colonial Constructs of Rurality in South–North Horticultural Trades', *Journal of Rural Studies* 19: 97–109.

—— (2003c) 'Cleaning up down South: Supermarkets, Ethical Trade and African Horticulture', *Social and Cultural Geography* 4(1): 27–43.

—— (2004) *French Beans and Food Scares: Culture and Commerce in an Anxious Age*. New York: Oxford University Press.

Friedland, W. (1984) 'Commodity Systems Analysis: An Approach to the Sociology of Agriculture', in H. K. Schwarzweller (ed.), *Research in Rural Sociology and Development*. Greenwich, CT: JAI Press.

Furtado, C. (1970) *Economic Development of Latin America: A Survey from Colonial Times to the Cuban Revolution*. Cambridge: Cambridge University Press.

Gereffi, G. (1994a) 'The Organization of Buyer-Driven Global Commodity Chains: How US Retailers Shape Overseas Production Networks', in G. Gereffi and M. Korzeniewicz (eds.), *Commodity Chains and Global Capitalism*. Westport: Greenwood Press.

—— (1994b) 'The International Economy and Economic Development', in N. J. Smelser (ed.), *The Handbook of Economic Sociology*. Princeton and New York: Princeton University Press and Russell Sage Foundation.

—— (1995) 'Global Production Systems and Third World Development', in B. Stallings (ed.), *Global Change, Regional Response: The New International Context of Development*. Cambridge: Cambridge University Press.

—— (1999) 'International Trade and Industrial Up-Grading in the Apparel Commodity Chain', *Journal of International Economics* 48(1): 37–70.

Gereffi, G., J. Humphrey and T. Sturgeon (2005), 'The Governance of Global Value Chains', *Review of International Political Economy* 12(1): 78–104.

Gereffi, G. and M. Korzeniewicz (eds.) (1994) *Commodity Chains and Global Capitalism*. Westport: Greenwood Press.

Gereffi, G., M. Korzeniewicz and R. Korzeniewicz (1994) 'Introduction: Global Commodity Chains', in G. Gereffi and M. Korzeniewicz (eds.), *Commodity Chains and Global*

Capitalism. Westport: Greenwood Press.

Gibbon, P. (2001) 'Upgrading Primary Production: A Global Commodity Chain Approach', *World Development* 29(2): 345–63.

—— (2003) 'Commodities, Donors, Value-Chain Analysis and Upgrading'. Geneva: UNCTAD.

—— (2004) 'The Commodity Question: New Thinking on Old Problems,' background paper prepared for the 2005 UNDP *Human Development Report*. Copenhagen: Danish Institute for International Studies.

Gibbon, P. and S. Ponte (2005) *Trading Down: Africa, Value Chains and the Global Economy*. Philadelphia: Temple University Press.

Gilbert, C. L. (1996) 'International Commodity Agreements: An Obituary', *World Development* 24(1): 1–19.

—— (1998) 'What Kind of Economic Clauses Could Generally Be Acceptable in a New International Coffee Agreement?' *ICO Coffee Newsletter* (7). London: ICO.

Giovannucci, D. (2001) 'Sustainable Coffee Survey of the North American Specialty Coffee Industry'. Long Beach, CA: Specialty Coffee Association of America.

Giovannucci, D. and F. J. Koekoek (2003) *The State of Sustainable Coffee: A Study of Twelve Major Markets*. London and Winnipeg: ICO and IISD.

Giovannucci, D. and S. Ponte (2005) 'Standards as a New Form of Social Contract? Sustainability Initiatives in the Coffee Industry', *Food Policy* (forthcoming).

Goodman, D. (2003) 'The "Quality Turn" and Alternative Food Practices: Reflections and Agenda', *Journal of Rural Studies* 19: 1–7.

—— (2004) 'Rural Europe Redux? Reflections on Alternative Agro-Food Networks and Paradigm Change', *Sociologia Ruralis* 44(1): 3–16.

Goodman, D. and E. M. DuPuis (2002) 'Knowing Food and Growing Food: Beyond the Production–Consumption Debate in the Sociology of Agriculture', *Sociologia Ruralis* 42(1): 6–23.

Gorter, H. de and J. Swinnen (2002) 'Political Economy of Agricultural Policy,' in G. C. Rausser (ed.), *Handbook of Agricultural Economics 2B*. Amsterdam and New York: Elsevier.

Gorz, A. (2003) *L'immatériel: Connaissance, valeur et capital*. Paris: Galilée.

Greenhill, R. (1977) 'The Brazilian Coffee Trade,' in D. C. M. Platt (ed.), *Business Imperialism, 1840–1930*. Oxford: Clarendon Press.

Grossman, G. M. and C. Shapiro (1988) 'Foreign Counterfeiting of Status Goods', *Quarterly Journal of Economics* 103(1): 79–100.

Guthman, J. (2002) 'Commodified Meanings, Meaningful Commodities: Rethinking Production–Consumption Links through the Organic System of Provision', *Sociologia Ruralis* 42(4): 295–311.

—— (2003) 'Fast Food/Organic Food: Reflexive Tastes and the Making of "Yuppie Chow"', *Social and Cultural Geography* 4(1): 45–58.

Hadass, Y. S. and J. G. Williamson (2001) 'Terms of Trade Shocks and Economic Performance 1870–1940: Prebisch and Singer Revisited'. NBER Working Papers, Cambridge, MA: NBER.

Hall, C. (1976) *El café y el desarrollo historico-geografico de Costa Rica*. San Jose, Editorial Costa Rica.

Hardt, M. (1999) 'Affective Labor', *Boundary 2* 26(2): 89–100.

Hardt, M. and A. Negri (2000) *Empire*. Cambridge, MA: Harvard University Press.

Hartwick, E. (1998) 'Geographies of Consumption: A Commodity Chain Approach', *Environment and Planning D: Society and Space* 16: 423–37.

Hayami, Y. (1996) 'The Peasant Economic Modernization', *American Journal of Agricultural Economics* 78(5): 1157–67.

Herrman, R., K. Burger and H. P. Smit (1993) *International Commodity Policy: A Quantitative Analysis*. London and New York: Routledge.

Hill, P. (1999) 'Tangibles, Intangibles and Services: A New Taxonomy for the Classification of Output', *Canadian Journal of Economics* 32(2): 426–46.

Hirschman, A. O. (1968) 'The Political Economy of Import-substituting Industrialization in

Latin America', *Quarterly Journal of Economics* 82(1): 1–32.

Holloway, T. H. (1978) 'Creating the Reserve Army: The Immigration Program of Sao Paolo 1886–1930', *International Migration Review* 12(2): 187–209.

Holt Stone, A. (1915) 'The Cotton Factorage System of the Southern States', *The American Historical Review* 20(3): 557–65.

Hopkins, T. K. and I. Wallerstein (1986) 'Commodity Chains in the World Economy Prior to 1800', *Review* 10(1): 157–70.

—— (1994) 'Commodity Chains: Construct and Research', in G. Gereffi and M. Korzeniewicz (eds.), *Commodity Chains and Global Capitalism*. Westport: Greenwood Press.

Hopp, H. (1954) *A lei da oferta e da procura em relacao ao preco do café*. Rio de Janeiro: IBC.

Huebner, G. G. (1911) 'The Coffee Market', *Annals of the American Academy of Political and Social Science* 38: 610–20.

Hughes, A. (2000) 'Retailers, Knowledges and Changing Commodity Networks: The Case of the Cut Flower Trade', *Geoforum* 31: 175–90.

Humphrey, J. (2003) 'Upgrading in Global Value Chains', background paper for the World Commission on the Social Dimensions of Globalization. Brighton: IDS-Sussex.

—— (2004) 'Commodities, Diversification and Poverty Reduction', paper presented to the FAO Symposium on the state of agricultural commodity market research, Rome, 15–16 December 2003.

Humphrey, J. and H. Schmitz (2002), 'Developing Country Firms in the World Economy: Governance and Upgrading in Global Value Chains', *INEF Report* 61/2002. Duisburg: INEF-University of Duisburg.

ICARD and Oxfam (2002) *The Impact of the Global Coffee Trade on Dak Lak Province, Viet Nam: Analysis and Policy Recommendations*. London: ICARD.

ICO (2000) *Coffee Profile: Italy*. London: International Coffee Organization.

ICO, ITC and CFC (2000) *The Gourmet Coffee Project: Adding Value to Green Coffee* (2 volumes). London, Geneva and Amsterdam: International Coffee Organization, International Trade Centre (UNCTAD/WTO), and Common Fund for Commodities.

Ilbery, B. and M. Kneafsey (1999) 'Niche Markets and Regional Specialty Food Products in Europe', *Environment and Planning A* 31: 2223–38.

IMF (2003) International Financial Statisitics 2003. Washington, DC: International Monetary Fund.

ITC (2002) *Coffee: An Exporter's Guide*. Geneva: International Trade Centre.

Jackson, P. and N. Thrift (1995) 'Geographies of Consumption', in D. Miller (ed.), *Acknowledging Consumption: A Review of New Studies*. London: Routledge.

Johnson, D. G. (1973) *World Agriculture in Disarray*. London: Macmillan.

Kaldor, N. (1963a) 'Stabilizing the Terms of Trade of Underdeveloped Countries', *Economic Bulletin for Latin America* 8: 1–7.

—— (1963b) 'Taxation for Economic Development', *Journal of Modern African Studies* 1(1): 7–23.

Kaplan, C. (1995) '"A World without Boundaries": The Body Shop's Trans/national Geographies', *Social Text* 43: 45–66.

Kaplinsky, R. (1993) 'Export Processing Zones in the Dominican Republic: Transforming Manufactures into Commodities', *World Development* 21(11): 1851–65.

Kautsky, K. (1988) *The Agrarian Question* (two volumes). London and Winchester, MA: Zwan Publications.

Keynes, J. M. (1942/1980) *The International Regulation of Primary Products: Collected Writings of J. M. Keynes*, Vol. 27. D. Moggridge (ed.). London: Macmillan.

Kindelberger, C. P. (1943) 'Planning for Foreign Investments', *American Economic Review*, 33.

—— (1950) *The Dollar Shortage*. Cambridge, MA: New York and London: Technology Press of Massachusetts Institute of Technology, John Wiley and Chapman and Hall.

—— (1956) *The Terms of Trade: A European Case Study*. New York: Technology Press of Massachusetts Institute of Technology and John Wiley.

—— (1983) 'Standards as Public, Collective and Private Goods', *Kyklos* 36: 377–96.

Koerner, J. (2002) 'The Dark Side of Coffee: Price War in the German Market for Roasted

Coffee', Department of Food Economics and Consumption Studies, University of Kiel, Working Paper EWP 0204.

Kolchin, P. (1993) *American Slavery, 1619–1877*. New York: Hill and Wang.

Kopytoff, I. (1986) 'The Cultural Biology of Things: Commoditization as Process,' in A. Appadurai (ed.), *The Social Life of Things: Commodities in Cultural Perspective*. Cambridge: Cambridge University Press.

Kozul-Wright, R. and P. Rayment (2004) 'Globalization Reloaded: An UNCTAD Perspective', *UNCTAD Discussion Papers*, No. 167. Geneva: UNCTAD.

Kruger, D., A. Mason, and R. Vakis (2003) 'The Coffee Crisis in Central America', *Spectrum* (3): 16–19, World Bank: Washington.

Kuznesof, E. (1986) 'Comentarios sobre "La Costa Rica cafetalera: Economia, sociedad y estructura de poder"', *Revista de Historia* 14: 31–9.

Laan, L. van der (1997) *The Trans-Oceanic Marketing Channel*. New York: The International Business Press.

Laerne, C. F. van Delden (1885) *Brazil and Java, Report on Coffee Culture in America, Asia and Africa*. London: W. H. Allen and Co.

Lagrange, L., H. Briand and L. Trogon (2000) 'Importance économique des filières agro-alimentaires de produits sous signes officiels de qualité', *Economie Rurale* 258: 6–18.

Lalière, A. (1909) *Le café dans l'état de Saint Paul (Brésil)*. Paris: Augustin Challamel.

Levy, T. (2002) 'The Theory of Conventions and a New Theory of the Firm', in E. Fullbrook (ed.), *Intersubjectivity in Economics*. London and New York: Routledge.

Lewin, B., D. Giovannucci and P. Varangis (2004) 'Coffee Markets: New Paradigms in Global Supply and Demand', *Agriculture and Rural Development Discussion Paper 3*. Washington, DC: World Bank.

Lewis, W. A. (1954) 'Economic Development with Unlimited Supplies of Labour,' *Manchester School* 22: 139–91.

Leys, C. (1996) *The Rise and Fall of Development Theory*. Nairobi, Bloomington, IN and Oxford: EAEP, Indiana University Press and James Currey.

Lockie, S. (2002) '"The Invisible Mouth": Mobilizing "the Consumer" in Food Production–Consumption Networks', *Sociologia Ruralis* 42(4): 278–94.

Lodder, C. A. (1997) 'The Just-in-Time Policy: Some Conditions for Success', *ICO Coffee Newsletter* (5). London: ICO.

Losch, B. (1999) *Le Complexe Café–Cacao de la Côte d'Ivoire* (two volumes). Thèse de Doctorat. Montpellier: Université Montpellier I.

Love, R. (2001) 'The Ethiopian Coffee Filière and Its Institutions: Cui Bono?' *Review of African Political Economy* (88): 225–40.

—— (2002) *Political Economy of the Coffee Filière in Ethiopia*. Ph.D. thesis. Leeds: Institute for Politics and International Studies, University of Leeds.

Mace, B. (1998) 'Global Commodity Chains, Alternative Trade and Small-Scale Coffee Production in Oaxaca, Mexico'. MA thesis. Oxford, OH: Miami University.

Machado, A. (1988) *El café: De la aparceria al capitalismo*. Bogota, Tercer Mundo Editores.

Marsden, T. and A. Arce (1995) 'Constructing Quality: Emerging Food Networks in the Rural Transition', *Environment and Planning A* 27: 1261–79.

Marsden, T., J. Banks and G. Bristow (2000) 'Food Supply Chain Approaches: Exploring Their Role in Rural Development', *Sociologia Ruralis* 40(4): 424–38.

Mason, E. S. (1952) 'An American view of Raw Materials Problems: The Report of the President's Materials Policy Commission', *Journal of Industrial Economics* 1(1): 1–20.

McClumpha, A. D. (1988) 'The Trading of Green Coffee', in R. J. Clarke and R. Macrae (eds.), *Coffee* (Volume 6): *Commercial and Technico-Legal Aspects*. London and New York: Elsevier Applied Science.

McCreery, D. (2003) 'Coffee and Indigenous Labor in Guatemala, 1871–1980', in W. G. Clarence-Smith and S. Topik (eds.), *The Global Coffee Economy in Africa, Asia and Latin America, 1500–1989*. Cambridge, Cambridge University Press.

McMichael, P. (2000) *Development and Social Change: A Global Perspective* (second edition). Thousand Oaks, CA: Pine Forge Press.

Means, G. C. (1935) 'Price Inflexibility and the Requirements of a Stabilizing Monetary Policy', *Journal of American Statistical Association* 30(190): 401–13.

Mitchell, D. and C. Gilbert (1997) 'Do Hedge Funds and Commodity Funds Affect Commodity Prices?' *Development Economics Notes* No. 29. Washington DC: World Bank.

Moran, W. (1993) 'The Wine Appellation as Territory in France and California', *Annals of the Association of American Geographers* 83(4): 694–717.

Morisset, J. (1997) 'Unfair Trade: Empirical Evidence in World Commodity Markets over the Past 25 Years', *Policy Working Paper*, No. 1825. Washington, DC: World Bank.

Murdoch, J. and M. Miele (1999) '"Back to Nature": Changing "Worlds of Production" in the Food Sector', *Sociologia Ruralis* 39(4): 465–83.

Murdoch, J., T. Marsden, and J. Banks (2000) 'Quality, Nature and Embeddedness: Some Theoretical Considerations in the Context of the Food Sector', *Economic Geography* 76: 107–25.

Murray, D., L. T. Raynolds and P. L. Taylor (2003) *One Cup at a Time: Poverty Alleviation and Fair Trade Coffee in Latin America*. Colorado State University.

Myrdal, G. (1956) *An International Economy: Problems and Prospects*. London: Routledge & Kegan Paul.

—— (1957) *Economic Theory and Underdeveloped Regions*. London: Gerald Duckworth.

—— (1960) *Beyond the Welfare State: Economic Planning and Its International Implications*. New Haven: Yale University Press.

Ndjieunde, G., S. Fambon, E. Ebollo, E. Ngongang and G. Etoundi (2002) 'Ajustement monetaire, liberalisation et performance des filières agricoles camerounaises: cas du café, du cacao, et du coton', mimeo. University of Yaoundé II, Faculty of Economics and Management.

Neilson, J. (2004) 'Geographical Specificity as a Mode of Ordering: Coffee Trade Networks from Toraja to Tokyo', in N. Fold and B. Pritchard (eds.), *Cross-continental Agro-food Chains: Structures, Actors and Dynamics in the Global Food System*. London: Routledge.

Nelson, P. (1970) 'Information and Consumer Behaviour', *Journal of Political Economy* 78(2): 311–29.

Netto, D. (1979) *O Problema do Café*. Rio de Janeiro: Fundacao Getulio Vargas.

Newbery, D. M. G. and J. E. Stiglitz (1981) *The Theory of Commodity Price Stabilization: A Study in the Economics of Risk*. Oxford and New York: Clarendon Press and Oxford University Press.

Northrup, D. (1995) *Indentured Labour in the Age of Imperialism, 1834–1922*. Cambridge and New York: Cambridge University Press.

Nurkse, R. (1959) *Patterns of Trade and Development*. Stockholm: Almqvist and Wiksell.

Nyangito, H. O. (2000) 'Delivery of Services to Smallholder Coffee Farmers and Impacts on Production under Liberalization in Kenya', Discussion Paper Series DP/04/2000, Nairobi: Kenya Institute for Public Policy Research and Analysis (KIPPRA).

Odle, T. (1964) 'Entrepreneurial Cooperation on the Great Lake: The Origin of the Methods of American Grain Marketing', *Business History Review* 38(4): 441–5.

OECD (2003) *Agricultural Policies in OECD Countries: Monitoring and Evaluation, 2003*. Paris: Organization for Economic Cooperation and Development.

Ostrom, V. and E. Ostrom (1977) 'Public Goods and Public Choices', in E. S. Savas (ed.), *Alternatives for Delivering Public Services: Toward Improved Performance*. Boulder, CO: Westview Press.

Oxfam (2002a) *Rigged Rules and Double Standards: Trade, Globalization and the Fight against Poverty*. Oxford: Oxfam.

—— (2002b) *Mugged: Poverty in Your Coffee Cup*. Oxford: Oxfam.

—— (2004) 'The Commodity Challenge: Towards an EU Action Plan'. Oxford: Oxfam.

Palacios, M. (1983) *Coffee in Colombia, 1850–1970: An Economic, Social, and Political History*. Cambridge and New York: Cambridge University Press.

Pelupessy, W. (1999) 'Coffee in Côte d'Ivoire and Costa Rica: National and Global Aspects of Competitiveness', in H. L. van der Laan, T. Dijkstra and A. van Tilburg (eds.), *Agricultural Marketing in Tropical Africa: Contributions from the Netherlands*. Leiden: African

Studies Centre Research Series 15/1999; Ashgate: Aldershot.

Pendergrast, M. (2001) *Uncommon Grounds: The History of Coffee and How It Transformed Our World*. New York: Basic Books.

Platt, D. C. M., A. J. H. Latham, and R. Michie (1993) *Decline and Recovery in Britain's Overseas Trade, 1873–1914*. Basingstoke: Macmillan.

Ploeg, J. D. van der, and H. Renting (2000) 'Impact and Potential: A Comparative Review of European Development Practices', *Sociologia Ruralis* 4(4): 529–43.

Ploeg, J. D. van der, H. Renting, G. Brunori, K. Knickel, J. Mannion, T. Marsden, K. de Roost, E. Sevilla-Guzman and F. Ventura (2000) 'Rural Development: From Practices and Policies Towards Theory', *Sociologia Ruralis* 4(4): 391–408.

Ponte, S. (2002a) 'Brewing a Bitter Cup? Deregulation, Quality and the Re-organization of the Coffee Marketing Chain in East Africa', *Journal of Agrarian Change*, 2(2), 248–72.

—— (2002b) 'The "Latte Revolution"? Regulation, Markets and Consumption in the Global Coffee Chain', *World Development* 30(7): 1099–122.

—— (2002c) 'Standards, Trade and Equity: Lessons from the Specialty Coffee Industry', CDR Working Paper 02.13, Copenhagen: Centre for Development Research.

—— (2002d) *Farmers and Markets in Tanzania: How Policy Reforms Affect Rural Livelihoods in Africa*. London, Portsmouth, NH and Dar es Salaam: James Currey, Heinemann and Mkuki na Nyota.

—— (2004) 'The Politics of Ownership: Tanzanian Coffee Policy in the Age of Liberal Reformism', *African Affairs* 103/413: 615–33.

Ponte, S. and P. Gibbon (2005) 'Quality Standards, Conventions and the Governance of Global Value Chains', *Economy and Society* 34(1): 1–31.

Ponte, S. and F. Kawuma (2003) 'Coffee Certification in Uganda: Feasibility Study,' report for the Department for International Development (DfID, UK) and the Uganda Coffee Development Authority, Kampala, Uganda.

Porter, R. C. (1970) 'Some Implications of Post-War Primary Product Trends', *Journal of Political Economy* 78: 586–97.

Potts, J. (2003) 'Policy Tools for Sustainability'. Mimeo. Winnipeg: International Institute for Sustainable Development.

Prebisch, R. (1949) 'El desarrollo economico de la American Latina y algunos de sus principales problemas', in CEPAL (ed.), *Estudio Economico de la America Latina, 1948*. Santiago: CEPAL.

—— (1950) 'Crecimiento, desequilibrio y disparidades: interpretacion del proceso de desarrollo economico', in CEPAL (ed.), *Estudio economico de la America Latina, 1949*. Santiago: CEPAL.

—— (1964) *Towards a New Trade Policy For Development*. New York: United Nations.

Raikes, P., M. F. Jensen and S. Ponte (2000) 'Global Commodity Chain Analysis and the French *Filière* Approach: Comparison and Critique', *Economy and Society* 29(3): 390–417.

Rangnekar, D. (2004) 'The Socio-Economics of Geographical Indications', issue paper, UNCTAD–ICTSD Project on IPRs and Sustainable Development, Geneva.

Raoul, E. (1897) *Culture du Caféier*. Paris: Augustin Challamel.

Ray, C. (1998) 'Culture, Intellectual Property and Territorial Rural Development', *Sociologia Ruralis* 38(1): 3–20.

Raynolds, L. T. (2000) 'Re-embedding Global Agriculture: The International Organic and Fair Trade Movements', *Agriculture and Human Values* 17: 297–309.

—— (2002) 'Consumer/Producer Links in Fair Trade Coffee Networks', *Sociologia Ruralis* 42(4): 404–24.

—— (2004) 'The Globalization of Organic Agro-Food Networks', *World Development* 32(5): 725–43.

Raynolds, L. T., D. Murray and P. L. Taylor (2004) 'Fair Trade Coffee: Building Producer Capacity via Global Networks', *Journal of International Development* 16: 1109–21.

Rees, G. L. (1972) *Britain's Commodity Markets*. London: Paul'Elek Books.

Reich, R. B. (1992) *The Work of Nations: Preparing Ourselves for Twenty-first Century Capitalism*. New York: Vintage Books.

Renard, M. C. (2003) 'Fair Trade: Quality, Market and Conventions', *Journal of Rural Studies* 19: 87–96.

Réviron, S., J. M. Chappuis and D. Barjolle (2003) 'Vertical Alliance for Origin Labelled Food Products: What Is the Most Relevant Economic Model of Analysis?', paper presented at the 80th EAAE Seminar 'New Policies and Institutions for European Agriculture', Ghent.

RIAS (2002) 'Identification and Assessment of Proposals by the International Private Coffee Sector Regarding the Poor Income Situation of Coffee Farmers'. Utrecht: Rabobank.

Rice, P. D. and J. McLean (1999) 'Sustainable Coffee at the Crossroads'. Consumer's Choice Council.

Rifkin, J. (2000) *The Age of Access: The New Culture of Hypercapitalism, Where All of Life Is a Paid-for Experience*. New York: J. P. Tarcher/Putnam.

Robbins, P. (2003) *Stolen Fruit: The Tropical Commodities Disaster*. London: Zed Books.

Roberts, N. (1984) 'Testing Oligopolistic Behaviour', *International Journal of Industrial Organisation* 2: 367–83.

Roest, K. and A. Menghi (2000) 'Reconsidering "Traditional" Food: The Case of Parmigiano Reggiano Cheese', *Sociologia Ruralis* 40(4): 439–51.

Rondet, M. (1997) 'La normalisation du caoutchouc naturel dans la gestion de la qualité'. *Document de travail en économie des filières*. Montpellier : CIRAD.

Rothstein, M. (1983) 'The Rejection and Acceptance of a Market Innovation: Hedging in the Late Nineteenth Century', *Review of Research in Futures Markets* 2(2): 201–14.

Rowe, J. W. F. (1963) *The World's Coffee: A Study of the Economics and Politics of the Coffee Industries of Certain Countries and of the International Problem*. London: Her Majesty's Stationery Office.

Rufenacht, C. (1955) *Le café et les principaux marchés de matières premières*. Le Havre : Société Commerciale Interocéanique.

Rundgren, G. and P. Lustig (2002) 'Feasibility Study for the Establishment of Certification Bodies for Organic Agriculture in Eastern and Southern Africa'. Grolink: Sweden.

Salais, R. (1989) 'L'analyse économique des conventions de travail', *Revue Economique* 40(2):199–240.

Salais, R. and M. Storper (1992) 'The Four "Worlds" of Contemporary Industry', *Cambridge Journal of Economics* 16: 169–93.

Scherer, F. M. (1970) *Industrial Market Structure and Economic Performance*. Chicago: Rand McNally College Publishing Company.

Schmid, O. (2002) 'Codex Alimentarius', in M. Yussefi and H. Willer (eds.), *The World of Organic Agriculture 2003: Statistics and Future Prospects*. Tholey-Theley: International Federation of Organic Agriculture Movements (IFOAM).

Schmidt, B. (2002) *Fair Trade Coffee: Incorporating Sustainability from Crop to Cup*. MSc thesis, Copenhagen: Copenhagen Business School.

Scholer, M. (2004) 'Bitter or Better Future for Coffee Producers?' *International Trade Forum* No. 2. Geneva: International Trade Centre.

Schultz, T. W. (1945) *Agriculture in an Unstable Economy*. New York: McGraw-Hill.

—— (1961) 'Economic Prospects of Primary Products', in H. S. Ellis and H. C. Wallich (eds.), *Economic Development for Latin America*. New York: St Martin's Press.

Sheingate, A. (2001) *The Rise of the Agricultural Welfare State: Institutions and Interest Group Power in the United States, France and Japan*. Princeton: Princeton University Press.

Sheridan, R. B. (1969) 'The Plantation Revolution and the Industrial Revolution', *Caribbean Studies* 9(3): 5–25.

Simmel, G. (1957) 'Fashion', *American Journal of Sociology* LXII/6: 541–58.

Singer, H. W. (1950) 'The Distribution of Gains between Investing and Borrowing Countries', *American Economic Review* 40(2): 473–85.

Smith, M. (1996) 'The Empire Filters Back: Consumption, Production and the Politics of Starbucks Coffee', *Urban Geography* 17: 502–24.

Specialty Coffee Association of America (SCAA) (1999) '1999 Coffee Market Summary'. Long Beach, CA: SCAA.

Spooner, B. (1986) 'Weavers and Dealers: The Authenticity of an Oriental Carpet', in A. Appadurai (ed.), *The Social Life of Things: Commodities in Cultural Perspective*. Cambridge: Cambridge University Press.

Spraos, J. (1980) 'The Statistical Debate on the Net Barter Terms of Trade between Primary Commodities and Manufactures', *The Economic Journal* 90(357): 107–28.

Storper, M. and R. Salais (1997) *Worlds of Production: The Action Frameworks of the Economy*. Cambridge, MA and London: Harvard University Press.

Sweigart, J. (1987) *Coffee Factorage and the Emergence of a Brazilian Capital, 1850–1888*. New York: Garland Publishing, Inc.

Talbot, J. M. (1997a) 'Where Does Your Coffee Dollar Go? The Division of Income and Surplus along the Coffee Commodity Chain', *Studies in Comparative International Development* 32(1): 56–91.

—— (1997b) 'The Struggle for Control of a Commodity Chain: Instant Coffee from Latin America', *Latin American Research Review* 32(2) 117–35.

Tallontire, A. M. (1999) 'Making Trade Fair? An Examination of the Relationship between Cafédirect and a Coffee Co-operative in Tanzania.' PhD thesis, Bradford: University of Bradford.

—— (2000) 'Partnerships in Fair Trade: Reflections from a Case Study of Cafédirect', *Development in Practice* 10(2): 166–77.

—— (2001) 'Challenges Facing Fair Trade: Which Way Now?' paper presented at the 2001 DSA conference, Manchester, 10–12 September.

Taylor, P. L. (2005) 'In the Market but not of It: Fair Trade Coffee and Forest Stewardship Council Certification as Market-Based Social Change', *World Development* 33(1): 129–47.

TechnoServe (2003) 'Business Solutions to the Coffee Crisis'. Norwalk, CT: Technoserve.

Temu, A. (2001) 'Market Liberalization, Vertical Integration and Price Behaviour in Tanzania's Coffee Auction', *Development Policy Review* 19(2): 207–24.

TerraChoice Environmental Services (2000) 'Environmental and Other Labelling of Coffee: The Role of Mutual Recognition'. Commission for Environmental Cooperation.

Thévenot, L. (1995) 'Des marchés aux normes', in G. Allaire and R. Boyer (eds.), *La grande transformation de l'agriculture: Lectures conventionnalistes et regulationnistes*. Paris: INRA–Economica.

Thomsen, F. L. (1951) *Agricultural Marketing*. New York: McGraw-Hill.

Tirole, J. (1988) *The Theory of Industrial Organization*. Cambridge, Mass: MIT Press.

Topik, S. (1998) 'Coffee', in S. Topik and A. Wells (eds.), *The Second Conquest of Latin America: Coffee, Henequen, and Oil during the Export Boom, 1850–1930*. Austin: University of Texas Press.

—— (2003) 'The Integration of the World Coffee Market,' in W. G. Clarence-Smith and S. Topik (eds.), *The Global Coffee Economy in Africa, Asia and Latin America, 1500–1989*. Cambridge: Cambridge University Press.

Toye, J. F. J. (1987) *Dilemmas of Development: Reflections on the Counter–revolution in Development Theory and Policy*. Oxford and New York: Blackwell.

Ukers, W. (1935) *All About Coffee*. New York: The Tea and Coffee Trade Journal Company.

UNCTAD (1982) *Trade and Development Report*. Geneva: United Nations Conference on Trade and Development.

—— (2002) *Trade and Development Report*. Geneva: United Nations Conference on Trade and Development.

UNCTAD and R. Prebisch (1964) 'Towards a New Trade Policy for Development: Report by the Secretary-General of the United Nations Conference on Trade and Development'. New York: United Nations.

USDA (2004) *Tropical Products: World Markets and Trade*. Washington, DC: United States Department of Agriculture.

USDC (1973) *Long-Term Economic Growth, 1860–1970*. Washington, DC: United States Department of Commerce.

Valceschini, E. and A. Mazé (2000) 'La politique de la qualité agro-alimentaire dans le contexte international', *Economie Rurale* 258: 30–41.

Varangis, P. and D. Larson (1996) *Dealing with Commodity Price Uncertainty*. Washington, DC: World Bank.

Vellema, S. and D. Boselie (eds.) (2003) *Cooperation and Competence in Global Food Chains: Perspectives on Food Quality and Safety*. Maastricht: Shaker Publishers.

Vercellone, C. (ed.) (2003) *Sommes-nous sortis du capitalisme industrial?* Paris: La Dispute.

Vioti da Costa, E. (1982) *Da senzala a colonia*. São Paulo: Livraria Ciéncias Humanas Ltda.

Vorley, B. (2003) *Corporate Concentration from Farm to Consumer*. Report for the UK Food Group. London: International Institute for Environment and Development (IIED).

Wallace, H. A. (1934) *New Frontiers*. New York: Reynal and Hitchcock.

Waridel, L. (2001) *Coffee with Pleasure: Just Java and World Trade*. Black Rose Books and Oxfam America.

Weber, M. (1927) *General Economic History*. New York: Greenberg.

Wilkinson, J. (1997) 'A New Paradigm for Economic Analysis?' *Economy and Society* 26(3): 305–39.

Wilkinson, J. (2002) 'The Final Foods Industry and the Changing Face of the Global Agro-Food System', *Sociologia Ruralis* 42(2): 329–46.

Williams, R. G. (1994) *States and Social Evolution: Coffee and the Rise of National Governments in Central America*. Chapel Hill and London: University of North Carolina Press.

Winter-Nelson, A. and A. Temu (2002) 'Institutional Adjustment and Transaction Costs: Product and Inputs Markets in the Tanzanian Coffee System', *World Development* 30(4): 561–74.

Woodman, H. D. (1966) 'The Decline of Cotton Factorage after the Civil War', *American Historical Review* 71(4): 1219–36.

—— (1968) *King Cotton and His Retainers: Financing and Marketing the Cotton Crop of the South, 1800–1925*. Lexington, KY: University of Kentucky Press.

World Bank (1986) *World Development Report 1986*. New York: Oxford University Press.

Wrigley, G. (1988) *Coffee*. Harlow: Longman Scientific and Technical.

Wrigley, N. and M. S. Lowe (eds.) (1996) *Retailing, Consumption and Capital: Towards the New Retail Geography*. Harlow: Longman.

Wrigley, N. and M. S. Lowe (2002) *Reading Retail: A Geographical Perspective on Retailing and Consumption Spaces*. London: Arnold.

Wrigley, N. and T. Marsden (1996) 'Retailing, the Food System and the Regulatory State,' in N. Wrigley and M. S. Lowe (eds.), *Retailing, Consumption and Capital: Towards the New Retail Geography*. Harlow: Longman.

Wunderlich, C. (2002) 'The Environmental Significance of Coffee Certification Programmes in Mexico'. Consumer's Choice Council.

Index

Puerto Rico 57

quality control/management xi, xiii, xv–xvi, 9–11, 26, 30–47, 50, 52–3, 69, 71, 102, 104, 119, 130–9, 149, 154–5, 175, 183, 185–7, 190–1, 193–4, 197–8, 216–17, 220–4, 230–4, 237, 239–40, 242, 243n, 245, 250, 253, 257–8, 262–5, 270, 271; *see also (under coffee)* in-person service qualities, material qualities, symbolic qualities
quinine 67

Rabobank 255
railways 4–5, 7, 57
Rainforest Alliance 164, 168, 177–81, 187, 189–92, 198, 203n
Rapunzel Pure Organics 164, 193; E-Blend 164; E-Espresso 164
regulation/deregulation xiv–xvi, 12, 20–1, 25, 34, 39, 42, 50, 74, 80, 83–123, 131–3, 137–9, 154, 168–70, 196, 199, 220, 230–2, 235–8, 242, 245–53, 255–6, 258, 262–3, 266, 269, 270, 271
reputation 37–8, 41, 127, 131, 135–6, 139–41, 154, 160
retailers xi, xvi, 2, 22, 25, 28, 43, 56, 74–9, 90, 93, 128–9, 140, 145, 148, 152, 155, 160, 166, 171, 173, 183, 192–3, 205, 208–19, 221, 235, 237–42, 257, 268–9, 270, 271; *see also* café chains, supermarkets
Réunion 57, 69
Ribeirao Preto 72
rice 174
Rio de Janeiro 63, 71
Rio Preto 72
Rothfos 124n
Royal Ahold 182
rubber 8–11, 19, 47–9n
Russia 254

Safeway 183
Saimaza 92
Saint Domingue *see* Haiti
San Francisco 53
San Francisco Bay Gourmet Coffee 156
Santander province, Colombia 67
Santo Domingo 57
Santos 69, 71–3
São Paulo 63–5, 68, 72, 84, 236
São Tome 8
Sara Lee 92, 124n, 168, 183, 195–6
Scandinavia 74, 117, 143–4
Seattle 77
Seattle Coffee Company 78

sebsabies 102, 108–9, 138
Second World War 1, 11, 14–15, 51, 56, 67–8, 73, 85–6, 113, 120, 142, 149, 151, 161
Segafredo Zanetti 144–5, 147
Senseo 92
services 12, 43–7
sharecropping 7–8, 65, 67
SICAFE 124n
Sidamo 99
Singer, H. W. 15–17, 19, 30–1
slavery 2–4, 7, 60–1, 63–5, 67–8, 80
smallholders 60, 63, 65–8, 70, 72, 79–80, 81n, 99, 101, 105, 119, 123, 129–30, 136, 151, 154, 158–9, 174, 180, 189, 193, 202n, 203n, 229, 235, 243n, 246, 254, 257, 259, 261–2, 265, 270, 272
Smithsonian Migratory Bird Centre (SMBC) 177–81, 188–9, 190–1
social justice 231, 234–5
Sociedade Protetora de Imigração 65
Soconusco 63
soil conservation 177–80, 182, 186, 189–91
Somalia 124n
South Africa 222
South America 60, 71, 176
Soviet Union 8
Spain 39, 65, 75, 149
Specialty Coffee Association of America (SCAA) 151–2, 155, 157–8, 161, 163n, 184, 221
Specialty Coffee Association of Europe (SCAE) 163n
speculation 6, 90
Splendid 92; Splendid/Kraft 144
Sri Lanka 57–9
St Louis 5
STABEX (Stabilization of Export Earnings) 251
standards 1–2, 4–6, 8–11; and auctions 134; and commodity fetishism 225, 229; and consumption 11; cosmetic 199; cross-sector 196; and diversion of responsibility 257; and entry barriers 158–9, 192, 261; evolution of 69–74; and exchange 225; and exports 102, 106, 129, 131–8, 245, 250; and Good Agricultural Practices 182–3; and fair trade coffee 173–4; and governance 11; and imports 168–70; and indications of geographical origin (IGOs) 235; and in-person service qualities 43–7; investment in 192; and market transactions xiii, 36–7, 42; and material qualities 34–7, 130, 221; national bureaus of 270; and

(UCDA) 106, 135-6
Uganda xv-xvi, 25, 57, 59-62, 73, 83, 95,
   97-102, 106-7, 119, 123n, 125n, 133,
   135-7, 143, 172, 184, 187, 189, 207-9,
   235, 254-5
United Airlines 79
United Kingdom (UK) 4, 57, 70, 73, 75-6,
   117, 144, 163n, 170, 177, 182-3, 238-9
United Nations (UN) 182, 196; Universal
   Declaration of Human Rights 182
United Nations Conference on Trade and
   Development (UNCTAD) 17-18, 25,
   249, 272n
United States (US) xv-xvi, 3-5, 7-9, 14, 22,
   24, 40, 45-6, 53, 56, 70-1, 75-7, 84, 86-
   7, 91, 114-17, 128, 140-4, 146-9, 151-3,
   165, 168-9, 176, 178-9, 205-7, 214-18,
   222, 236-7, 246, 249, 251, 267; Agricul-
   tural Adjustment Act (1938) 14; Civil
   War 4, 7; Department of Agriculture
   (USDA) 14, 169; Farm Security and
   Rural Investment Bill 22; National
   Organic Programme (NOP) 169;
   Organic Foods Production Act (OFPA)
   169; Rubber Manufacturers' Association
   9; State Department 14; US Agency for
   International Development (USAID) 159

Van der Bosch, J. 66
vanilla 254

vending machines 144
Venezuela 67, 123n
Venice Biennale 150
Vermont 156
Vietnam x, xviiin, 57-62, 80, 81n, 100,
   123n, 143, 189, 196, 207, 237, 247
Volcafé 91, 195-6

Wal-Mart 76-7
Washington 265
waste 182, 194
water 177, 194
wheat 4-5, 23
Wildlife Trust 194
wine/spirits 39, 41, 130, 132, 150, 174,
   222, 230-6, 253, 266-8, 270
wood products 180
World Bank 20, 247, 253, 255
World Health Organization (WHO) 168
World Trade Organization (WTO) 1, 12,
   21-3, 41, 222, 236-7, 247, 251-3, 266,
   270; dispute settlement process 22, 237;
   Doha Round 12, 21-2, 252

Yemen 69
Yrgacheffe 99

Zaïre 143
Zambia 189, 202n, 243n
Zanzibar 69

CTA

partageons les connaissances au profit des communautés rurales

sharing knowledge, improving rural livelihoods

The Technical Centre for Agricultural and Rural Cooperation (CTA) was established in 1983 under the Lomé Convention between the ACP (African, Caribbean and Pacific) Group of States and the European Union Member States. Since 2000, it has operated within the framework of the ACP–EC Cotonou Agreement.

CTA's tasks are to develop and provide services that improve access to information for agricultural and rural development, and to strengthen the capacity of ACP countries to produce, acquire, exchange and utilise information in this area. CTA's programmes are designed to: provide a wide range of information products and services and enhance awareness of relevant information sources; promote the integrated use of appropriate communication channels and intensify contacts and information exchange (particularly intra-ACP); and develop ACP capacity to generate and manage agricultural information and to formulate ICM strategies, including those relevant to science and technology. CTA's work incorporates new developments in methodologies and cross-cutting issues such as gender and social capital.

CTA
Postbus 380
6700 AJ Wageningen
The Netherlands

Printed in the United States
125781LV00001B/1-90/P